Individual and Group
Privacy

Individual and Group Privacy

EDWARD J. BLOUSTEIN

Transaction Books
New Brunswick, New Jersey

Library of Congress Catalog Number: 77-28972
ISBN: 0-87855-286-3 (cloth)
Printed in the United States of America

Library of Congress Cataloging in Publication Data

Bloustein, Edward J.
  Individual and Group Privacy
    1. Privacy, Right of—United States—Addresses, essays, lectures. 2. Press law—United States—Addresses, essays, lectures. I. Title.
KF1262.A75B55   343'.73'0998   77-28972
ISBN: 0-87855-286-3

Reprinted by permission from:

Chapter 1—*New York University Law Review*, vol. 39, no. 6 (December 1964):962-1007.
Chapter 2—*Texas Law Review* (April 1968):611-29.
Chapter 3—*Rutgers Law Review*, vol. 28, no. 1 (Fall 1974):41-95.
Chapter 4—*Rutgers-Camden Law Journal*, vol. 8, no. 2 (Winter 1977):219-83.

CONTENTS

INTRODUCTION

The four essays on privacy presented in this book were completed over a thirteen-year period and represent distinct stages in the development of my thinking on the subject. I believe that the development of my own views parallels in an instructive fashion the development of the stages of thoughtful concern about privacy in society at large. Moreover, the sequence of development, no less than the substantive views presented, is especially appropriate to discussions of privacy and the right to know in the post-Watergate era.

The earliest conceptual stage presented in these essays centers on privacy as a tort, as a wrong done to one individual by another. My 1964 essay (chapter 1) attempts to bring some doctrinal clarity to what was then—and in some measure still is—a hodgepodge of ideas. It establishes grave insult to individual dignity, to individuals' freedom to be themselves, as the gravamen of the privacy tort.

As the privacy tort continued to be discussed and dealt with in the courts after 1964, its constitutional dimension—discussed briefly in Brandeis' and Warren's article of 1890—began to emerge more and more clearly. Many aspects of this constitutional dimension to privacy have emerged since then; two of them are dealt with at length in these essays. The first is freedom of expression as protected by the First Amendment: Does Constitutional protection of freedom of expression preclude legal liability for any publication which invades an individual's privacy? In my 1968 essay (chapter 2) I defend the importance of the privacy tort against claims that it is petty, and I also begin to deal with the First Amendment issue, as presented in a case involving a *Time* magazine story about a family held hostage by escaped convicts. The United States Supreme Court had held that a recovery of damages against *Time* magazine, without a showing of actual malice, was an unconstitutional abridgement of freedom of expression. I conclude that the Court erred in this case, and that privacy could be protected against incursions of mass publicity without impairing valued First Amendment rights.

I develop this view at length in my 1974 study on "The First Amendment and Privacy" (chapter 3). Some years previously, Alexander Meikeljohn had expounded the view that the purpose of the First Amendment was *not* protection for "the words of the speakers"; this is provided under the "reasonableness" test of the due process clause of the Constitution. The First Amendment rather provides protection, said Meikeljohn, for "the minds of the hearers." The First Amendment is "absolute" or "unlimited"—not subject to the test of "reasonableness"—but it only applies "to speech which bears, directly or indirectly, upon issues with which voters have to deal—only, therefore, to consideration of matters of public interest."

My 1974 article expands and relies upon the Meikeljohn thesis to support limitations on the right to publish in those cases where the publication substantially impairs an individual's privacy without contributing "to consideration of matters of public interest." Thus, I urge that in the *Sidis* case and the case of *Hill v. Time Inc.*—two classic cases in which the individual right to privacy and the First Amendment clashed—the public interest intended to be protected by the First Amendment would have been fully vindicated had the publishers been required to suppress the identity of the individuals whose private lives were exposed, but been otherwise free to publish the articles concerned.

The final—and most recent—article in the book is on group privacy (chapter 4). It explores a second important area of constitutional conflict, this one between the public interest in being informed and the right to privacy. Here the right to privacy which is at issue is the right of individuals to huddle or associate with one another in private. Besides defining "group privacy" and distinguishing it from "individual privacy," this most recent article identifies varied forms of legal protection of group privacy afforded currently, and it concludes that, in Robert Merton's terms, they are essential to a properly functioning social structure. The article warns that it would be disastrous if this principle of social structure were to be neglected as part of an overreaction to the misuse of group confidences which characterized the Nixon era.

Individual and Group
Privacy

1

PRIVACY AS AN ASPECT OF HUMAN DIGNITY: AN ANSWER TO DEAN PROSSER

I

INTRODUCTION

THREE-QUARTERS of a century have passed since Warren and Brandeis published their germinal article, "The Right of Privacy."[1] In this period many hundreds of cases, ostensibly founded upon the right to privacy, have been decided,[2] a number of statutes expressly embodying it have been enacted,[3] and a sizeable scholarly literature has been devoted to it.[4] Remarkably enough, however, there remains to this day considerable confusion concerning the nature of the interest which the right to privacy is designed to protect. The confusion is such that in 1956 a distinguished federal judge characterized the state of the law of privacy by likening it to a "haystack in a hurricane."[5] And, in 1960, the dean of tort scholars wrote a comprehensive article on the subject which, in effect, repudiates Warren and Brandeis by suggesting that privacy is not an independent value at all but rather a composite of the interests in reputation, emotional tranquility and intangible property.[6]

Edward J. Bloustein is Professor of Law at New York University School of Law.

This article was prepared for the Special Committee on Science and Law of the Association of the Bar of the City of New York and an early version of the paper was delivered at the Committee's Conference on the Impact of Technological Advances on the Law of Privacy held at Sterling Forest, New York in May 1964. Although the author is indebted to the members of the Committee, especially its Chairman, Oscar Ruebhausen, its Secretary, Bevis Longstreth, and its Research Director, Allan Westin, for many valuable suggestions, the views expressed are the author's and not those of the Committee on Science and Law.

1. Warren & Brandeis, The Right of Privacy, 4 Harv. L. Rev. 193 (1890) [hereinafter cited as Warren & Brandeis].

2. See, e.g., Annot., 138 A.L.R. 22 (1942); Annot., 168 A.L.R. 446 (1947); Annot., 14 A.L.R.2d 750 (1950).

3. N.Y. Civ. Rights Law §§ 50-51; Okla. Stat. Ann. tit. 30, §§ 839-40 (1951); Utah Code Ann. §§ 76-4-7, 76-4-9 (1953); Va. Code Ann. § 8-650 (1950).

4. E.g., Feinberg, Recent Developments in the Law of Privacy, 48 Colum. L. Rev. 713 (1948); Green, Right of Privacy, 27 Ill. L. Rev. 237 (1932); Lisle, Right of Privacy (A Contra View), 19 Ky. L.J. 137 (1931); Nizer, Right of Privacy: A Half Century's Developments, 39 Mich. L. Rev. 526 (1941); O'Brien, The Right of Privacy, 2 Colum. L. Rev. 437 (1902); Winfield, Privacy, 47 L.Q. Rev. 23 (1931); Yankwich, Right of Privacy: Its Development, Scope and Limitations, 27 Notre Dame Law. 499 (1952).

5. Ettore v. Philco Television Broadcasting Co., 229 F.2d 481 (3d Cir. 1956) (Biggs, C.J.).

6. Prosser, Privacy, 48 Calif. L. Rev. 383 (1960) [hereinafter cited as Prosser, Privacy].

My purpose in this article is to propose a general theory of individual privacy which will reconcile the divergent strands of legal development—which will put the straws back into the hay-stack. The need for such a theory is pressing. In the first place, the disorder in the cases and commentary offends the primary canon of all science that a single general principle of explanation is to be preferred over a congeries of discrete rules. Secondly, the conceptual disarray has had untoward effects on the courts; lacking a clear sense of what interest or interests are involved in privacy cases has made it difficult to arrive at a judicial consensus concerning the elements of the wrong or the nature of the defenses to it. Thirdly, analysis of the interest involved in the privacy cases is of utmost significance because in our own day scientific and technological advances have raised the spectre of new and frightening invasions of privacy.[7] Our capacity as a society to deal with the impact of this new technology depends, in part, on the degree to which we can assimilate the threat it poses to the settled ways our legal institutions have developed for dealing with similar threats in the past.

The concept of privacy has, of course, psychological, social and political dimensions which reach far beyond its analysis in the legal context;[8] I will not deal with these, however, except incidentally. Nor do I pretend to give anything like a detailed exposition of the requirements for relief and the character of the available defenses in the law of privacy. Nor will my analysis touch on privacy problems of organizations and groups. My aim is rather the more limited one of discovering in the welter of cases and statutes the interest or social value which is sought to be vindicated in the name of individual privacy.

I propose to accomplish this by examining in some detail Dean Prosser's analysis of the tort of privacy and by then suggesting the conceptual link between the tort and the other legal contexts in which privacy finds protection. My reasons for taking this route rather than another, for concentrating initially on the tort cases and Dean Prosser's analysis of them, are that privacy began its modern history as a tort and that Dean Prosser

---

7. See, e.g., Brenton, The Privacy Invaders (1964); Dash, Knowlton & Schwartz, The Eavesdroppers (1959); Gross, The Brain Watchers (1962); Packard, The Naked Society (1964); Big Brother 7074 is Watching You, Popular Science, March 1963; 1410 Is Watching You, Time, Aug. 1963; Hearings Before the Subcommittee on the Use of Polygraphs as "Lie Detectors" By the Federal Government of the House Committee on Government Operations, 88th Cong., 2d Sess., pt. 3 (1964).

8. See, e.g., Arendt, The Human Condition (1958); Hoffer, The True Believer: Thoughts on the Nature of Mass Movements (1951); Orwell, 1984 (1949).

is by far the most influential contemporary exponent of the tort. Warren and Brandeis who are credited with "discovering" privacy thought of it almost exclusively as a tort remedy. However limited and inadequate we may ultimately consider such a remedy, the historical development in the courts of the concept of privacy stems from and is almost exclusively devoted to the quest for such a civil remedy. We neglect it, therefore, only at the expense of forsaking the valuable insights which seventy-five years of piecemeal common law adjudication can provide.

The justification for turning my own search for the meaning of privacy around a detailed examination of Dean Prosser's views on the subject is simply that his influence on the development of the law of privacy begins to rival in our day that of Warren and Brandeis.[9] His concept of privacy is alluded to in almost every decided privacy case in the last ten years or so,[10] and it is reflected in the current draft of the Restatement of Torts.[11] Under these circumstances, if he is mistaken, as I believe he is, it is obviously important to attempt to demonstrate his error and to attempt to provide an alternative theory.

---

9. Dean Wade, writing in the Virginia Law Weekly Dicta, Oct. 8, 1964, p. 1, col. 1, described the influence of Dean Prosser in this fashion:

> Another event took place some four years ago which may quickly bring the state of the law to maturity, and may also modify the habit of referring to the Warren-Brandeis article as both the origin and the true description of the nature of the right [to privacy]. This was the publication by William L. Prosser of an article entitled very simply *Privacy*, in 48 California Law Review 383, in August 1960.

10. See, e.g., Norris v. Moskin Stores, Inc., 272 Ala. 174, 176, 132 So. 2d 321, 323 (1961); Gill v. Curtis Publishing Co., 38 Cal. 2d 273, 239 P.2d 630 (1952); Carlisle v. Fawcett Publishing, Inc., 201 Cal. App. 2d 733, 734, 20 Cal. Rptr. 405, 411 (Dist. Ct. App. 1962); Werner v. Times-Mirror Co., 193 Cal. App. 2d 111, 118, 14 Cal. Rptr. 208, 214 (Dist. Ct. App. 1961); Felly v. Johnson Publishing Co., 160 Cal. App. 2d 718, 720, 325 P.2d 659, 661 (Dist. Ct. App. 1959); Barbieri v. News Journal Publishing Co., 189 A.2d 773, 774 (Del. 1963); McAndrews v. Roy, 131 So. 2d 256, 261 (Fla. 1961); Harms v. Miami Daily News, Inc., 127 So. 2d 715, 717 (Fla. 1961); Ford Motor Co. v. Williams, 108 Ga. App. 21, 29-30 nn.6 & 7, 132 S.E.2d 206, 211 nn.6 & 7 (1964); Peterson v. Idaho First Nat'l Bank, 83 Idaho 578, 583, 367 P.2d 284, 287 (1961); Yoder v. Smith, 253 Iowa 506, 507, 112 N.W.2d 862 (1962); Bremmer v. Journal-Tribune Publishing Co., 247 Iowa 817, 821, 76 N.W.2d 762, 764 (1956); Carr v. Watkins, 227 Md. 578, 583, 585-86, 177 A.2d 841, 843, 845-46 (1962); Hawley v. Professional Credit Bureau, 245 Mich. 500, 514, 325 P.2d 659, 671 (1956); Hubbard v. Journal Publishing Co., 67 N.M. 473, 475, 368 P.2d 147, 148-49 (1961); Spahn v. Messner, Inc., 43 Misc. 2d 219, 221, 250 N.Y.S.2d 529, 532 (Sup. Ct. 1964).

11. "[T]here is every reason to expect that when the second edition of the Restatement on Torts is completed and adopted by the American Law Institute, [Dean Prosser's] analysis will be substituted for the very generalized treatment now to be found in section 867." Wade, supra note 9. Dean Prosser, it should be noted, is the Reporter for the Restatement of the Law Second, Torts, and Dean Wade is one of his advisers.

II
DEAN PROSSER'S ANALYSIS OF THE PRIVACY CASES

Although it is not written in the style of an academic exposé of a legal myth, Dean Prosser's 1960 article on privacy has that effect; although he does not say it in so many words, the clear consequence of his view is that Warren and Brandeis were wrong, and their analysis of the tort of privacy a mistake. For, after examining the "over three hundred cases in the books,"[12] in which a remedy has ostensibly been sought for the same wrongful invasion of privacy, he concludes that, in reality, what is involved "is not one tort, but a complex of four."[13] A still more surprising conclusion is that these four torts involve violations of "four different interests,"[14] none of which, it turns out, is a distinctive interest in privacy.[15]

The "four distinct torts" which are discovered in the cases are described by Dean Prosser as follows:

1. Intrusion upon the plaintiff's seclusion or solitude, or into his private affairs.
2. Public disclosure of embarrassing facts about the plaintiff.
3. Publicity which places the plaintiff in a "false light" in the public eye.
4. Appropriation, for the defendant's advantage, of the plaintiff's name or likeness.[16]

The interest protected by each of these torts is: in the intrusion cases, the interest in freedom from mental distress,[17] in the public disclosure and "false light" cases, the interest in reputation,[18] and in the appropriation cases, the proprietary interest in name and likeness.[19]

Thus, under Dean Prosser's analysis, the much vaunted and discussed right to privacy is reduced to a mere shell of what it has pretended to be. Instead of a relatively new, basic and independent legal right protecting a unique, fundamental and relatively neglected interest, we find a mere application in

---

12. Prosser, Privacy 388.
13. Id. at 389.
14. Ibid. Actually, Dean Prosser subsequently identifies only three distinct interests since, in his view, both the public disclosure and the "false light" cases involve the same interest in reputation. See note 18 infra and accompanying text.
15. Prosser, Privacy 389-407, 422-23.
16. Id. at 389.
17. Id. at 392, 422.
18. Id. at 398, 401, 422-23; see note 14 supra.
19. Id. at 406, 423.

novel circumstances of traditional legal rights designed to protect well-identified and established social values. Assaults on
privacy are transmuted into a species of defamation, infliction
of mental distress and misappropriation. If Dean Prosser is
correct, there is no "new tort" of invasion of privacy, there are
rather only new ways of committing "old torts." And, if he is
right, the social value or interest we call privacy is not an independent one, but is only a composite of the value our society
places on protecting mental tranquility, reputation and intangible
forms of property.

III
Dean Prosser's Analysis Appraised

A. Consistency with the Warren and Brandeis Analysis

One way of testing Dean Prosser's analysis and of illuminating the concept of privacy itself, is to compare it with the
Warren-Brandeis article.[20] Did those learned authors propose
a "new tort" or merely a new name for "old torts"?

We may begin by noting the circumstances which stimulated the writing of the article. "On January 25, 1883," Brandeis'
biographer writes,

> Warren had married Miss Mabel Bayard, daughter of Senator
> Thomas Francis Bayard, Sr. They set up housekeeping in Boston's
> exclusive Back Bay section and began to entertain elaborately. The
> *Saturday Evening Gazette*, which specialized in "blue blood items"
> naturally reported their activities in lurid detail. This annoyed
> Warren who took the matter up with Brandeis. The article was
> the result.[21]

The article itself presents an intellectualized and generalized
account of the plight of the Warrens beleaguered by the yellow
journalism of their day.

> Instantaneous photographs and newspaper enterprise have
> invaded the sacred precincts of private and domestic life; and
> numerous mechanical devices threaten to make good the prediction
> that "what is whispered in the closet shall be proclaimed from the
> house tops."[22]
> The press is overstepping in every direction the obvious
> bounds of propriety and of decency. Gossip is no longer the re-
> source of the idle and of the vicious, but has become a trade,
> which is pursued with industry as well as effrontery. To satisfy
> a prurient taste the details of sexual relations are spread broad-
> cast in the columns of the daily papers. To occupy the indolent,

20. Warren & Brandeis.
21. Mason, Brandeis: A Free Man's Life 70 (1960).
22. Warren & Brandeis 195.

column upon column is filled with idle gossip, which can only be procured by intrusion upon the domestic circle.[23]

Thus, Warren and Brandeis were disturbed by lurid newspaper gossip concerning private lives. But what, in their view, made such gossip wrongful? What value or interest did such gossip violate to give it a tortious character? How, in other words, were people hurt by such gossip?

On more than one occasion in their article, they allude to the "distress" which "idle gossip" in newspapers causes. "[M]odern enterprise and invention," they write, "have, through invasions . . . [of man's] privacy, subjected him to mental pain and distress, far greater than could be inflicted by mere bodily injury."[24] And they mention "the suffering of those who may be made the subjects of journalistic or other enterprise."[25]

These allusions to mental distress seem to afford support for Dean Prosser's view that, in one of its aspects, at least, the right to privacy protects against intentionally inflicted emotional trauma; that the gravaman of an action for the invasion of privacy is really hurt feelings.[26] Such a conclusion, however, cannot be justified by the Warren and Brandeis article because, in fact, they expressly disown it. They point out that, although "a legal remedy for . . . [invasion of privacy] seems to involve the treatment of mere wounded feelings,"[27] the law affords no remedy for "mere injury to feelings. However painful the mental effects upon another of an act, though purely wanton or even malicious, yet if the act is otherwise lawful the suffering inflicted is without legal remedy."[28] And they then go on to distinguish invasion of privacy as "a legal *injuria*" or "act wrongful in itself" from "mental suffering" as a mere element of damages.[29]

Thus, in Warren and Brandeis' view, idle gossip about private affairs may well cause mental distress, but this is not what makes it wrongful; the mental distress is, for them, parasitic of an independent tort, the invasion of privacy. Nor did they believe, as evidently Dean Prosser believes, that "public

---

23. Id. at 196.
24. Ibid.
25. Ibid.
26. It should be noted, however, that Dean Prosser regards the Warren & Brandeis article as devoted primarily to one of the four torts he identifies, namely to "public disclosure of embarrassing facts," and he regards the interest invaded in this tort as being that of reputation. Prosser, Privacy 392.
27. Warren & Brandeis 197.
28. Ibid.
29. Id. at 197-98, 213.

disclosure of private facts" constitutes a species of defamation and an injury to reputation.[30]

"The principle on which the law of defamation rests," they say, "covers . . . a radically different class of effects from those for which attention is now asked."[31] Defamation concerns "injury done to the individual in his external relations to the community," injury to the estimation in which others hold him; the wrong involved in defamation is "material."[32] The invasion of privacy, by contrast, involves a "spiritual" wrong, an injury to a man's "estimate of himself" and an assault upon "his own feelings."[33] Moreover, invasion of privacy does not rest upon falsity as does defamation; the right to privacy exists not only "to prevent inaccurate portrayal of private life, but to prevent its being depicted at all."[34]

The third interest or value which Warren and Brandeis examine as the possible basis of the wrongfulness of newspaper gossip concerning private lives is a proprietary or property interest. Here as well, their conclusion is the negative one that, although the invasion of privacy may involve, on occasion, a misappropriation of something of pecuniary value, this is not the essence of the wrong.

This conclusion is the more striking because the legal precedents upon which they rely for the erection of a right to privacy are cases enforcing so-called common law property rights in literary and artistic works and cases involving trade secrets.[35] It is also a strong argument against Dean Prosser's identification of a "distinct" tort of appropriation of name or likeness as involving the protection of a proprietary interest[36] because, although they primarily concentrate on publicity cases, they expressly take account of the cases involving an unconsented use of a photographic likeness.[37]

Warren and Brandeis announce at the outset of their article that they believe that "the legal doctrines relating to infraction of what is ordinarily termed the common-law right to *intellectual and artistic property*" can, "properly understood," provide "a remedy for the evils under consideration."[38] They distinguish, however, between the common law protection of such property

---

30. Prosser, Privacy 398, 422-23.
31. Warren & Brandeis 197.
32. Ibid.
33. Ibid.
34. Id. at 218.
35. E.g., id. at 198-205, 211-12.
36. Prosser, Privacy 406, 423.
37. See e.g., Warren & Brandeis 195, 208, 210, 214.
38. Id. at 198. (Emphasis added.)

and that secured by forms of copyright statutes. The common law right allows a man "to control absolutely the act of publication, and in the exercise of his own discretion, to decide whether there shall be any publication at all."[39] The statutory right, by contrast, aims "to secure to the author, composer or artist the entire profits arising from publication."[40]

This distinction between the purposes of common law and statutory protection of literary and artistic property provides, in the Warren and Brandeis analysis, a key to the underlying significance of common law rights to literary and artistic property. They are really nothing but "instances and applications of a general right to privacy"[41] because "the value of the production [of a work subject to *common law* property right] is found not in the right to take the profits arising from publication, but in the peace of mind or the relief afforded by the ability to prevent any publication at all."[42] This being so, "it is difficult to regard the [common law] right as one of property."[43]

It is admitted that the courts which erected the legal remedy which "secures to each individual the right of determining, ordinarily, to what extent his thoughts, sentiments, and emotions shall be communicated to others,"[44] had, for the most part, "asserted that they rested their decisions on the narrow grounds of protection of property."[45] Yet, according to Warren and Brandeis, no thing of pecuniary value, no right of property "in the narrow sense," is to be found at issue in many of the cases. The concept of "property" was put forward by the courts as a fiction to rationalize a form of legal relief which was really founded on other grounds of policy. In other words, what we mean by saying there is common law property in literary and artistic works is not that violation of the right involves destruction or appropriation of something of monetary value but rather only that the law affords a remedy for the violation.[46]

In sum, as far as Warren and Brandeis were concerned,

---

39. Id. at 200.
40. Ibid.
41. Id. at 198.
42. Id. at 200.
43. Ibid.
44. Id. at 198.
45. Id. at 204.
46. I omit extended discussion of the theory that common law literary and artistic property rights rest on theories of breach of contract or breach of trust. Warren and Brandeis found here, as with the "property theory," that a fiction of sorts was involved, that courts implied a term of contract or a condition of trust as a form of "judicial declaration that public morality, private justice, and general convenience demand the recognition of . . . [the] rule [proscribing publication]." Warren & Brandeis 210.

newspaper gossip about private lives was not a wrong because it destroyed character, caused mental distress, or constituted a misappropriation of property—a taking of something of pecuniary value. Although the yellow journalism which feeds luridly upon the details of private lives may incidentally accomplish each of these results, they are not the essence of the wrong. Mrs. Warren's reputation could have been completely unaffected, her equanimity entirely unruffled, and her fortune wholly undisturbed; the publicity about her and her husband would nevertheless be wrongful, nevertheless be in violation of an interest which the law should protect.

What then is the basis of the wrong? Unfortunately, the learned authors were not as successful in describing the interest violated by publicity concerning private lives as in saying what it was not. This explains, in part, the fact that after hundreds of cases enforcing Warren and Brandeis' "right to privacy," Dean Prosser, Harper and James,[47] the Restatement of Torts,[48] and other learned authorities[49] predicate the right on bases expressly rejected by Warren and Brandeis.

Warren and Brandeis obviously felt that the term "privacy" was in itself a completely adequate description of the interest threatened by an untrammeled press; man, they said, had a right to his privacy, a right to be let alone, and this was, for them, a sufficient description of the interest with which they were concerned. This right, although violated by publication of information about a person's life and character, much in the same way the right to reputation is violated, is not the same as the right to reputation. Nor is the interest in being let alone like that of being protected against attempts to inflict mental trauma, even though distress is the frequent accompaniment of intrusions on privacy. And, although the common law property right to literary and artistic products is an instance of the right to privacy, privacy is not to be confused with something of pecuniary value.

Warren and Brandeis went very little beyond thus giving "their right" and "their interest" a name and distinguishing it from other rights or interests. It is only in asides of characterization and passing attempts at finding a verbal equivalent of the principle of privacy that we may find any further clues to the interest or value they sought to protect. Thus, at one

---

47. Harper & James, Torts § 9.6 (1956).
48. Restatement, Torts § 867 (1939).
49. See, e.g., Davis, What Do We Mean by "Right of Privacy"?, 4 S.D.L. Rev. 1 (1959); Green, The Right of Privacy, 27 Ill. L. Rev. 237 (1932); Pound, Interests of Personality, 28 Harv. L. Rev. 343 (1915).

point they remark, as I have indicated above, that, unlike reputation which is a "material" value, privacy is a "spiritual" one.[50] And they make repeated suggestions that the invasion of privacy, in some way, involves man's mentality,[51] that it involves an "effect upon . . . [a man's] estimate of himself and upon his own feelings."[52]

The most significant indication of the interest they sought to protect, however, is in their statement that "the principle which protects personal writings and all other personal productions . . . against publication in any form is in reality not the principle of private property, but that of *inviolate personality*."[53] I take the principle of "inviolate personality" to posit the individual's independence, dignity and integrity; it defines man's essence as a unique and self-determining being. It is because our Western ethico-religious tradition posits such dignity and independence of will in the individual that the common law secures to a man "literary and artistic property"—the right to determine "to what extent his thoughts, sentiments, emotions shall be communicated to others."[54] The literary and artistic property cases led Warren and Brandeis to the concept of privacy because, for them, it would have been inconsistent with a belief in man's individual dignity and worth to refuse him the right to determine whether his artistic and literary efforts should be published to the world. He would be less of a man, less of a master over his own destiny, were he without this right.

Thus, I believe that what provoked Warren and Brandeis to write their article was a fear that a rampant press feeding on the stuff of private life would destroy individual dignity and integrity and emasculate individual freedom and independence. If this is so, Dean Prosser's analysis of privacy stands clearly at odds with "the most influential law review article ever published," one which gave rise to a "new tort,"[55] not merely to a fancy name for "old torts."

As I have already indicated,[56] Dean Prosser's analysis of the privacy cases is remarkable for two propositions; the first, that there is not a single tort of the invasion of privacy, but rather "four distinct torts"; the second, that there is no distinctive single value or interest which these "distinct torts" protect and

50. See text accompanying notes 32 & 33 supra.
51. See, e.g., Warren & Brandeis 196.
52. Id. at 197.
53. Id. at 205. (Emphasis added.)
54. Id. at 198.
55. Gregory & Kalven, Cases on Torts 883 (1959).
56. See text accompanying notes 13-19 supra.

that, in fact, they protect three different interests, no one of which can properly be denominated an interest in privacy. I have considerable doubt that the cases support either of these conclusions.

B. The Intrusion Cases

This category of cases comprises instances in which a defendant has used illegal or unreasonable means to discover something about the plaintiff's private life.[57] Included in the category, thus, is a case in which a defendant was an unwanted spectator to the plaintiff giving birth to her child.[58] The Michigan court, writing nine years before Warren and Brandeis, declared the wrong was actionable in tort because "to the plaintiff the occasion was a most sacred one and no one had a right to intrude unless invited or because of some real and pressing necessity."[59]

Another illustrative case is *Rhodes v. Graham*,[60] where the defendant tapped the plaintiff's telephone wires without authorization. In upholding the cause of action for damages the court declared that "the evil incident to the invasion of the privacy of the telephone is as great as that accompanied by unwarranted publicity in newspapers and by other means of a man's private affairs."[61] In still another case of the same type, where a home was illegally entered, a cause of action for damages was upheld on the theory of a violation of state constitutional search and seizure provisions.[62]

What interest or value is protected in these cases? Dean Prosser's answer is that "the gist of the wrong [in the intrusion cases] is clearly the intentional infliction of mental distress."[63]

The fact is, however, that in no case in this group is mental distress said by the court to be the basis or gravamen of the cause of action. Moreover, all but one of these decisions predate the recognition in the jurisdictions concerned of a cause of action for intentionally inflicted mental distress[64] and, in most instances, the lines of authority relied upon in the intrusion cases are quite different from those relied upon in the mental distress cases.[65]

---

57. For the relevant cases, see Prosser, Privacy 389-90 nn.60-73.
58. De May v. Roberts, 46 Mich. 160, 9 N.W. 146 (1881).
59. Id. at 165, 9 N.W. at 149.
60. 238 Ky. 225, 37 S.W.2d 46 (1931).
61. Id. at 228-29, 37 S.W.2d at 47.
62. Young v. Western & A.R. Co., 39 Ga. App. 761, 766-67, 148 S.E. 414, 417 (1929).
63. Prosser, Privacy 422.
64. The exception is West Virginia. Roach v. Harper, 143 W. Va. 869, 105 S.E.2d 564 (1958); Monteleone v. Cooperative Transit Co., 128 W. Va. 340, 36 S.E.2d 475 (1945) (dictum).
65. In at least two instances, however, courts have cited privacy cases for

Furthermore, special damages in the form of "severe emotional distress" is recognized by Dean Prosser[66] and other authorities[67] as a requisite element of the cause of action for intentionally inflicted emotional distress. Yet, many of the cases allowing recovery for an intrusion expressly hold that special damages are not required.[68] Except in a small number of the cases of this group, there does not even seem to have been an allegation of mental illness or distress, certainly not an allegation of serious mental illness. And even in one of the rare cases in which serious mental distress was alleged, the court expressly says that recovery would be available without such an allegation.[69]

The most important reason, however, for disputing Dean Prosser's thesis in regard to the intrusion cases is that, in my judgment, he neglects the real nature of the complaint; namely that the intrusion is demeaning to individuality, is an affront to personal dignity. A woman's legal right to bear children without unwanted onlookers does not turn on the desire to protect her emotional equanimity, but rather on a desire to enhance her individuality and human dignity. When the right is violated she suffers outrage or affront, not necessarily mental trauma or distress. And, even where she does undergo anxiety or other symptoms of mental illness as a result, these consequences themselves flow from the indignity which has been done to her.

The fundamental fact is that our Western culture defines individuality as including the right to be free from certain types of intrusions. This measure of personal isolation and personal control over the conditions of its abandonment is of the very essence of personal freedom and dignity, is part of what our culture means by these concepts. A man whose home may be entered at the will of another, whose conversation may be overheard at the will of another, whose marital and familial intimacies may be overseen at the will of another, is less of a man,

---

the proposition that there may be recovery for mental suffering without physical impact or physical injury. State Rubbish Collector Ass'n v. Siliznoff, 38 Cal. 2d 330, 240 P.2d 282 (1952); Kuhr Bros. v. Spakas, 89 Ga. App. 885, 81 S.E.2d 491 (1954).
    66. Prosser, Insult and Outrage, 44 Calif. L. Rev. 40, 43 (1956). See also, Prosser, Privacy 422.
    67. See, e.g., Sams v. Eccles, 11 Utah 2d 289, 358 P.2d 344 (1961); Magruder, Mental and Emotional Disturbances in the Law of Torts, 49 Harv. L. Rev. 1033 (1936); Restatement, Torts § 46 (Supp. 1948).
    68. E.g., Young v. Western & A.R. Co., 39 Ga. App. 761, 148 S.E. 414 (1929); Rhodes v. Graham, 238 Ky. 225, 228, 37 S.W.2d 46, 47 (1931); Welsh v. Pritchard, 125 Mont. 517, 525, 241 P.2d 816, 820 (1959); Sutherland v. Kroger Co., 144 W. Va. 673, 684-85, 110 S.E.2d 716, 724 (1959); Roach v. Harper, 143 W. Va. 869, 877, 105 S.E.2d 564, 568 (1958).
    69. Young v. Western & A.R. Co., supra note 68.

has less human dignity, on that account. He who may intrude upon another at will is the master of the other and, in fact, intrusion is a primary weapon of the tyrant.[70]

I contend that the gist of the wrong in the intrusion cases is not the intentional infliction of mental distress but rather a blow to human dignity, an assault on human personality. Eavesdropping and wiretapping, unwanted entry into another's home, may be the occasion and cause of distress and embarrassment but that is not what makes these acts of intrusion wrongful. They are wrongful because they are demeaning of individuality, and they are such whether or not they cause emotional trauma.

This view of the gravamen of the wrong of intrusion finds support in cases in which courts have expressly rested the right to recover damages for the intrusion on violation of constitutional prohibitions against search and seizure.[71] To be sure, these cases do not say that an unwanted intrusion strikes at one's dignity and offends one's individuality. But the suggestion of this constitutional basis of the right to damages is a step in that direction; at the very least, the cases contradict the view that mental distress is the gist of the action.

Cases in which some form of relief other than damages is sought for an intrusion violating the constitutional prohibition against unreasonable searches and seizures are even closer to the point. The Supreme Court of the United States has declared plainly that the fourth amendment to the federal constitution is designed to protect against intrusions into privacy and that the underlying purpose of such protection is the preservation of individual liberty.[72] These cases represent, it seems to me, a recognition that unreasonable intrusion is a wrong because it involves a violation of constitutionally protected liberty of the person.

Thus, from the early *Boyd* case[73] to the recent case of

---

70. See Arendt, The Human Condition (1958); Hoffer, The True Believer: Thoughts on the Nature of Mass Movements (1951); Orwell, 1984 (1949).

71. Young v. Western & A.R. Co., 39 Ga. App. 761, 148 S.E. 414 (1929); cf. Walker v. Whittle, 83 Ga. App. 445, 64 S.E.2d 87 (1951).

72. See, e.g., Silverman v. United States, 365 U.S. 505 (1961); Wolf v. Colorado, 338 U.S. 25 (1949); United States v. Lefkowitz, 285 U.S. 452 (1932); Gouled v. United States, 255 U.S. 298 (1921); Boyd v. United States, 116 U.S. 616 (1886); Lopez v. United States, 373 U.S. 427, 439 (1963) (Brennan, Douglas, and Goldberg, JJ., dissenting); Poe v. Ullman, 367 U.S. 497, 549-50 (1961) (Harlan, J., dissenting); OnLee v. United States, 343 U.S. 747, 763 (1952) (Douglas, J., dissenting); Goldman v. United States, 316 U.S. 129, 136-37 (1942) (Murphy, J., dissenting); Olmstead v. United States, 277 U.S. 438, 469, 476-79 (1928) (Brandeis, J., dissenting); cf. Public Utilities Comm'n v. Pollak, 343 U.S. 451, 467 (1952) (Douglas, J., dissenting).

73. Boyd v. United States, note 72 supra.

Silverman v. United States,[74] the Supreme Court has made clear that the "Fourth Amendment gives a man the right to retreat into his own home and there be free from unreasonable governmental intrusion"[75] and that this right is of "the very essence of constitutional liberty and security."[76] "The Fourth Amendment," the Court has declared, "forbids every search that is unreasonable and is construed to safeguard the right of privacy."[77] Moreover, the Court has proclaimed that "the security of one's privacy against arbitrary intrusion by the police . . . is basic to a free society."[78]

In all of these cases, the intruder was an agent of government and, without doubt, the forms of relief available against a government officer are to be distinguished from those available against intrusions by a private person.[79] This is not to say, however, that intrusion is a different wrong when perpetrated by an FBI agent and when perpetrated by a next door neighbor; nor is it to say that the gist of the wrong is different in the two cases. The threat to individual liberty is undoubtedly greater when a policeman taps a telephone than when an estranged spouse does, but a similar wrong is perpetrated in both instances. Thus, the conception of privacy generated by the fourth amendment cases may rightly be taken, I would urge, as being applicable to any instance of intrusion even though remedies under the fourth amendment are not available in all such instances.

Brandeis' dissent in the *Olmstead* case[80] is especially instructive in this regard.[81] In that case—decided before the enactment of Section 605 of the Federal Communications Act—the federal government had gained evidence of a violation of the Prohibition Act by tapping a telephone, and the defendant sought to preclude use of the evidence on the theory that it was gained in violation of the fourth amendment. The majority of the Court held that, since the wiretap did not involve a trespass, there was no violation of the fourth amendment and, therefore, the evidence so obtained was legally admissible. Brandeis and Holmes dissented.

---

74. 365 U.S. 505 (1961).
75. Id. at 511.
76. Boyd v. United States, 116 U.S. 616, 630 (1886).
77. United States v. Lefkowitz, 285 U.S. 452, 464 (1932).
78. Wolf v. Colorado, 338 U.S. 25, 27 (1949).
79. See, e.g., Burdeau v. McDowell, 256 U.S. 465 (1921); Imboden v. People, 46 Colo. 142, 90 Pac. 608 (1907); Sackler v. Sackler, 16 App. Div. 2d 423, 229 N.Y.S.2d 61 (2d Dep't 1962), aff'd 15 N.Y.2d 40, 255 N.Y.S.2d 83 (1964); Sutherland v. Kroger, 110 S.E.2d 716 (W. Va. 1959); Note, 72 Yale L.J. 1062 (1963).
80. 277 U.S. 438, 471 (1928).
81. It might be noted in passing that Dean Prosser's analysis of privacy neglects this phase of Brandeis' thinking on the subject.

It is apparent from Brandeis' dissent that, in the almost forty years which had passed since he had written his article on privacy, he had become as concerned about the evils of unbridled intrusion upon private affairs as he had once been about the evils of unreasonable publicity concerning private affairs. He had also begun to look upon the evils of wiretapping, eavesdropping and the like in the same perspective in which he regarded those attendant upon lurid journalistic exposés of private life.

Modesty seems to have kept him from citing his article, but he nevertheless "lifts" phrases out of it almost verbatim,[82] and the underlying conceptual scheme is identical. The article was written to thwart threats posed to privacy by "recent inventions and business methods,"[83] by "numerous mechanical devices";[84] the dissent is directed against "far-reaching means of invading privacy"[85] occasioned by "discovery and invention."[86] The article seeks to move the common law in the direction of protecting "man's spiritual nature,"[87] in the direction of recognizing "thoughts, emotions and sensations"[88] as objects of legal protection; the dissent attempts to enlarge the sphere of constitutionally protected liberty so as to encompass "man's spiritual nature," and so as "to protect Americans in their beliefs, their thoughts, their emotions and their sensations."[89]

The parallelism between the privacy article and the *Olmstead*

---

82. E.g., compare, "Discovery and invention have made it possible for the Government, by means far more effective than stretching upon the rack, to obtain disclosure in court of *what is whispered in the closet*," 277 U.S. at 473, with "numerous mechanical devices threaten to make good the prediction that '*what is whispered in the closet*' shall be proclaimed from the housetops." Warren & Brandeis 195. (Emphasis added.) Also compare

> The makers of our Constitution . . . *recognized* the significance of *man's spiritual nature, of his feelings and of his intellect.* They knew that *only part of the pain, pleasure and satisfactions of life are to be found in material things.* They sought to *protect Americans in their beliefs, their thoughts, their emotions and their sensations,*

277 U.S. at 478, with

> Later, there came a recognition [in the law] of *man's spiritual nature, of his feelings and his intellect* . . . . [It was] made . . . clear to men that *only part of the pain, pleasure and profit of life lay in physical things. Thoughts, emotions, and sensations demanded legal recognition* . . . . The common law *secures to each individual the right of determining, ordinarily, to what extent his thoughts, sentiments, and emotions shall be communicated to others.*

Warren & Brandeis 193, 195, 198. (Emphasis added.)
83. Warren & Brandeis 195.
84. Ibid.
85. 277 U.S. at 473.
86. Ibid.
87. Warren & Brandeis 193.
88. Id. at 195.
89. 277 U.S. at 478.

dissent is so close as to suggest strongly that Brandeis believed, at the time he wrote his dissent, that the fourth amendment was intended to protect the very principle of "inviolate personality" which he had earlier suggested was the principle underlying the common law right to privacy.[90] More recently, Justice Murphy of the Supreme Court has made this conceptual identification explicit. In his dissent in the *Goldman* case, he said that the "right of personal privacy [is] guaranteed by the Fourth Amendment" and in describing the right he relied upon the Warren-Brandeis article, as well as numerous tort cases.[91] The dissents of Brandeis and Murphy—and it should be noted that in each of these cases the Court divided over the scope of the protection of the fourth amendment rather than the analysis of the social value it embodies—provide authoritative support for believing that the social interest underlying the "intrusion cases" is that of liberty of the person, the same interest protected by the fourth amendment.

C.   The Public Disclosure Cases

The second group of privacy cases to which Dean Prosser addresses himself is that in which there is a public disclosure of facts concerning a person's private life.[92] Typically, these cases involve a newspaper story, a film, or a magazine article about some aspect of a person's private life. Two of the leading cases are *Melvin v. Reid*[93] and *Sidis v. F-R Publishing Corp.*[94] In the former case, the defendant had made a motion picture using the plaintiff's maiden name and depicting her as a prostitute who had been involved in a sensational murder trial. The scandalous and sensational behavior shown in the film took place many years before it was made and, when the picture was released, the plaintiff was living a conventionally respectable life. The California court upheld a cause of action for the violation of the plaintiff's right to privacy, relying upon the Warren-Brandeis article and upon a provision of the California constitution guaranteeing the "inalienable rights" of "enjoying and defending life and liberty; acquiring, possessing, and protecting property; and pursuing and obtaining safety and happiness."[95]

In the *Sidis* case, the New Yorker magazine had published

---

90. Ibid.
91. 316 U.S. at 136-37. It should be noted that Justice Murphy cites so-called "intrusion cases," "public disclosure cases," and "appropriation cases," as defining the right protected by the fourth amendment, without distinguishing between them conceptually.
92. See cases cited in Prosser, Privacy 392-93 nn.83-89.
93. 112 Cal. App. 285, 297 Pac. 91 (Dist. Ct. App. 1931).
94. 113 F.2d 806 (2d Cir. 1940).
95. 112 Cal. App. at 291, 297 Pac. at 93.

a "profile" of a young man who, years before, had been an infant prodigy, well known to the public, but who, at the time of the article, had retired of his own will and desire into a life of obscurity and seclusion. The article, although true and not unfriendly, was "merciless in its dissection of intimate details of its subject's personal life"[96] and the court plainly indicated that Sidis' privacy had been invaded.[97] Recovery was nevertheless denied. Relying on a suggestion in the Warren-Brandeis article that "the interest of the individual in privacy must inevitably conflict with the interest of the public in news," the court concluded that, since Sidis was a "public figure," the "inevitable conflict" had to be resolved in favor of the public interest in news.[98]

After discussing *Melvin v. Reid,* the *Sidis* case and dozens of others like them, Dean Prosser concludes that "this branch of the tort is evidently something quite distinct from intrusion" and that the interest protected in these cases "is that of reputation."[99] As I have shown above, this analysis is completely at odds with that of Warren and Brandeis.[100] It is also, I believe, at odds with the cases.

What Warren and Brandeis urged, even before the decision of any of the public disclosure cases, about the differences between privacy and defamation makes eminent good sense in the light of the cases themselves,[101] and Dean Prosser nowhere attempts to meet it. The public disclosure cases rest on a "radically different principle" than the defamation cases because the former class of cases involves an affront to "inviolate personality" while the latter class of cases involves an impairment of reputation.[102] Moreover, the one class of cases rests on unreasonable publicity, the other on falsity. The right to privacy exists not only "to prevent inaccurate portrayal of private life, but to prevent its being depicted at all."[103]

To be sure, *Melvin v. Reid*[104] and many other of the cases of this type contain express allegations of loss of reputation, of being exposed to public contempt, obloquy, ridicule and scorn

---

96. 113 F.2d at 807.
97. Id. at 811.
98. Id. at 809.
99. Prosser, Privacy 398, 422.
100. See text accompanying notes 30-34 supra.
101. This is not accidental, of course, since most, if not all, of these cases rely on Warren and Brandeis' analysis.
102. Warren & Brandeis 197; cf. Themo v. New England Newspaper Publishing Co., 306 Mass. 54, 27 N.E.2d 753 (1940).
103. Warren & Brandeis 218.
104. 112 Cal. App. 285, 297 Pac. 91 (Dist. Ct. App. 1931).

as a result of the public disclosure. To my mind, however, such allegations are only incidental to the real wrong complained of, which is the intrusion on privacy, and this wrong, as the *Sidis* case[105] makes apparent, is made out even if the public takes a sympathetic rather than a hostile view of the facts disclosed. What the plaintiffs in these cases complain of is not that the public has been led to adopt a certain attitude or opinion concerning them—whether true or false, hostile or friendly—but rather that some aspect of their life has been held up to public scrutiny at all. In this sense, the gravamen of the complaint here is just like that in the intrusion cases; in effect, the publicity constitutes a form of intrusion, it is as if 100,000 people were suddenly peering in, as through a window, on one's private life.

When a newspaper publishes a picture of a newborn deformed child,[106] its parents are not disturbed about any possible loss of reputation as a result. They are rather mortified and insulted that the world should be witness to their private tragedy. The hospital and the newspaper have no right to intrude in this manner upon a private life. Similarly, when an author does a sympathetic but intimately detailed sketch of someone, who up to that time had only been a face in the crowd,[107] the cause for complaint is not loss of reputation but that a reputation was established at all. The wrong is in replacing personal anonymity by notoriety, in turning a private life into a public spectacle.

The cases in which undue publicity was given to a debt[108] and in which medical pictures were published[109] are founded on a similar wrong. The complaint is not that people will take a different attitude towards the plaintiff because he owes a debt or has some medical deformity—although they might do so—but rather that publicity concerning these facets of private life represents an imposition upon and an affront to the plaintiff's human dignity.

The essential difference between the cause of action for invasion of privacy by public disclosures and that for defamation is exhibited forcefully by examining how the fact of publication fits into each of the actions. In defamation, publication to

---

105. 113 F.2d 806 (2d Cir. 1940).
106. Bazemore v. Savannah Hosp., 171 Ga. 257, 155 S.E. 194 (1930); Douglas v. Stokes, 149 Ky. 506, 149 S.W. 849 (1912).
107. Cason v. Baskin, 155 Fla. 198, 20 So. 2d 243 (1944).
108. Trammell v. Citizen's News Co., 285 Ky. 529, 148 S.W.2d 708 (1941); Brederman's of Springfield, Inc. v. Wright, 322 S.W.2d 892 (Mo. 1941).
109. Banks v. King Features Syndicate, 30 F. Supp. 353 (S.D.N.Y. 1939); Feeney v. Young, 191 App. Div. 501, 181 N.Y. Supp. 481 (2d Dep't 1920); Griffin v. Medical Soc'y, 11 N.Y.S.2d 109 (Sup. Ct. 1939).

even one person is sufficient to make out the wrong.[110] In privacy, unless the information was gained by wrongful prying or unless its communication involves a breach of confidence or the violation of an independent duty, some form of mass publication is a requisite of the action. As Dean Prosser himself points out, citing cases in support,

> It is an invasion of the right [of privacy] to publish in a newspaper that the plaintiff does not pay his debts, or to post a notice to that effect in a window on the public street or cry it aloud in the highway; but except for one decision of a lower Georgia court which was reversed on other grounds, it has been agreed that it is no invasion to communicate that fact to the plaintiff's employer, or to any other individual, or even to a small group, unless there is is some breach of contract, trust or confidential relation which will afford an independent basis for relief.[111]

What at first seem like exceptions to the requirement of mass publication in privacy are easily explained. Where private information is wrongfully gained and subsequently communicated, the wrong is made out independently of the communication. Communication in such a case, whether to one person or many, is not of the essence of the wrong and only goes to enhance damages. This, then, is not an exception to the rule of mass communication at all. Where, however, a person chooses to give another information of a personal nature on the understanding it will be held private and the confidence is broken, publication is indeed a requisite of recovery and even limited publication is sufficient to support the action. But the wrong here is not the disclosure itself, but rather the disclosure in violation of a relationship of confidence. Disclosure, whether to one person or many, is equally wrongful as a breach of the condition under which the information was initially disclosed.

It is in cases where public disclosure of personal and intimate facts is made without any breach of confidence that the rule of mass disclosure applies in full force. Why should it make a difference in such cases—other than in the amount of damages recoverable, as it does in defamation actions—whether a statement is published to one or many? Why should it make a difference in determining if an invasion of privacy is made out whether I tell a man's employer he owes me money or whether I shout it from the rooftops? In defamation, a statement is either actionable or not depending upon its subject matter and irrespective of the extent of publication. Why should actionability in privacy sometimes depend upon the extent of publication?

---

110. Prosser, Torts 597 (2d ed. 1955).
111. Prosser, Privacy 393-94.

The reason is simply that defamation is founded on loss of reputation while the invasion of privacy is founded on an insult to individuality. A person's reputation may be damaged in the minds of one man or many. Unless there is a breach of a confidential relationship, however, the indignity and outrage involved in disclosure of details of a private life, only arise when there is a massive disclosure, only when there is truly a disclosure to the public.

If a woman who had always lived a life of rectitude were called a prostitute, she could succeed in defamation even if the charge had been made to only one individual. The loss of the respect of that single individual is the wrong complained of. However, absent a breach of confidentiality, if a respectable woman who had once been a prostitute was described as such to a single friend or small group of friends, no cause of action would lie, no matter how radically her friends' opinions changed as a result. The wrong in the public disclosure cases is not in changing the opinions of others, but in having facts about private life made public. The damage is to an individual's self-respect in being made a public spectacle.

The gravamen of a defamation action is engendering a false opinion about a person, whether in the mind of one other person or many people. The gravamen in the public disclosure cases is degrading a person by laying his life open to public view. In defamation a man is robbed of his reputation; in the public disclosure cases it is his individuality which is lost.

It is admitted that no court has expressed such a view of the series of cases Dean Prosser identifies as public disclosure cases.[112] But then no court has adopted Dean Prosser's view of these cases either. The analysis I offer is, however—as I showed above—suggested by the Warren-Brandeis article.[113] Moreover, it finds support in the fact that *Melvin v. Reid*, one of the leading cases of this type, relied upon a constitutional provision guaranteeing life, liberty and happiness.[114] Even if this suggestion of a constitutional conceptual basis for privacy is considered "vague,"[115] it nevertheless points away from reputation and

112. But see the discussion of Pavesich v. New England Life Ins. Co., 122 Ga. 190, 50 S.E. 68 (1905) in text accompanying notes 130-33 infra.

113. See text accompanying notes 53-54 supra.

114. 112 Cal. App. 285, 291, 297 Pac. 91, 93 (Dist. Ct. App. 1931).

115. Dean Prosser states that reliance on this "vague constitutional provision . . . has since disappeared from the California cases." Prosser, Privacy 392-93. The suggestion of a constitutional ground for the privacy cases was reaffirmed by the California District Court of Appeals in Gill v. Curtis Publishing Co., 231 P.2d 565 (Dist. Ct. App. 1951), twenty years after Melvin v. Reid, supra note 114, was decided. But in the opinion of the California Supreme Court in the same case

towards personal dignity and integrity as the gist of the wrong.

Further support for this analysis of the public disclosure cases is found in the fact that it brings these cases into the same framework of theory as the intrusion cases. Many of the intrusion cases rely upon the authority of the public disclosure cases and vice versa.[116] If Dean Prosser were correct, such reliance would be mistaken or, at the least, misleading. All else being equal, a theory of the intrusion and public disclosure cases which explains their interdependence and provides a single rationale for them is, I suggest, to be preferred. Physical intrusion upon a private life and publicity concerning intimate affairs are simply two different ways of affronting individuality and human dignity. The difference is only in the means used to threaten the protected interest.

Consider the childbirth situation involved in the *De May* case,[117] discussed above. The cause of action there, it will be recalled, was based upon the defendant's having been an unwanted and unauthorized spectator to the plaintiff's birth pangs. To the Michigan court, this was a defilement of what was "sacred."[118] But the same sense of outrage, of defilement of what was "sacred," would have ensued if the defendant had been authorized to witness the birth of the plaintiff's child and had subsequently described the scene in detail in the public press. An unwanted report in a newspaper of the delivery room scene, including the cries of anguish and delight, the sometimes abusive, sometimes profane, sometimes loving comments voiced under sedation and the myriad other intimacies of childbirth, would be an insult and an affront of the same kind as an unauthorized physical intrusion upon the scene. The publicity would constitute the same sort of blow to our moral sensibility as the intrusion.

The parallelism which can be constructed in the *De May* case cannot be constructed in all of the intrusion and publicity cases. Sometimes public disclosure of what is seen or overheard can be offensive and, perhaps, actionable even though the intrusion itself may not be, as, for example, where a reporter "crashes" a private social gathering. Sometimes the details of private life which are publicly reported are not subject to being seen or over-

---

six months later, no mention is made of the constitutional basis of the right. Gill v. Curtis Publishing Co., 38 Cal. 2d 273, 239 P.2d 630 (1952).

116. See, e.g., McDaniel v. Atlanta Coca-Cola Bottling Co., 60 Ga. App. 92, 2 S.E.2d 810 (1939); Pritchett v. Board of Comm'rs, 42 Ind. App. 3, 85 N.E. 32 (1908); Rhodes v. Graham, 238 Ky. 225, 37 S.W.2d 46 (1931); Roach v. Harper, 143 W. Va. 869, 105 S.E.2d 564 (1958).

117. 46 Mich. 160, 9 N.W. 146 (1881).

118. Id. at 165, 9 N.W. at 149.

heard in a secret or unauthorized fashion at all, as in the case of a debt or a sordid detail of someone's past which is recorded in a public record. However, the fact that public disclosure of information might be actionable even though gaining the information by physical intrusion might not be, or vice versa, is not a ground for believing that the interest protected in each instance is different. The only thing it proves is that publicity concerning personal affairs and physical intrusions upon private life may each be the cause of personal indignity and degradation in ways the other cannot.

The underlying identity of interest in these two branches of the tort was lost sight of, I would suggest, because menacing technological means for intruding upon privacy developed at a later period than threatening forms of public disclosure. Lurid journalism became a fact of American life before the "private eye," the "bug" and the "wiretap." At the time Warren and Brandeis wrote, the common neighborhood snoop was not a sufficient cause for public concern to arouse their interest and the uncommon snoop who uses electronic devices had not yet made his appearance. This possibly explains why their article neglects the three earliest forms of protection against physical intrusions upon privacy, the action in trespass quare clausum fregit, "peeping tom" statutes[119] and the fourth amendment.[120] However, by the time Brandeis wrote his dissent in the *Olmstead* case,[121] involving a telephone wiretap, the technology of intrusion had developed to the point where he saw that it presented the same threat to individuality as did lurid journalism. As I have already indicated,[122] Brandeis then drew the necessary consequences for his theory of privacy.

Another aspect of our social history which teaches us something about the gravamen of the public disclosure cases is that Warren and Brandeis did not write their article until 1890, when the American metropolitan press had turned to new forms of sensational reporting and when the social pattern of American life had begun to be set by the mores of the metropolis instead of the small town. A number of writers have recently pointed out that gossip about the private affairs of others is surely as old as human society and that the small town gossip spread the

---

119. See, e.g., La. Rev. Stat. Ann. § 14:284 (1950); N.Y. Pen. Law § 721; Bishop, Criminal Law §§ 1122-24 (9th ed. 1923); 4 Blackstone, Commentaries § 168(6) (Cooley ed. 1889); Wharton, Criminal Law and Procedure § 1718 (12th ed. 1932).

120. See notes 72-91 supra and accompanying text.

121. See note 72 supra.

122. See text accompanying notes 80-89 supra.

intimacies of one's life with the same energy, skill and enthusiasm as the highest paid reporter of the metropolitan press.[123] Why then did it take "recent inventions" and "numerous mechanical devices," the advent of yellow journalism where "gossip . . . has become a trade,"[124] to awaken Warren and Brandeis to the need for the right to privacy?

Although the distinction should not be drawn too sharply— the mythology of ruralism is already too deeply embedded—the small town gossip did not begin to touch human pride and dignity in the way metropolitan newspaper gossip mongering does. Resources of isolation, retribution, retraction and correction were very often available against the gossip but are not available to anywhere near the same degree, against the newspaper report. The whispered word over a back fence had a kind of human touch and softness while newsprint is cold and impersonal. Gossip arose and circulated among neighbors, some of whom would know and love or sympathize with the person talked about. Moreover, there was a degree of mutual interdependence among neighbors which generated tolerance and tended to mitigate the harshness of the whispered disclosure.

Because of this context of transmission, small town gossip about private lives was often liable to be discounted, softened and put aside. A newspaper report, however, is spread abroad as part of a commercial enterprise among masses of people unknown to the subject of the report and on this account it assumes an imperious and unyielding influence. Finally, for all of these reasons and others as well, the gossip was never quite believed or was grudgingly and surreptitiously believed, while the newspaper tends to be treated as the very fount of truth and authenticity, and tends to command open and unquestioning recogniton of what it reports.

Thus, only with the emergence of newspapers and other mass means of communication did degradation of personality by the public disclosure of private intimacies become a legally significant reality. The right to sue for defamation has ancient origins because reputation could be put in peril by simple word of mouth or turn of the pen. The right to privacy in the form we know it, however, had to await the advent of the urbanization of our way of life including, as an instance, the institutionalization of mass publicity, because only then was a significant and everyday threat to personal dignity and individuality realized.

---

123. Hicks, The Limits of Privacy, The American Scholar, Spring, 1959, p. 185; Ruebhausen, Book Review, N.Y.L.J. Vol. 151, No. 106, p. 4 (May 29, 1964).
124. Warren & Brandeis 195-96.

D. *The Use of Name or Likeness*

The third "distinct tort" involving a "distinct interest" which Dean Prosser isolates turns on the commercial exploitation of a person's name or likeness.[125] This group of cases is designed, he says, to protect an interest which "is not so much a mental as a proprietary one, in the exclusive use of the plaintiff's name and likeness as an aspect of identity."[126]

In 1902, a flour company circulated Abigail Roberson's photograph, without her consent, as part of an advertising flier and, as a result, she was "greatly humiliated by the scoffs and jeers of persons who recognized her face and picture . . . and her good name had been attacked, causing her great distress and suffering in body and mind."[127] The New York Court of Appeals, in a 4 to 3 decision, refused recovery because they could find no legal precedent for Warren and Brandeis' right to privacy, on which Abigail relied.[128] To succeed, the majority indicated, the plaintiff in such a case had to prove either "a breach of trust or that plaintiff had a property right in the subject of litigation which the court could protect,"[129] and here the plaintiff could show neither.

Three years after the *Roberson* case was decided the same issue came before the Georgia Supreme Court which reached the opposite result. In *Pavesich v. New England Life Ins. Co.*,[130] the plaintiff's photograph was used, without his consent, in a newspaper advertisement for life insurance, which proclaimed to the world that Pavesich had bought life insurance and was the better man for it. There was no suggestion in the case that the plaintiff sought to vindicate a proprietary interest, that he sought recompense for the commercial value of the use of his name; since he was not well known, the use of his name or picture could hardly command even a fraction of the cost of the lawsuit. Nor did Pavesich claim, as the plaintiff in the *Roberson* case did, that he suffered severe nervous shock as a result of the publication.

The basis of recovery in the case was rather "a trespass upon Pavesich's right of privacy."[131] Relying heavily on the

---

125. Illustrative cases are set out in Prosser, Privacy 401-06.
126. Prosser, Privacy 406.
127. Roberson v. Rochester Folding Box Co., 171 N.Y. 538, 542-43, 64 N.E. 442, 448 (1902) (dissenting opinion).
128. Id. at 543, 64 N.E. at 443.
129. Id. at 550, 64 N.E. at 445.
130. 122 Ga. 190, 50 S.E. 68 (1905).
131. Id. at 222, 50 S.E. at 81. Actually, the case could have been decided, but was not, on the narrow ground that the publication involved a breach of trust by one Adams, a photographer who had taken Pavesich's picture.

Warren-Brandeis article, the Georgia court recognized the right as derivative of natural law and "guaranteed . . . by the constitutions of the United States and State of Georgia, in those provisions which declare that no person shall be deprived of liberty except by due process of law."[132] The use of the photograph, declared the court, was an "outrage":

> The knowledge that one's features and form are being used for such a purpose and displayed in such places as such advertisements are often liable to be found brings not only the person of an extremely sensitive nature, but even the individual of ordinary sensibility, to a realization that his liberty has been taken away from him, and as long as the advertiser uses him for these purposes, he cannot be otherwise than conscious of the fact that he is, for the time being, under the control of another, and that he is no longer free, and that he is in reality a slave without hope of freedom, held to service by a merciless master; and if a man of true instincts, or even of ordinary sensibilities, no one can be more conscious of his complete enthrallment than he is.[133]

The *Pavesich* case has probably been cited more often than any other case in the history of the development of the right to privacy, and it has been cited not only in cases involving use of name or likeness but also in the so-called intrusion cases[134] and the public disclosure cases.[135] To my mind, *Pavesich* and the other use of name or likeness cases are no different in the interest they seek to protect than the intrusion and public disclosure cases. That interest is not, as Dean Prosser suggests,[136] a "proprietary one," but rather the interest in preserving individual dignity.

The use of a personal photograph or a name for advertising purposes has the same tendency to degrade and humiliate as has publishing details of personal life to the world at large; in the *Pavesich* court's words, the use of a photograph for commercial purposes brings a man "to a realization that his liberty has been taken away from him" and "that he is no longer free."[137] Thus, a young girl whose photograph was used to promote the sale of dog food complained of "humiliation," "loss of respect and admiration" and co-incident "mental anguish," and the Illinois court which upheld her cause of action cited the Illinois constitutional guarantee of life, liberty and pursuit of happiness as

---

132. Id. at 197, 50 S.E. at 71.
133. Id. at 220, 50 S.E. at 80.
134. See note 116 supra.
135. See, e.g., Bazemore v. Savannah Hosp., 117 Ga. 257, 155 S.E. 194 (1930); Brents v. Morgan, 221 Ky. 765, 299 S.W. 967 (1927); Housch v. Peth, 165 Ohio St. 35, 133 N.E.2d 340 (1956).
136. Prosser, Privacy 406.
137. Pavesich v. New England Life Ins. Co., 122 Ga. 190, 220, 50 S.E. 68, 80 (1905).

the basis of recovery.[138] Similarly, where a lawyer's name was used for the purposes of advertising photocopy equipment,[139] where a young woman's picture in a bathing suit was used to advertise a slimming product,[140] or where the plaintiff's photograph was used to advertise Doan's pills,[141] the wrong complained of was mortification, humiliation and degradation rather than any pecuniary or property loss.

The only difference between these cases and the public disclosure cases is the fact that the sense of personal affront and indignity is provoked by the association of name or likeness with a commercial product rather than by publicity concerning intimacies of personal life. In the public disclosure cases what is demeaning to individuality is being made a public spectacle by disclosure of private intimacies. In these cases what is demeaning and humiliating is the commercialization of an aspect of personality.

One possible cause for confusion concerning the interest which underlies these cases is that the use of name or likeness is held to be actionable in many of the cases precisely because it is a use for commercial or trade purposes. This seems to suggest that the value or interest threatened is a proprietary or commercial one. Such a conclusion is mistaken, however, because, in the first place, as I noted above, the name or likeness which is used in most instances has no true commercial value, or it has a value which is only nominal and hardly worth the lawsuit. In fact, it has been held that general rather than special damages are recoverable and this, in itself, is a refutation of the conclusion that the interest concerned is a proprietary one.[142]

In the second place, the conclusion that the plaintiff seeks to vindicate a proprietary right in these cases overlooks the true role of the allegation that the plaintiff's name or picture was used commercially. The reason that the commercial use of a personal photograph is actionable, while—under many circumstances, such as where consent to publication is implied from the fact the photograph was taken in a public place—the use

138.   Eick v. Perk Dog Food Co., 347 Ill. App. 293, 106 N.E.2d 742 (1952).
139.   Fairfield v. American Photocopy Equip. Co., 138 Cal. App. 2d 82, 291 P.2d 194 (Dist. Ct. App. 1955).
140.   Flake v. Greensboro News Co., 212 N.C. 780, 195 S.E. 55 (1938).
141.   Foster-Milburn Co. v. Chinn, 134 Ky. 424, 120 S.W. 364 (1909).
142.   See, e.g., Fairfield v. American Photocopy Equip. Co., 138 Cal. App. 2d 82, 291 P.2d 194 (Dist. Ct. App. 1955); Eick v. Perk Dog Food Co., 347 Ill. App. 293, 106 N.E.2d 742 (1952); Kunz v. Allen, 102 Kan. 883, 172 Pac. 532 (1918); Foster-Milburn Co. v. Chinn, supra note 141; Munden v. Harris, 153 Mo. App. 652, 134 S.W. 1076 (1911); Flake v. Greensboro News Co., 212 N.C. 780, 195 S.E. 55 (1938); State ex rel. La Follette v. Hinkle, 131 Wash. 86, 229 Pac. 317 (1924).

of the same photograph in a news story would not be,[143] is that it is the very commercialization of a name or photograph which does injury to the sense of personal dignity. As one court has stated, "the right protected is the right to be protected against the commercial exploitation of one's personality."[144]

No man wants to be "used" by another against his will, and it is for this reason that commercial use of a personal photograph is obnoxious. Use of a photograph for trade purposes turns a man into a commodity and makes him serve the economic needs and interest of others. In a community at all sensitive to the commercialization of human values, it is degrading to thus make a man part of commerce against his will.[145]

Another reason which has possibly led Dean Prosser and others[146] to the conclusion that the interest involved in the use of name or likeness cases is a proprietary one, is that in some few of the cases,[147] the plaintiffs are well known figures whose name or photograph does indeed command a commercial price. In these cases, as Judge Frank has pointed out, the plaintiffs, "far from having their feelings bruised through public exposure of their likenesses, would feel sorely deprived if they no longer received money for authorizing advertisements, popularizing their countenances, displayed in newspapers, magazines, busses, trains and subways."[148]

The conclusion to be drawn from such cases, however, is

---

143. See, e.g., Berg v. Minneapolis Star & Tribune Co., 79 F. Supp. 957 (D. Minn. 1948); Gill v. Hearst Publishing Co., 40 Cal. 2d 224, 253 P.2d 441 (1953); Lyles v. State, 330 P.2d 734 (Okla. Crim. 1958).

144. Hill v. Hayes, 18 App. Div. 2d 485, 488, 240 N.Y.S.2d 286, 290 (1st Dep't 1963). See also Birmingham Broadcasting Co. v. Bell, 266 Ala. 266, 96 So. 2d 263 (1957); Gautier v. Pro-Football, 304 N.Y. 354, 358, 107 N.E.2d 485, 487-88 (1952); Spahn v. Messner, Inc., 43 Misc. 2d 219, 226, 250 N.Y.S.2d 529, 537 (Sup. Ct. 1964).

145. Dean Wade, in Virginia Law Weekly Dicta, Oct. 8, 1964, p. 1, col. 1, has suggested that these appropriation cases really involve "an action for unjust enrichment which the defendant has wrongfully obtained." This view was presented and rejected in Birmingham Broadcasting Co. v. Bell, 259 Ala. 656, 661, 68 So. 2d 314, 319 (1953), on the ground that commercial use of name or likeness did not fit any of the well-defined categories of recovery in quasi-contract. Moreover, the measure of recovery in the cases is not "what defendant may have gained, nor what plaintiff may have lost, but the recovery is as for other forms of tort." Id. at 662, 68 So. 2d at 320.

146. See, e.g., Nimmer, The Right of Publicity, 19 Law & Contemp. Prob. 203 (1954); Note, 62 Yale L.J. 1123 (1953).

147. Uproar Co. v. National Broadcasting Co., 8 F. Supp. 358 (D. Mass. 1934); Birmingham Broadcasting Co. v. Bell, 259 Ala. 656, 68 So. 2d 314 (1953); cf. Haelan Labs., Inc. v. Topps Chewing Gum, Inc., 202 F.2d 866 (2d Cir.), cert. denied, 346 U.S. 816 (1953); Gautier v. Pro-Football, Inc., 304 N.Y. 354, 107 N.E.2d 485 (1952) (Desmond, J. concurring); Spahn v. Messner, Inc., 43 Misc. 2d 219, 226, 250 N.Y.S.2d 529, 537 (Sup. Ct. 1964).

148. Haelan Labs., Inc. v. Topps Chewing Gum, Inc., supra note 147, at 868; Gautier v. Pro-Football, Inc., supra note 147, at 361, 107 N.E.2d at 489.

simply that, under special circumstances, as where the plaintiff is a public figure, the use of his likeness or name for commercial purposes involves the appropriation of a thing of value. But it is important to note that, in this respect, such cases are distinguishable from cases like *Pavesich*[149] and *Eick*,[150] for instance, where the plaintiff had no public renown. In other words, the use of name or likeness only involves an appropriation of a thing of value in a limited class of cases where the plaintiff is known to the public and where his name or likeness commands a price.

Some have said that in such cases a "right of publicity" rather than a right of privacy is involved.[151] It is a mistake, however, to conclude from these "right of publicity" cases that all the cases involving commercial use of name or likeness are founded on a proprietary interest.[152] Moreover, the very characterization of these cases as involving a "right to publicity" disguises the important fact that name and likeness can only begin to command a commercial price in a society which recognizes that there is a right to privacy, a right to control the conditions under which name and likeness may be used. Property becomes a commodity subject to be bought and sold only where the community will enforce an individual's right to maintain use and possession of it as against the world. Similarly, unless an individual has a right to prevent another from using his name or likeness commercially, even where the use of that name or likeness has no commercial value, no name or likeness could ever command a price.

Thus, there is really no "right to publicity"; there is only a right, under some circumstances, to command a commercial price for abandoning privacy. Every man has a right to prevent the commercial exploitation of his personality, not because of its commercial worth, but because it would be demeaning to human dignity to fail to enforce such a right. A price can be had in the market place by some men for abandoning it, however. If a commercial use is made of an aspect of the personality of such a man without his consent, he has indeed suffered a pecuniary loss, but the loss concerned is the price he could command for abandoning his right to privacy. The so-called "right to publicity" is merely a name for the price for which some men can sell their right to maintain their privacy.

---

149. See Pavesich v. New England Life Ins. Co., 122 Ga. 190, 50 S.E. 68 (1905).

150. See Eick v. Perk Dog Food Co., 347 Ill. App. 293, 106 N.E.2d 742 (1952).

151. See authorities cited supra note 146; cf. Haelan Labs., Inc. v. Topps Chewing Gum, Inc., 202 F.2d 866 (2d Cir. 1953).

152. See Prosser, Privacy 406-07.

Undoubtedly, there will be cases in which the publication of a name or likeness without consent is a boon and not a burden. Rather than suffering humiliation and degradation as a result, the beautiful but unknown girl pictured on the cover of a nationally circulated phonograph record might be delighted at having been transfigured into a modern Cinderella. Suddenly, she is a national figure, glowing in the limelight, and her picture and name have become sought after commodities as a result. Has privacy been violated when there is no personal sense of indignity and the commercial values of name or likeness have been enhanced rather than diminished?

I believe that in such a case there is an invasion of privacy, although it is obviously not one which will be sued on and not one which is liable to evoke community sympathy or command anything but a nominal jury award. The case is very much like one in which a physician successfully treats a patient but is held liable for the technical tort of battery because the treatment extended beyond the consent.[153] However beneficient the motive, or successful the result, the "touching" is considered wrongful. As I view the matter, using a person's name or likeness for a commercial purpose without consent is a wrongful exercise of dominion over another even though there is no subjective sense of having been wronged, even, in fact, if the wrong was subjectively appreciated, and even though a commercial profit might accrue as a result. This is so because the wrong involved is the objective diminution of personal freedom rather than the infliction of personal suffering or the misappropriation of property.

I agree with Dean Prosser that, in one sense, it is "quite pointless to dispute over whether such a right is to be classified as 'property' ";[154] as Warren and Brandeis long ago pointed out, there is a sense in which there inheres "in all . . . rights recognized by the law . . . the quality of being owned or possessed—and (as that is the distinguishing attribute of property) there may be some propriety in speaking of those rights as property."[155]

But in one sense it is very important, as Warren and Brandeis saw, to decide whether the right to damages for the commercial use of name or likeness is called a property right. The importance resides in finding the common ground between the use of name and likeness cases, the public disclosure cases and the intrusion cases. In Dean Prosser's view the interest vindi-

---

153. Cf. Mohr v. Williams, 95 Minn. 261, 263, 104 N.W. 12, 16 (1905); Prosser, Torts 83-84 (2d ed. 1955).
154. Prosser, Privacy 406.
155. Warren & Brandeis 205.

cated in each of these classes of cases is a different one. In my view the interest protected in each is the same, it is human dignity and individuality or, in Warren and Brandeis' words, "inviolate personality."

E. The "False Light" Cases

The fourth and final distinct group of cases which Dean Prosser identifies within the overall rubric of privacy are cases which he describes as involving "publicity falsely attributing to the plaintiff some opinion or utterance,"[156] cases in which "the plaintiff's picture [is used] to illustrate a book or an article with which he has no reasonable connection"[157] or in which "the plaintiff's name, photograph and fingerprints [are included] in a public 'rogues' gallery' of convicted criminals, when he has not in fact been convicted of any crime."[158] He says these cases all involve reputation and "obviously differ from those of intrusion, or disclosure of private facts [or appropriation]."[159]

I agree with Dean Prosser that all of these cases involve reputation, but I am persuaded, though he is not, that they also involve the assault on individual personality and dignity which is characteristic of all the other privacy cases. The slur on reputation is an aspect of the violation of individual integrity.

Two California cases in which Mr. and Mrs. Gill sued for damages illustrate the point. They were photographed embracing in their place of business and the photograph was used in two different articles in the public press on the subject of love. In one of the articles, the photograph was used to illustrate the "wrong kind of love" consisting "wholly of sexual attraction and nothing else." In the other article, the photograph was used without any particular portion of the text referring to it. The plaintiffs succeeded against the publisher who characterized their love as being of the "wrong kind,"[160] but their complaint was dismissed as against the other publisher.[161]

The use of a photograph taken in a public place and published without comment in a news article could not be considered offensive to personal dignity because consent to such a publication, to the abandonment of privacy, is implied from the fact the Gills embraced in public. Use of the same photograph ac-

---

156. Prosser, Privacy 398.
157. Id. at 399.
158. Ibid.
159. Id. at 400, 422-23.
160. Gill v. Curtis Publishing Co., 38 Cal. 2d 273, 239 P.2d 630 (1952).
161. Gill v. Hearst Publishing Co., 40 Cal. 2d 224, 253 P.2d 441 (1953). Leave to amend the complaint was granted.

companied by false and derogatory comment is another matter, however. Although the comment may not be defamatory and, therefore, not actionable as such, when combined with the public exploitation of the photograph, it turns the otherwise inoffensive publication into one which is an undue and unreasonable insult to personality. It is the combination of false and stigmatic comment on character with public exhibition of the photograph which constitutes the actionable wrong.

Publishing a photograph in a "false light" serves the same function in constituting the wrong as does a use of the photograph for advertising purposes. The picture of Mr. and Mrs. Gill embracing could no more be used to cast aspersions on the character of their love than it could be used to advertise the aphrodisiac effects of a perfume. In both instances, such publicity "violates the ordinary decencies"[162] and impinges on their right to maintain their identity as individuals. (Significantly, the California District Court of Appeals which upheld the Gills' action cited a section of the California constitution guaranteeing the right to pursue and gain happiness[163] which is almost identical to the section of the Georgia constitution cited in the *Pavesich* case,[164] involving an unauthorized use of a photograph for advertising purposes.)

The use of a name in a "false light" is actionable for the same reasons as the use of a name for a commercial purpose. The "false light" in which the name is used makes the use wrongful for the same reason that the use of the name for advertising purposes does. And, in fact, many of the cases which Dean Prosser cites as actionable for "falsely attributing to the plaintiff some opinion or utterance"[165]—including the leading *Pavesich* case[166]—are cases in which a name has been used for advertising purposes.

I suspect that the reason which leads Dean Prosser to distinguish the "false light" cases from the use of name and likeness cases is that, as I indicated above,[167] he mistakenly regards the latter group of cases as turning on a proprietary interest in name or likeness. If you believe the use for advertising purposes of a photograph of two ordinary people embracing is wrongful

---

162. Gill v. Curtis Publishing Co., 38 Cal. 2d 273, 239 P.2d 630 (1952).

163. Gill v. Curtis Publishing Co., 231 P.2d 565 (Dist. Ct. App. 1951). But see note 115 supra.

164. Pavesich v. New England Life Ins. Co., 122 Ga. 190, 203, 50 S.E. 68, 73 (1905).

165. Prosser, Privacy 398.

166. See note 112 supra.

167. See notes 136-52 supra and accompanying text.

because it violates their pecuniary interest in their name or likeness, you will regard the use of the same photograph in a "false
light"—illustrating a depraved kind of lovemaking, for instance—as involving a fundamentally different kind of wrong.
However, once it is recognized that the use of a name for advertising purposes is wrongful because it is an affront to personal
dignity,[168] the underlying similarity between the advertising and
"false light" cases becomes apparent. The "false light" and the
advertising use are merely two different means of publishing a
person's name or likeness so as to offend his dignity as an
individual.

There is a recent tendency in the law of defamation which
has extended the interest protected by that cause of action beyond
the traditional reaches of character to include aspects of personal
humiliation and degradation.[169] The cases pointing in this direction are those, for instance, in which recovery in libel has been
allowed to a man whose published photograph represented him
as grossly deformed[170] and in which recovery was allowed for
publishing a photograph of an English sports amateur so as to
suggest that he was commercially advertising chocolate.[171] These
cases, it has been said, "have made it possible to reach certain
indecent violations of privacy by means of the law of libel, on
the theory that any writing is a libel that discredits the plaintiff
in the minds of any considerable and respectable class in the
community though no wrongdoing or bad character is imputed
to him."[172]

This tendency in the law of defamation is consistent with,
is, in fact, the counterpart of, the growth of the "false light"
category of recovery in the law of privacy. It strongly suggests
that the law of privacy may provide a valuable avenue or development for the law of defamation.[173] In this sense, however, it
is the law of privacy which helps explain the defamation cases,
rather than vice versa, as Dean Prosser suggests.

IV

PRIVACY IN NON-TORT CONTEXTS

Besides introducing four principles to explain the tort cases
involving privacy where one will suffice, Dean Prosser's analysis

---

168. See text accompanying notes 137-41 supra.
169. See Wade, Defamation and the Right of Privacy, 15 Vand. L. Rev
1093 (1963).
170. Burton v. Crowell Publishing Co., 82 F.2d 154 (2d Cir. 1936).
171. Tolley v. J.S. Fry & Sons Ltd., [1931] A.C. 333.
172. Themo v. New England Publishing Co., 306 Mass. 54, 55, 27 N.E.2d
753, 754 (1940).
173. Wade, supra note 169, at 1094-95.

also has the unfortunate consequence that it makes impossible the reconciliation of privacy in tort and non-tort contexts. If privacy in tort is regarded as an amalgam of the infliction of emotional distress, defamation and misappropriation, it is impossible to find any common link between the tort cases and various forms of protection of privacy which are found in constitutions, statutes and common law rules which do not involve tort claims.

Actually, however, there is a common thread of principle and an identical interest or social value which runs through the tort cases as well as the other forms of legal protection of privacy. Thus, for instance, as I have already shown,[174] the fourth amendment to the federal constitution erects a barrier against unreasonable governmental entries into a man's home or searches of his person, and the Supreme Court has indicated on many occasions that this protection is of the very essence of constitutional liberty and security.[175] If the gravamen of intrusion as a tort is said to be the intentional infliction of emotional distress, the conceptual link between the tort and the fourth amendment is lost. But if the intrusion cases in tort are regarded as involving a blow to human dignity or an injury to personality, their relation to the constitutional protection of the fourth amendment becomes apparent.

The difference between the *De May* case,[176] involving an unauthorized witness to childbirth, and the *Silverman* case,[177] involving the use of a "spike" microphone in a criminal investigation to overhear a conversation in a home, is that the former involved an intrusion by a private person and a tort remedy was sought, while the latter involved an intrusion by a government agent and the remedy sought was the suppression of the use of the fruits of the intrusion. But the underlying wrong in both instances was the same; the act complained of was an affront to the individual's independence and freedom. A democratic state which values individual liberty can no more tolerate an intrusion on privacy by a private person than by an officer of government and the protections afforded in tort law, like those afforded under the Constitution, are designed to protect this same value.

A similar analysis may also be made of the public disclosure cases, the use of name or likeness cases and the "false light"

---

174. See text accompanying notes 72-91 supra.
175. See, e.g., Silverman v. United States, 365 U.S. 505 (1961), and cases cited in note 72 supra.
176. DeMay v. Roberts, 46 Mich. 160, 9 N.W. 146 (1881).
177. Silverman v. United States, 365 U.S. 505 (1961).

cases. In these cases the individual's dignity has been subject to challenge just as it was in the *Silverman* case, the *De May* case and the other intrusion cases. Respect for individual liberty not only commands protection against intruders into a person's home but also against making him a public spectacle by undue publicity concerning his private affairs or degrading him by commercializing his name or likeness or using it in a "false light." Each of these wrongs constitutes an intrusion on personality, an attack on human dignity.

It is true, of course, that the fourth amendment only protects against invasions of privacy perpetrated by state or federal officers.[178] This does not mean, however, that the wrong against which the amendment was erected is different from that which is involved where one private citizen intrudes upon another's home or subjects his person to an unwarranted search. Moreover, each state has a search and seizure provision comparable to that of the fourth amendment[179] and, in some states at least, it has been held that the provision applies to private persons.[180]

Thus, the protection which the fourth amendment secures against the enforcement of the criminal law by means of unreasonable searches and seizures involves the same underlying interest as that secured by the right of privacy in tort law. Although there are undoubtedly other considerations of policy involved in the fourth amendment cases,[181] they, like the tort cases, are intended to preserve individual dignity.

This same value is also enforced in numerous statutes which make intrusions on privacy a crime. The oldest of such are the so-called "peeping tom" statutes, which make it a misdemeanor to peer into the window of another's home.[182] The introduction of new means of "peeping," of electronic means of eavesdropping, has brought forth modern versions of the older "peeping tom" statutes. The Federal Communications Act makes it a crime to listen in to a telephone conversation without consent by tapping the telephone and subsequently disclosing what is heard.[183] And in New York, Illinois and Nevada it is a crime to eavesdrop "by

---

178. See note 79 supra.

179. Frankfurter, J., dissenting in Monroe v. Pape, 365 U.S. 167, 209 (1961), sets forth a complete list of these state search and seizure provisions.

180. See, e.g., Lebel v. Swincicki, 354 Mich. 427, 93 N.W.2d 281 (1958); Young v. Western & A.R. Co., 39 Ga. App. 761, 148 S.E. 414 (1929). But see Sutherland v. Kroger Co., 144 W. Va. 673, 683, 110 S.E.2d 716, 723 (1959).

181. One of them, at least, was mentioned by Brandeis in his dissent in the Olmstead case: "If government becomes a lawbreaker, it breeds contempt for law." 277 U.S. 438, 485 (1928).

182. See authorities cited supra note 119.

183. 48 Stat. 1103-04 (1934), 47 U.S.C. § 605 (1958).

means of instrument" on any conversation, telephonic or other-wise, or even to possess eavesdropping equipment.[184]

These statutes are obviously aimed at the same wrong against which the common law intrusion cases discussed above are directed.[185] Some of them provide for a civil remedy as well as a criminal penalty and thereby expressly enlarge the tort right to privacy.[186] Some courts have engrafted a civil remedy on the criminal prohibition, using the criminal statute—as is frequently done in the law of tort[187]—to define the wrong for which recompense in damages may be sought.[188]

Thus, for instance, in *Reitmaster v. Reitmaster*,[189] the defendants had violated the provisions against wiretapping in Section 605 of the Federal Communications Act and the plaintiff sued for damages. Although a jury verdict in favor of the defendant based on a finding of consent was affirmed, Judge Learned Hand, writing for the Second Circuit Court of Appeals, plainly indicated that a civil suit for damages would lie for a breach of section 605. He said:

> Although the Act does not expressly create any civil liability, we can see no reason why the situation is not within the doctrine which, in the absence of contrary implications, construes a criminal statute, enacted for the benefit of a specified class, as creating a civil right in members of the class, although the only express sanctions are criminal.[190]

Such judicial creation of a civil remedy on the basis of the criminal wrong of wiretapping or eavesdropping, read together with the eavesdropping statutes which expressly provide co-ordinate civil and criminal remedies,[191] proves the identity of interest behind the civil and criminal remedies. It also provides

---

184. See Ill. Stat. Ann. ch. 38, §§ 14-1 to 14-7 (1961); Nev. Rev. Stat. § 200.650 (1957); N.Y. Pen. Law § 738. It should be noted that, under the New York statutes, evidence gained by means of illegal eavesdropping is inadmissible in a civil suit. See N.Y.C.P.L.R. § 4506.
185. See note 116 supra and accompanying text.
186. Ill. Stat. Ann. ch. 38, §§ 14-1 to 14-7 (1961); cf. Pa. Stat. Ann. tit. 72, § 2443 (1958).
187. See, e.g., Martin v. Herzog, 228 N.Y. 164, 126 N.E. 814 (1920); Thayer, Public Wrong and Private Action, 27 Harv. L. Rev. 317 (1914).
188. See, e.g., Pugach v. Dollinger, 277 F.2d 739 (2d Cir. 1960), aff'd, 365 U.S. 458 (1961); Reitmaster v. Reitmaster, 162 F.2d 691 (2d Cir. 1947); United States v. Goldstein, 120 F.2d 485 (2d Cir. 1941); Newfield v. Ryan, 91 F.2d 700 (5th Cir. 1937); McDaniel v. Atlanta Coca-Cola Bottling Co., 60 Ga. App. 92, 2 S.E.2d 810 (1939); Sander v. Pendleton Detectives, 88 So. 2d 716 (La. Ct. App. 1956); cf. People v. Trieber, 163 P.2d 492 (Cal. Dist. Ct. App. 1945).
189. See note 188 supra.
190. Id. at 694.
191. See Ill. Stat. Ann. ch. 38, §§ 14-1 to 14-7 (1961); cf. Pa. Stat. Ann. tit. 72, § 2443 (1958).

an added reason for disputing Dean Prosser's contention[192] that the wrong in such intrusion cases is the intentional infliction of mental distress; if it were, the civil remedy would only be available on a showing of such distress, but, in fact, there is no such requirement. Finally, it should be noted that the theory expressed by Judge Hand in *Reitmaster* would provide an easy avenue for extending the civil right of privacy in New York, where it is a creature of a statute which limits recovery of damages to the use of name or likeness for purposes of trade or advertising.[193]

Another important class of statutes which are intended to protect against degradation of individuality are those which prohibit the disclosure of confidential information of various sorts. Thus, for instance, we are all required by law to divulge a great deal of information—of a personal as well as of a business nature—to the United States Government for the purpose of the census.[194] But all such information is made confidential by statute and unauthorized disclosure of it is a crime.[195] Although it is not as comprehensive, a similar prohibition against disclosure of data concerning personal lives and business affairs given for purposes of tax collection is to be found in the Internal Revenue Code.[196] And, in Title 18 of the United States Code, there is a broad prohibition, backed by criminal penalty, against disclosure by a federal officer of a wide range of confidential information concerning the operation of businesses.[197]

Similar statutes are to be found in state law. New York, for example, has a provision in its Public Officer's Law, which is not enforced by a criminal penalty, forbidding any public officer from disclosing confidential information acquired in the course of his official duties.[198] In the Penal Law, there are provisions making it a crime for an employee of a telegraph or telephone company to divulge information gained in the course of his employment.[199] In another section of the Penal Law, disclosure by an election officer or poll watcher of the name of the candidate for

---

192. See text accompanying note 63 supra.
193. See N.Y. Civ. Rights Law §§ 50-51 (1948). See also, e.g., Gautier v. Pro-Football, 304 N.Y. 354, 107 N.E.2d 485 (1952); Kimmerle v. New York Evening J., 262 N.Y. 99, 186 N.E. 217 (1933).
194. Census Act, 13 U.S.C. §§ 221-24 (1954); cf. Hearings on the "Confidentiality of Census Reports" Before the House Committee on Post Office and Civil Service, 87th Cong., 2d Sess. (1962).
195. Census Act, 13 U.S.C. §§ 8, 9, 214 (1954).
196. Fed. Tax Reg. § 301.6103(a) (1964).
197. 18 U.S.C. § 1905 (1948).
198. N.Y. Pub. Officers Law § 74.
199. N.Y. Pen. Law §§ 553, 554, 734(1).

whom a person has voted is made a misdemeanor.[200] In the Social
Welfare Law, publication of the names of people receiving or applying for public assistance is made a crime, and all information
obtained by and communications to a public welfare official, as
well as all records of abandoned or delinquent children, are made
confidential.[201]

The same pattern of protection is found in still other New
York statutes. Thus, the Correction Law contains provisions intended to preserve the confidential character of criminal identification records and statistics.[202] The General Business Law forbids an employee of a licensed private investigator to divulge
information gathered by his employer.[203] The Civil Rights Law
forbids the publication of testimony taken in private by certain
state investigative agencies.[204] And, finally, the Education Law
forbids soliciting, receiving or giving information concerning persons applying for vocational rehabilitation training.[205]

This brief survey of federal and New York State statutes
regulating disclosure of confidential information is not, of course,
intended to be exhaustive. My purpose is rather to demonstrate
by these statutes—and it should be noted that there are undoubtedly untold administrative regulations on the federal and
state level which have a similar purport—that the same impetus
which moved the common law courts to erect a civil cause of
action founded on public disclosure of aspects of private life[206]
also provoked action by the national and state legislatures intending to serve the same purpose.

Following Warren and Brandeis' lead, the common law
courts responded to the threat posed to privacy by lurid journalism and demeaning advertising. Legislatures have responded to
threats to personal dignity which were not yet manifest when
Warren and Brandeis wrote. It was only after the turn of the
century that the telephone and telegraph became instruments of
everyday life, used to confide personal intimacies and business
secrets. Unless some security could be found against people il-
licitly breaking in upon these private communications and divulging what was learned, an important area of private life would

---

200. N.Y. Pen. Law § 762.
201. N.Y. Soc. Welfare Law §§ 136, 372, 258(2). These provisions are evidently mandated by § 402(a)(8) of the federal Social Security Act. See Pennsyl-
vania Dep't of Pub. Assistance, People in Need 88-90 (1947).
202. N.Y. Correc. Law § 615, 616 (2i)(3).
203. N.Y. Gen. Bus. Law § 82.
204. N.Y. Civ. Rights Law § 73(8).
205. N.Y. Educ. Law § 1007.
206. See text accompanying notes 92-98 supra.

be subject to degrading public scrutiny, and public confidence in these instruments of communication would be destroyed. Section 605 of the Federal Communications Act[207] and various state statutes[208] were intended to prevent this consequence. Whether they were successful or not is, of course, another question.

Another avenue for impairing the privacy of our lives— again one which only became a cause for public concern after Warren and Brandeis wrote—was the increasing accumulation of information about each of us which finds its way into government records and files. Of course, the very fact that a government agency requires such information under the compulsion of law,[209] whether for the purposes of providing social welfare benefits, taking the census, or collecting taxes, is itself an intrusion upon our persons. Most of us have agreed, however, that the social benefits to be gained in these instances require the information to be given and that the ends to be achieved are worth the price of diminished privacy.

But this tacit agreement is founded upon an assumption that information given for one purpose will not be used for another.[210] We are prepared to tell the tax collector and the census taker what they need to know, but we are not prepared to have them make a public disclosure of what they have learned. The intrusion is tolerable only if public disclosure of the fruits of the intrusion is forbidden. This explains why many of the statutes which require us to tell something about ourselves to a government agency contain an express provision against disclosure of such information.[211] It also explains why there are general provisions prohibiting disclosure of information of a personal nature gained in an official capacity.[212] Again, I note that my purpose here is

---

207. 48 Stat. 1103-04 (1934), 47 U.S.C. § 605 (1958).

208. The earliest New York provisions, limited to telephone and telegraphic eavesdropping, were to be found in §§ 552-54 of the Penal Law. They have, for the most part, since been superseded by the broader provisions against eavesdropping cited in note 184 supra.

209. See, e.g., notes 181 & 188 supra.

210. This "condition" is stated very broadly for the purposes of my main argument. It should be noted, however, that, for instance, income tax information given to one federal agency is available, under certain conditions, to other governmental agencies and to state governments. 26 C.F.R. §§ 301.6103(a)-(1)(f) (1961), 301.6103(b) (1961), 301.6103(d). To what degree this is true of other government records is not known. A provocative case in this regard is St. Regis Paper Co. v. United States, 368 U.S. 208 (1961), in which the Supreme Court upheld the right of the Federal Trade Commission to subpoena a copy of a report submitted to the Census Bureau, even though the Commission was forbidden by statute to obtain the report directly from the Census Bureau.

211. See notes 195, 196, 201, & 205 supra.

212. See notes 197, 198, 200, 201, 202, & 204 supra.

not to comment upon the effectiveness of these anti-disclosure statutes; it is only to describe their broad aims.

The parallelism between the intrusion and the disclosure statutes, on the one hand, and the intrusion and disclosure tort cases, on the other, illuminates, I believe, the common conceptual character of privacy which runs through all of them. Intrusion and public disclosure are merely alternative forms of injury to individual freedom and dignity. The common law courts provide civil relief against turning a man's private life into a public spectacle as well as against impairing his private intimacies by intruding upon them.[213] Similarly, legislatures have been impelled to prevent both eavesdropping *and* divulgence[214] or, where the intrusion is socially sanctioned, as in the census and tax fields, disclosure for other than sanctioned purposes. The disclosure provisions of the statutes, like the tort disclosure cases, preserve dignity by restricting publicity, by assuring a man that his life is not the open and indiscriminate object of all eyes. And, as the comparable tort cases do in relation to the tort intrusion cases, the statutory disclosure provisions complement the statutory intrusion provisions by making a man secure in his person, not only against prying eyes and ears, but against the despair of being the subject of public scrutiny and knowledge.

V

CONCLUSION: THE INVASION OF PRIVACY AS AN AFFRONT TO HUMAN DIGNITY

Dean Prosser has described the privacy cases in tort as involving "not one tort, but a complex of four,"[215] as "four disparate torts under . . . [a] common name."[216] And he believes that the reason the state of the law of privacy is "still that of a haystack in a hurricane," as Chief Judge Biggs said in *Ettore v. Philco Television Broadcasting Co.*,[217] is that we have failed to "separate and distinguish" these four torts.[218]

I believe to the contrary that the tort cases involving privacy are of one piece and involve a single tort. Furthermore, I believe that a common thread of principle runs through the tort

---

213. See text accompanying notes 57-62, 92-98 supra.
214. The federal crime under § 605 of the Communications Act requires divulgence to make out any violation. Pugach v. Klein, 193 F. Supp. 630 (S.D.N.Y. 1961). The state prohibitions against eavesdropping are generally distinct from those against divulgence. See note 184 supra.
215. Prosser, Privacy 389.
216. Id. at 408.
217. 229 F.2d 481 (3d Cir. 1956).
218. Prosser, Privacy 407. See also notes 181 & 188 supra.

cases, the criminal cases involving the rule of exclusion under the fourth amendment, criminal statutes prohibiting peeping toms, wiretapping, eavesdropping, the possession of wiretapping and eavesdropping equipment, and criminal statutes or administrative regulations prohibiting the disclosure of confidential information obtained by government agencies.

The words we use to identify and describe basic human values are necessarily vague and ill-defined. Compounded of profound human hopes and longings on the one side and elusive aspects of human psychology and experience on the other, our social goals are more fit to be pronounced by prophets and poets than by professors. We are fortunate, then, that some of our judges enjoy a touch of the prophet's vision and the poet's tongue.

Before he ascended to the bench, Justice Brandeis had written that the principle which underlies the right to privacy was "that of an inviolate personality."[219] Some forty years later, in the *Olmstead* case,[220] alarmed by the appearance of new instruments of intrusion upon "inviolate personality," he defined the threatened interest more fully.

> The makers of our Constitution undertook to secure conditions favorable to the pursuit of happiness. They recognized the significance of man's spiritual nature, of his feeling and of his intellect. . . . They sought to protect Americans in their beliefs, their thoughts, their emotions and their sensations. They conferred as against the government, the right to be let alone—the most comprehensive of rights and the right most valued by civilized men.[221]

Other Justices of our Supreme Court have since repeated, elucidated and expanded upon this attempt to define privacy as an aspect of the pursuit of happiness.[222]

More obscure judges, writing in the more mundane context of tort law, have witnessed this same connection. In two of the leading cases in the field, *Melvin v. Reid*[223] and *Pavesich v. New England Life Ins. Co.*[224]—one a so-called public disclosure case, the other a so-called appropriation or "false light" case—the right to recovery was founded upon the state constitutional pro-

---

219. Warren & Brandeis 205.
220. Olmstead v. United States, 277 U.S. 438 (1928).
221. Id. at 478.
222. See, e.g., Poe v. Ullman, 367 U.S. 497, 522 (1961) (dissenting opinion of Harlan, J.); Public Util. Comm'n v. Pollak, 343 U.S. 451, 467 (1952) (dissenting opinion of Douglas, J.); Goldman v. United States, 316 U.S. 129, 136 (1942) (dissenting opinion of Murphy, J.).
223. 112 Cal. App. 285, 297 Pac. 91 (Dist. Ct. App. 1931).
224. 122 Ga. 190, 50 S.E. 68 (1905).

vision insuring the pursuit of happiness.[225] Judge Cobb, writing
in *Pavesich*, declared:

> An individual has a right to enjoy life in any way that may be
> most agreeable and pleasant to him, according to his temperament
> and nature, provided that in such enjoyment he does not invade
> the rights of his neighbor or violate public law or policy. The right
> of personal security is not fully accorded by allowing an individual
> to go through his life in possession of all his members and his body
> unmarred; nor is his right to personal liberty fully accorded by
> merely allowing him to remain out of jail or free from other
> physical restraints. . . .
>
> Liberty includes the right to live as one will, so long as that
> will does not interfere with the rights of another or of the public.
> One may desire to live a life of seclusion; another may desire to
> live a life of publicity; still another may wish to live a life of
> privacy as to certain matters and of publicity as to others. . . . Each
> is entitled to a liberty of choice as to his manner of life, and
> neither an individual nor the public has a right to arbitrarily take
> away from him his liberty.[226]

Some may find these judicial visions of the social goal
embodied in the right to privacy vague and unconvincing. I find
them most illuminating. Unfortunately, the law's vocabulary of
mind is exceedingly limited. Our case law too often speaks of
distress, anguish, humiliation, despair, anxiety, mental illness,
indignity, mental suffering, and psychosis without sufficient dis-
crimination of the differences between them. Justice Brandeis and
Judge Cobb help us see, however, that the interest served in
the privacy cases is in some sense a spiritual interest rather
than an interest in property or reputation. Moreover, they also
help us understand that the spiritual characteristic which is at
issue is not a form of trauma, mental illness or distress, but rather
individuality or freedom.

An intrusion on our privacy threatens our liberty as individuals to do as we will, just as an assault, a battery or imprisonment of our person does. And just as we may regard
these latter torts as offenses "to the reasonable sense of personal
dignity,"[227] as offensive to our concept of individualism and the
liberty it entails, so too should we regard privacy as a dignitary
tort.[228] Unlike many other torts, the harm caused is not one

---

225. 112 Cal. App. 285, 297 Pac. 91 (Dist. Ct. App. 1931); 122 Ga. 190, 50
S.E. 68 (1905).
226. 122 Ga. 190, 195-96, 50 S.E. 68, 70 (1905).
227. The phrase is used in the Restatement of Torts to describe an "offensive
battery," i.e., one not involving bodily harm. Restatement, Torts § 18 (1934).
228. Gregory and Kalven describe privacy as a dignitary tort in the index
to their casebook, but seem to treat it as within the mental distress category in the
text. See Gregory & Kalven, Cases on Torts 883-99, 1307 (1959).

which may be repaired and the loss suffered is not one which may be made good by an award of damages. The injury is to our individuality, to our dignity as individuals, and the legal remedy represents a social vindication of the human spirit thus threatened rather than a recompense for the loss suffered.

What distinguishes the invasion of privacy as a tort from the other torts which involve insults to human dignity and individuality is merely the means used to perpetrate the wrong. The woman who is indecently petted[229] suffers the same indignity as the woman whose birth pangs are overseen.[230] The woman whose photograph is exhibited for advertising purposes[231] is degraded and demeaned as surely as the woman who is kept aboard a pleasure yacht against her will.[232] In all of these cases there is an interference with individuality, an interference with the right of the individual to do what he will. The difference is in the character of the interference. Whereas the affront to dignity in the one category of cases is affected by physical interference with the person, the affront in the other category of cases is affected, among other means, by physically intruding on personal intimacy and by using techniques of publicity to make a public spectacle of an otherwise private life.

The man who is compelled to live every minute of his life among others and whose every need, thought, desire, fancy or gratification is subject to public scrutiny, has been deprived of his individuality and human dignity. Such an individual merges with the mass. His opinions, being public, tend never to be different; his aspirations, being known, tend always to be conventionally accepted ones; his feelings, being openly exhibited, tend to lose their quality of unique personal warmth and to become the feelings of every man. Such a being, although sentient, is fungible; he is not an individual.

The conception of man embodied in our tradition and incorporated in our Constitution stands at odds to such human fungibility. And our law of privacy attempts to preserve individuality by placing sanctions upon outrageous or unreasonable violations of the conditions of its sustenance. This, then, is the social value served by the law of privacy, and it is served not only in the law of tort, but in numerous other areas of the law as well.

To be sure, this identification of the interest served by the

229. Hatchett v. Blacketer, 162 Ky. 266, 172 S.W. 533 (1915).
230. DeMay v. Roberts, 46 Mich. 160, 9 N.W. 146 (1881).
231. Flake v. Greensboro News Co., 212 N.C. 780, 195 S.E. 55 (1938).
232. Whittaker v. Sanford, 110 Me. 77, 85 Atl. 399 (1912).

law of privacy does not of itself "solve" any privacy problems; it does not furnish a ready-made solution to any particular case of a claimed invasion of privacy. In the first place, not every threat to privacy is of sufficient moment to warrant the imposition of civil liability or to evoke any other form of legal redress. We all are, and of necessity must be, subject to some minimum scrutiny of our neighbors as a very condition of life in a civilized community. Thus, even having identified the interest invaded, we are left with the problem whether, in the particular instance, the intrusion was of such outrageous and unreasonable character as to be made actionable.

Secondly, even where a clear violation of privacy is made out, one must still face the question whether it is not privileged or excused by some countervailing public policy or social interest. The most obvious such conflicting value is the public interest in news and information which, of necessity, must sometimes run counter to the individual's interest in privacy.[233] Again, identification of the nature of the privacy interest does not resolve the conflict of values, except insofar as it makes clear at least one of the elements which is to be weighed in the balance.

One may well ask, then, what difference it makes whether privacy is regarded as involving a single interest, a single tort, or four? What difference whether the tort of invasion of privacy is taken to protect the dignity of man and whether this same interest is protected in non-tort privacy contexts?

The study and understanding of law, like any other study, proceeds by way of generalization and simplification. To the degree that relief in the law courts under two different sets of circumstances can be explained by a common rule or principle, to that degree the law has achieved greater unity and has become a more satisfying and useful tool of understanding. Conceptual unity is not only fulfilling in itself, however; it is also an instrument of legal development.

Dean Prosser complains of "the extent to which defenses, limitations and safeguards established for the protection of the defendant in other tort fields have been jettisoned, disregarded, or ignored" in the privacy cases.[234] Because he regards intrusion as a form of the infliction of mental distress, it comes as a surprise and cause for concern that the courts, in the intrusion cases, have not insisted upon "genuine and serious mental harm," the

---

233. See, e.g., Sidis v. F-R Publishing Corp., 113 F.2d 806, 809 (2d Cir. 1940); Hubbard v. Journal Publishing Co., 69 N.M. 473, 475, 368 P.2d 147, 148 (1962); Franklin, *A Constitutional Problem in Privacy Protection: Legal Inhibitions on Reporting of Fact,* 16 Stan. L. Rev. 107 (1963).

234. Prosser, *Privacy* 422.

normal requirement in the mental distress cases.[235] Because he believes the public disclosure cases and the "false light" cases involve injury to reputation, he is alarmed that the courts in these cases have jettisoned numerous safeguards—the defense of truth and the requirement, in certain cases, of special damages, for instance—which were erected in the law of defamation to preserve a proper balance between the interest in reputation and the interest in a free press.[236] And because he conceives of the use of name and likeness cases as involving a proprietary interest in name or likeness comparable to a common law trade name or trademark, he is puzzled that there has been "no hint" in these cases "of any of the limitations which have been considered necessary and desirable in the ordinary law of trade-marks and trade names."[237]

The reason for Dean Prosser's concern and puzzlement in each instance is based on his prior identification of the interest the tort remedy serves. If the intrusion cases serve the purpose of protecting emotional tranquility, certain legal consequences concerning necessary allegations and defenses appropriate to the protection of that interest seem to follow. The same is true for the other categories of cases as well. If he is mistaken in his identification of the interest involved in the privacy cases, however, the development of the tort will take—actually, as I have shown above, it has already taken—an entirely different turn, and will have entirely different dimensions.

The interest served by the remedy determines the nature of the cause of action and the available defenses because it enters into the complex process of weighing and balancing of conflicting social values which courts undertake in affording remedies. Therefore, my suggestion that all of the tort privacy cases involve the same interest in preserving human dignity and individuality has important consequences for the development of the tort. If this, rather than emotional tranquility, reputation or the monetary value of a name or likeness is involved, courts will be faced by the need to compromise and adjust an entirely different set of values, values more similar to those involved in battery, assault and false imprisonment cases than in mental distress, defamation and misappropriation cases.

The identification of the social value which underlies the privacy cases will also help to determine the character of the development of new legal remedies for threats posed by some of

235. Ibid.
236. Id. at 422-23.
237. Id. at 423.

the aspects of modern technology. Criminal statutes which are intended to curb the contemporary sophisticated electronic forms of eavesdropping and evidentiary rules which forbid the disclosure of the fruits of such eavesdropping can only be assimilated to the common law forms of protection against intrusion upon privacy if the social interest served by the common law is conceived of as the preservation of individual dignity. These statutes are obviously not designed to protect against forms of mental illness or distress and to so identify the interest involved in the common law intrusion cases is to rob the argument for eavesdropping statutes of a valuable source of traditional common law analysis.

A similar argument may be made concerning other contempory tendencies in the direction of stripping the individual naked of his human dignity by exposing his personal life to public scrutiny. The personnel practices of government and large-scale corporate enterprise increasingly involve novel forms of investigation of personal lives. Extensive personal questionnaires, psychological testing and, in some instances, the polygraph have been used to delve deeper and deeper into layers of personality heretofore inaccessible to all but a lover, an intimate friend or a physician. And the information so gathered is very often stored, correlated and retrieved by electronic machine techniques. The combined force of the new techniques for uncovering personal intimacies and the new techniques of electronic use of this personal data threatens to uncover inmost thoughts and feelings never even "whispered in the closet" and to make them all too easily available "to be proclaimed from the housetops."[238]

The character of the problems posed by psychological testing, the polygraph and electronic storage of personal data can better be grasped if seen in the perspective of the common law intrusion and disclosure cases. The interest threatened by these new instruments is the same as that which underlies the tort cases. The feeling of being naked before the world can be produced by having to respond to a questionnaire or psychological test as well as by having your bedroom open to prying eyes and ears. And the fear that a private life may be turned into a public spectacle is greatly enhanced when the lurid facts have been reduced to key punches or blips on a magnetic tape accessible, perhaps, to any clerk who can throw the appropriate switch.

This is not to say, of course, that the same adjustments of conflicting values which have been made in the tort privacy cases can be assumed to apply without modification to resolve the

---

238. For a description of the threat, see the authorities cited in note 7 supra.

2

PRIVACY, TORT LAW, AND THE CONSTITUTION: IS WARREN AND BRANDEIS' TORT PETTY AND UNCONSTITUTIONAL AS WELL?

For many years courts and commentators have regarded Warren and Brandeis' article on "The Right to Privacy"[1] as the very fount of learning on the subject of privacy in tort law. A recent decision of the United States Supreme Court[2] and a recent law review article by Professor Harry Kalven[3] feed the irreverence and scepticism of our day by suggesting that Warren and Brandeis' tort of privacy[4] may be petty, wrong, or unconstitutional—probably all three.

Others before Professor Kalven have hinted that Warren and Brandeis' tort may not be all it has been taken to be by its legal devotees.[5] Still others have read the article to erect a tort Warren and Brandeis never intended.[6] Kalven is the first, as far as I know, to say in the face of the hundreds of court decisions that have followed or attempted to follow the Warren-Brandeis analysis, and in the face of the dozens of legislative acts that have embodied or were intended to embody that analysis into statute, that Warren and Brandeis were mistaken: They labored mightily, he says, but they gave birth to a trivial tort.[7]

This is an audacious and intellectually refreshing point of view.

---

[1] Warren & Brandeis, *The Right to Privacy*, 4 HARV. L. REV. 193 (1890).

[2] Time, Inc. v. Hill, 385 U.S. 374 (1967).

[3] Kalven, *Privacy In Tort Law—Were Warren and Brandeis Wrong?*, 31 LAW & CONTEMP. PROB. 326 (1966).

[4] Since the concept of privacy was introduced by Warren and Brandeis, it has been used to mean many things that they did not intend or anticipate. *See* W. PROSSER, TORTS § 97 (2d ed. 1955). In this article, I limit my discussion to the tort with which Warren and Brandeis were concerned, what I call the mass publication tort.

[5] *See, e.g.,* Davis, *What Do We Mean by Right to Privacy?*, 4 S.D.L. REV. 1 (1959).

[6] *See* cases cited by W. PROSSER, *supra* note 4, at 637 following his statement that the tort "appears in reality to be a complex of four distinct wrongs."

[7] *See* Kalven, *supra* note 3, at 337.

Coming from as brilliant a student of tort law as Professor Kalven, it invites careful reading, especially on the part of those who have thus far maintained a worshipful attitude towards the Warren and Brandeis article. Perhaps the emperor has no clothes on, after all.

Let me recall the main outlines of that unique law review article which launched a tort. After a brief and eloquent sketch of the development of the legal recognition of "man's spiritual nature, of his feelings and his intellect," Warren and Brandeis call attention to "the next step which must be taken for the protection of the person": legal recognition of the right "to be let alone."[8] This step must be taken because "instantaneous photographs and newspaper enterprise have invaded the sacred precincts of private and domestic life," because "the press is overstepping in every direction the obvious bounds of propriety and of decency."[9] The consequence of the press' impropriety has been not only that the individual has become subject to "mental pain and distress far greater than could be inflicted by mere bodily injury," but also that "each crop of unseemly gossip results in a lowering of social standard and morality."[10] Ultimately the result will be the destruction of "robustness of thought and delicacy of feeling" in the society at large.[11]

Having defined the substantive evil, Warren and Brandeis turn to the search for a legal principle that will guard against this evil. They find it in the doctrine of common-law copyright, in the protection that the law affords "to thoughts, sentiments, and emotions expressed through the medium of writing or of the arts"[12] when it prevents their publication without the consent of the author. This right of the individual to determine whether his literary or artistic work shall be published "is merely an instance of the enforcement of the more general right to be let alone,"[13] of the more "general right to privacy for thoughts, emotions and sensations . . . whether expressed in writing, or in conduct, in conversation . . . or in facial expression."[14] Here, then, in the very bosom of the common law, Warren and Brandeis find the legal principle of privacy that the common law in its "eternal youth" must enlarge to meet the danger posed to man and society by the organs of mass publicity.

Anyone who reads this seminal article must marvel at its sensi-

---

8 Warren & Brandeis, *supra* note 1, at 195.
9 *Id.* at 195-96.
10 *Id.* at 196.
11 *Id.*
12 *Id.* at 205.
13 *Id.*
14 *Id.* at 206.

bility to subtle wrongs, its array of legal learning, its philosophic sweep, and its literary distinction. Here is a brief before the court of legal opinion that seems to have won the day because of its magnificent craftsmanship. But now we hear profound rumblings that the day of Warren and Brandeis' tort is over, and—even more unsettling—that the day of the privacy tort should never have dawned.

Professor Kalven's attack[15] on the Warren-Brandeis tort is compounded of gentle but debunking aspersions and astute, thoughtful, but essentially erroneous legal analysis. He complains that the reception of the article owes more to the legal prominence of its authors and its lofty rhetoric than to the power of its argument. By endowing the discussion with a "touch of grandeur" and by emphasizing "the spiritual side of man," Warren and Brandeis gave the tort "class" and social status.[16] This, together with the fact that courts and legislatures recognized privacy as "a key value" and were excited with the thought of participating in law "at a point of growth," dulled the legal critical sense.[17] As a result, the legal world unthinkingly spawned a tort that is "an anachronism" founded on "a curious nineteenth century quaintness" at odds with "the more robust tastes or mores of today."[18]

Kalven feeds the sceptic's delight in learning that influences long heralded as heroic are indeed mundane. He is surely right in ascribing much of the impact of the Warren-Brandeis article to the glamour of their names and the intellectually seductive character of their prose. He is also right, I believe, in detecting in those learned authors a tone of personal prissiness that underlies their philosophic concern for "man's spiritual nature." Finally, Kalven hits the mark in suggesting that many courts and commentators alike have responded indiscriminately to the claimed tortious wrong described by Warren and Brandeis, as if what was really at issue was the deprivation of the more fundamental constitutional right to privacy.

But this brief and destructive excursion into the genesis of the influence of the Warren-Brandeis article should not be mistaken for an argument against its substance. And Kalven rightly turns from historical asides to direct his main attention to an analysis of the thesis Warren and Brandeis present.

He looks first to the logic of their argument and urges that their attempt to rest the right of privacy on the principle underlying com-

---

15 Kalven, *supra* note 3.
16 *Id.* at 328.
17 *Id.*
18 *Id.* at 329.

mon-law copyright is "simplistic" and constitutes an "incomplete argument."[19] But Warren and Brandeis never supposed that their mere
reference to the principle of common-law copyright would provide a
"complete" argument for recognition of the right to privacy. They did
all one can ever do in a legal argument by analogy: They delineated
the respect in which protecting a man's right to forbid publication of
his writing or his art is similar to his right to forbid publication of his
picture—both involve the individual's desire to be let alone, his desire
to fashion his own personality and determine for himself what he shall
be. Moreover, they suggested that the failure of the law to protect man
in his desire to avoid becoming a public spectacle, whether as a result of
the publication of his picture or of his art work, caused injury to the
individual as well as to the social fabric of thought and sensibility.

Thus Warren and Brandeis did not argue, as Kalven suggests, simply that the right to prevent publication of one's photograph should be
protected because the right to prevent publication of one's writing is;
rather, they urged that it should be protected because the two shared
a common property, which, when neglected by the law, was productive
of similar evils.

Fortunately, the main burden of Kalven's critique stands on firmer
ground. What he questions most seriously is whether privacy is really
a viable tort remedy,[20] and whether, even if it is viable, it is not a
"petty" or trivial remedy.[21] Suppose we grant that mass publicity concerning someone's personal life has a tendency to debase and demean
his sense of himself; how shall we distinguish between publicity that is
innocuous and harmless, petty in its effects, and publicity that should
invoke the legal remedy because it consummates the legal wrong? Shall
all publicity, no matter what its motive and no matter what care was
exercised by the publisher to avoid harm to the individual, be equally
vulnerable to the legal sanction? And how shall we measure the harm
to the individual for which damages shall be awarded?

These are extremely important questions, questions that must be
answered if we are to have a viable and effective tort remedy. Warren
and Brandeis almost completely neglected them, as have most of the
courts, legislatures, and commentators that have been active in fashion-
ing a tort remedy for the invasion of privacy. The tort, Kalven suggests,
"has no legal profile."[22]

---

19 *Id.* at 329-30.
20 *Id.* at 333.
21 *Id.* at 329, 336.
22 *Id.* at 333.

One reason for this neglect of the tort's profile is to be found, of course, in the very way in which our common law grows. Its growth is a hit-and-miss and rough-and-ready process, responsive to sporadic cries for relief by litigants, rather than a planned scheme of development intended to answer all problems at once in a systematic fashion. In this process Warren and Brandeis played the role of learned and articulate counsel urging a remedy rather than of detached scholars in search of a fully reasoned and developed legal theory.

There is a still more significant explanation for the failure of courts, legislatures, and commentators to address themselves in any great detail to issues concerning the threshold of wrongful publication, the care, intention, and motive of the publisher, and the measure of damages in privacy actions. These questions are so fundamental that the reason for neglecting them over so long a period of time can only be that the answers have seemed, as indeed I believe they are, obvious.

Kalven asks what less than "every unconsented-to reference" to a person in a mass media should constitute a legal wrong?[23] And he argues by indirection that failure to provide a detailed answer to this question renders the tort useless. But the obvious answer to the question is that there can be no precise or detailed formula for the threshold of liability in privacy cases any more than there can be a precise formula "in the large class of cases [in law] in which the reasonableness or unreasonableness of an act is made the test of liability."[24] The answer will always have to take into account "the varying circumstances of each case."[25] This is what Warren and Brandeis themselves said when they faced this problem,[26] only adding, what must also be plain, that "it is only the more flagrant breaches of decency and propriety that could in practice be reached."[27]

That courts and commentators have not been able to improve on Warren and Brandeis' formulation of the threshold of liability is, I contend, not at all an indication of a failure of thought or of an inadequate theory of liability. It is merely a reflection of the complexity and variety of the circumstances in which people's lives can become the subject of comment and scrutiny in the mass media.

Kalven's concern about the failure of courts and commentators to have discussed the motives, intentions, and standard of care of the

[23] *Id.*
[24] Warren & Brandeis, *supra* note 1, at 214.
[25] *Id.* at 215.
[26] *Id.* at 214-15.
[27] *Id.*

publisher carries more weight. But here also it must be said that the subject is only slightly open to doubt. What uncertainty there is on these questions is founded, for the most part, on a confusion between the way they arise in the context of defamation and privacy.

In the case of defamatory statements, it is sometimes possible that a publisher had no reason to believe that what he published was defamatory at all;[28] it is also possible that he might not have had reason to believe that the defamatory statement was false;[29] finally, it is possible that he might not have had reason to believe that the defamatory statement was defamatory of the plaintiff.[30] These possibilities—and a few others—have given rise to a great deal of discussion about whether, under the circumstances described, a publisher should be held liable even if he exercised all due care or whether he should be held liable only for failing to have taken the precautions he could reasonably have been expected to have taken.[31]

The reason the same kind of discussion has not been undertaken in the privacy field[32] is not that the issues are unclear or unresolvable, as Kalven intimates, but rather that carelessness simply cannot, as a matter of logic, play the same role in most privacy cases that it plays in defamation cases. A publisher always knows whether what he published is about the private life of another individual; it is not as if he could be unaware of the private and intimate character of what he utters in the same way he might lack good reason to know its defamatory character.

Moreover, since the Warren and Brandeis tort is founded on complaints about true statements concerning the private lives of individuals, the question whether the publisher had reason to believe that what he uttered was false does not arise. Whether a publisher had reason to believe that what he uttered was true is a question that can indeed arise, but it hardly seems likely to arise, except in theory. Even if it did arise, one could hardly argue that it is a defense to a privacy suit that the publisher uttered private details of someone's life believing them to be false or fictitious. If he believed his account of another's

---

28 See, e.g., Burton v. Crowell Publishing Co., 82 F.2d 154 (2d Cir. 1936); Braun v. Armair & Co., 254 N.Y. 514, 173 N.E. 845 (1930); Morrison v. John Ritchie & Co., 39 Scot. L.R. 432, 9 SCOTS L.T.R. 476, 4 Sess. Cas. 645 (1902).

29 See, e.g., Cassidy v. Daily Mirror Newspapers, Ltd., [1929] 2 K.B. 331; Bromage v. Prosser, 107 Eng. Rep. 1051 (K.B. 1825).

30 See, e.g., Clare v. Farrell, 70 F. Supp. 276 (D. Minn. 1947); E. Hulton & Co. v. Jones, [1910] A.C. 20.

31 See, e.g., 1 F. HARPER & F. JAMES, TORTS § 5.7 (1956); W. PROSSER, supra note 4, at 602-4; Smith, Jones v. Hulton: Three Conflicting Views as to a Question of Defamation, 60 U. PA. L. REV. 365 (1912).

32 See note 4 supra.

life to be false or fictitious, but presented it as true, and it turned out to be true, he has invaded the privacy of that person to the same extent as if he had believed the account to be true.

As far as I can see, only two circumstances exist in which the use of reasonable care could function as a possible defense in a privacy suit. The first arises when a publisher presents as a fiction what he supposes to be a fiction, but which turns out to be a true account of the personal life of someone unknown to him. The other arises when a publisher utters an account of another's personal life intending and attempting not to identify the person involved, but, in fact, the publication is identifiable as concerning him. In each of these cases we would be called upon to decide whether reasonable care on the part of the publisher excused the wrong.

In the nature of things, however, both of these kinds of cases are liable to occur rarely, and this surely explains, as much as anything else, why the problem they present is so little discussed. But, in any event, as difficult as is the problem of policy they present, I hardly see why they should constitute any more reason for concluding that invasion of privacy is a wrong-headed tort than they do for concluding the same of defamation.

The other questions Kalven raises concerning the publisher's conduct seem to raise no problems at all, unless we are to suppose that all it takes to raise a problem is merely to ask a question. Kalven asks, "does it matter whether the defendant knew the disclosure would be so offensive, or . . . whether he thought he was privileged by the public interest in the item?"[33] No one has discussed these questions at any length because, once again, the answers seem plain and incontrovertible. The settled rule concerning motive in intentional torts and in defamation actions is that, as long as the act constituting the wrong was intended, it is no defense that the consequence of the act was not.[34] Why should anyone suppose the rule would vary in right to privacy cases? The same must be said in relation to privilege. Why should mistake on the existence of a privilege constitute a defense here when the nearly universal rule in tort law is to the contrary?[35]

The final element of the "profile" of the tort of invasion of privacy that Professor Kalven finds lacking is a theory of damages. "The theory of damages is . . . vague and mysterious in so far as damages are sup-

---

[33] Kalven, *supra* note 3, at 334.
[34] *See* W. PROSSER, *supra* note 4, at 36, 601-02.
[35] *Id.* at 80-82.

posed to be compensatory,"[36] he says. And he adds, "it remains odd to give recovery for emotional disturbance without any showing that plaintiff suffered or was upset."[37]

Kalven's problems only arise, however, if we suppose that Warren and Brandeis' tort is intended to compensate for harm done to the emotional stability of the individual. In my view,[38] this mistakes the nature of the tort as Warren and Brandeis intended it and as, in fact, it has developed in the courts. Although I admit that there is far from a settled view of this matter, I believe invasion of privacy by mass publication is a dignitary tort, like assault and battery, rather than a compensatory tort like negligence. As such it involves general damages rather than special damages. And where recovery is given for emotional disturbance or any other element of special damage, that recovery is parasitic rather than at the root of the tort.

The theory of damages in privacy cases turns out to be no more murky or insoluble than the theories already examined concerning the basis of liability or the threshold of the tort. To be sure, there are some unresolved questions, and it is also quite possible that I am mistaken in some of my attempts to resolve others, but the questions are not unresolvable in principle, as Kalven suggests; in fact, they are not very different from the questions we face in other areas of tort law. Even if Kalven is unable to, *I* can see the profile of Warren and Brandeis' tort.

The reason Kalven fails to see the profile of the tort is that he does not want to see it. Of course I am not accusing him of a willful failure of intention; I am only urging that Kalven's position is somewhat like that of a man searching for a penny at dusk who winds up saying "I can't find it, but anyway, it's not important." He *could* find the penny if it were really that important to him.

Ultimately, Kalven's argument must rest not on the ground that Warren and Brandeis' tort is "unviable" or "wrong," but rather on the ground that there is really no point in making it viable because it is a "petty" or "trifling" tort. "The mountain," he concludes, "has brought forth a pretty small mouse," and why, after all, should we worry over a small mouse?

But is the Warren and Brandeis tort really "a small mouse"? Is it really a trivial tort? The answer depends on how much the interest the tort is designed to protect is valued—one man's trivia may be another man's treasure—and on how effectively the tort protects that interest.

---

[36] Kalven, *supra* note 3, at 334.
[37] *Id.*
[38] *See* Bloustein, *Privacy as an Aspect of Human Dignity: An Answer to Dean Prosser,* 39 N.Y.U.L. Rev. 962 (1964).

Kalven intimates at one point that mass publicity concerning the intimacies of a man's life threatens no more than an anachronistic nineteenth-century sense of gentility or propriety "hardly in keeping with the more robust tastes or mores of today."[39] And his discussion of some of the reported cases[40] suggests that the impact of mass publicity in our society simply does not present a grave problem to him. At most, the complaints that he finds in cases seem to amount to no more than "emotional upset,"[41] with few, if any, of them terribly significant at that.

Even if he were troubled by the harm that mass publicity threatens under some circumstances, the tort would still be trivial for Kalven because the remedy it offers seems ineffectual to him. He "surmises"—and that this is only a "guess" he makes clear—that the victims who need the remedy most do not use it and those who do use it very often have "shabby unseemly grievances."[42] Since bringing a lawsuit may be the cause of the very same kind of publicity that is the subject of complaint, people who are truly sensitive to publicity will shun the legal remedy, Kalven argues, leaving it to be pursued only by the thick-skinned and litigious.

My own estimate of the harm mass publicity threatens and of the effectiveness of the remedy that the Warren-Brandeis tort affords is at odds with Kalven's.[43] What is really at issue when, for instance, a magazine gives an account of the emotional crisis that a man faced in leaving his wife and children, is not merely the distress the individual suffers as a result of the reawakening of his agony, but the debasement of his sense of himself as a person that results because his life has become a public spectacle against his will. There is anguish and mortification, a blow to human dignity, in having the world intrude as an unwanted witness to private tragedy. The wrong is to be found in the fact that a private life has been transformed into a public spectacle.

The love and nurture of individuality, the projection of the self as an independent source of value and as the justification of all other social values, is our most profound philosophical commitment. Even were I capable of the insight and eloquence required to catalogue the myriad intersecting influences that determine the course of individuality in our culture, this would be neither the place nor the occasion to do it. It is enough for me to say in this context—what would be so obvious as to be trite in most other contexts—that the institutions of law must

---

39 Kalven, *supra* note 3, at 329.
40 *Id.* at 336-38.
41 *Id.* at 334.
42 *Id.* at 338.
43 Bloustein, *supra* note 38, at 979, 987, 995, 1001-03.

be recognized as among the most important social conditions for the sustenance of individuality. It is as part of the system of rules and sanctions that preserve the concept of man as a self-determining being that we must locate the privacy tort.

An intrusion on our privacy by mass publicity threatens our liberty as individuals "to be let alone"[44] and to do as we will, in the same way as does an assault or imprisonment of our person. It is an offense against the right of the individual to be self-determining, to decide for himself where he shall go and who he shall be, to decide for himself whether he wants to remain anonymous or become a public figure. To live a life of seclusion, free from the glare of publicity, is as valued an aspect of human individuality as any I know. And therefore, to the degree the tort remedy can help preserve such a life option in an age pervaded and dominated by the mass media of communication, it should be fostered and developed.

As to Kalven's fear that the tort remedy will be used only by those who love or can at least endure publicity rather than by those who truly cherish their privacy, the reply I offer is two-fold. First, as Kalven himself recognizes,[45] many of the cases that have actually been litigated deal with appealing rather than shoddy claims. The suit to recover damages evidently serves to vindicate pride in self rather than to debase still further the individual's self-esteem.

But secondly, even if "the wrong" plaintiffs do in fact use the remedy, we must recognize here, as in other areas of the law, that when the legal right has been vindicated by the application of a sanction, the true beneficiary is the public at large. We all vicariously benefit when a criminal successfully asserts fundamental constitutional principles in his own sordid defense. Similarly in the case of privacy, every award of damages, perhaps every lawsuit, is a vindication of the right for the entire community; it acts as a deterrent to the wrong and as a potent social symbol of the value embodied in the tort. Thus the meanest and most base of claimants to privacy serves the interest of all of us in preserving our freedom from unwanted publicity.

The final point that Kalven makes against the Warren-Brandeis tort is surely the most significant of all. It is a measure of his perceptiveness and scholarship that he anticipated a constitutional infirmity in the tort, which the Supreme Court recognized a year after he

---

[44] This phrase is, of course, from the Warren & Brandeis article, *supra* note 1, at 195, quoted by them from T. COOLEY, TORTS 29 (2d ed. 1888).
[45] Kalven, *supra* note 3, at 338.

wrote.[46] This constitutional issue is simply put: Is the first amendment privilege to publish what is newsworthy "so over-powering as virtually to swallow the tort?"[47]

Warren and Brandeis were themselves aware that "the right to privacy [should] not prohibit any publication of matter which is of public or general interest," and they recognized this privilege as being similar to the privilege of fair comment on matters of public and general interest in the law of defamation.[48] Even so, until recently the privileges of fair comment in defamation and of "public interest" or "newsworthiness" in the law of privacy were considered private law privileges. In the last few years, however, the dimensions of the privilege in both defamation and privacy have been radically enlarged and reconstituted as forms of constitutional limitation by the Supreme Court of the United States.

In *New York Times Company v. Sullivan*,[49] in 1964, the Supreme Court held that a defamatory comment concerning a public official fell within the protection of the first amendment and that an award of damages without a showing of actual malice was unconstitutional.[50] In the 1967 *Time, Inc.*[51] case, the Supreme Court extended the protection of the first amendment to a tort action for the invasion of privacy by mass publicity and held that the privacy action could not succeed without a showing by the plaintiff of actual malice on the part of the publisher.[52]

The *Time, Inc.* case involved an article that appeared in *Life* magazine describing a play entitled "The Desperate Hours." The play was an adaptation of a novel with the same title, and the novel was a fictionalization of an incident in which a family had been held hostage in its home by escaped prisoners. Although the novel and play were clearly fictionalized and did not mention the name of the family, the *Life* magazine article did. Published three years after the event, the article used the episode involving the family as a pivotal element of its story and commented, falsely as it turned out, that the family's story was "re-enacted" in the play.

---

46 Time, Inc. v. Hill, 385 U.S. 374 (1967). It should be noted that the problem raised in the *Time, Inc.* case was recognized at an early point by, among others, Franklin, *A Constitutional Problem in Privacy Protection*, 16 STAN. L. REV. 107 (1963).

47 Kalven, *supra* note 3, at 336.

48 Warren & Brandeis, *supra* note 1, at 214.

49 376 U.S. 254 (1964).

50 *Id.* at 279.

51 Time, Inc. v. Hill, 385 U.S. 374 (1967).

52 *Id.* at 387-88.

Under New York statutes and case law prior to the decision in the
Time, Inc. case, the settled rule had been that "the factual reporting
of newsworthy persons and events is in the public interest"; such reporting, therefore, was not considered wrongful or tortious conduct.[53]
Under New York law prior to the *Time, Inc.* case, however, the use of
a man's name or photograph in a false or fictionalized article or report
was considered a tortious invasion of privacy and subject to damages.[54]
It was under this latter rule of fictionalization that recovery was had
against Time, Inc. in the New York courts by the family whose privacy
was invaded. But the Supreme Court reversed and declared that there
could be no recovery against the publisher without proof of actual
malice—without proof that the publisher knowingly or recklessly published the false account.

Although the *Time, Inc.* decision is expressly limited to cases involving fictionalized reports or articles about newsworthy persons, there
can be little doubt that its logic would extend a fortiori to cases involving true accounts. If the first amendment protects fictionalized accounts
of private lives absent malice, why would it not protect true accounts?
The Supreme Court hints as much in the *Time, Inc.* case by citing
with approval a large number of cases in which true accounts of newsworthy persons and events were held not to be actionable.[55]

The full significance of the *Time, Inc.* case for the Warren-
Brandeis tort becomes apparent only if we look more closely at the concept of "newsworthiness." If what is "newsworthy" is identical to what
news media publish, if, as Kalven puts it, "the press in the nature of
things must be the final arbiter of 'newsworthiness,' "[56] there is indeed
little left of the Warren-Brandeis tort.[57] If "newsworthiness" is used by
the courts as an evaluative rather than merely a descriptive test,[58] however, the tort can continue to flourish and serve to prevent the debasement of human personality by mass publicity.

The two concepts of "newsworthiness" may be illustrated by reference to the *Time, Inc.* case itself. In the first draft of the *Life* magazine
article complained of, the play, "The Desperate Hours," had been de-

[53] *Id.* at 383. *See also* Sidis v. F-R Publishing Corp., 113 F.2d 806, 809 (2d Cir. 1940).
[54] *See, e.g.,* Spahn v. Julian Messner, Inc., 18 N.Y.2d 324, 328, 221 N.E.2d 543, 545, 234
N.Y.S.2d 877, 879, *rev'd on other grounds,* 387 U.S. 239 (1967).
[55] Time, Inc. v. Hill, 385 U.S. 374, 383 n.7 (1967).
[56] Kalven, *supra* note 3, at 336.
[57] The Supreme Court hints as much by quoting Kalven to this effect in Time, Inc.
v. Hill, 385 U.S. 374, 383 n.7 (1967).
[58] For the distinction between these two senses of "newsworthiness" see Comment,
*The Right to Privacy: Normative-Descriptive Confusion in the Defense of Newsworthi-
ness,* 30 U. CHI. L. REV. 722 (1963).

scribed as "a hair-raising report of a suburban Philadelphia family, held prisoner in their own home by three escaped convicts"; the name of the family was not mentioned in this draft. The trial record shows that the family name was inserted into the second draft of the article by a senior editor of the magazine because he found that the first draft was not "newsy enough."[59]

I have no doubt that the senior editor "knew his business"; he knew what he was doing and he was right in believing that the draft of the article that did not mention the name of the family was not as readable, nor as provocative as the draft that identified the family. In this sense, the second draft was more "newsworthy," more attractive to the reading public.

But was the second draft really that much more informative than the first for having mentioned the name of the family involved in the real-life episode? (For that matter, would my account of this case have been more informative if I had mentioned the name of the family involved in it?) Did it contribute at all to public enlightenment about the play, about play-writing, or about crime to use the name of the family in the *Life* article? Surely the article would have been no less a contribution to public understanding generally and, in this sense, it would have been no less "newsworthy," had it omitted all reference to the name of the family. Identification of the family merely pandered to the public taste for emotional color, gossip, and sensation without serving in the least to inform the public of any matter of legitimate concern.

In his opinion for the majority in the *Time, Inc.* case, Justice Brennan expressed the rationale of the Court's decision when he declared that the first amendment guarantees "are not for the benefit of the press so much as for the benefit of all of us. [They assure] the maintenance of our political system and an open society."[60] And he added, "We have no doubt that . . . the opening of a new play linked to an actual incident, is a matter of public interest."[61]

The curious thing is that the majority of the Court never asked itself whether it was important to the "maintenance of our political system and an open society" to use the name of the family linked to the play or whether that purpose could have been accomplished equally well without identifying the family; the majority never asked itself

---

59 Record at 220-21 ex. 21, 342-46, Time, Inc. v. Hill, 385 U.S. 374 (1967).
60 385 U.S. at 389.
61 *Id.* at 388.

whether the "public interest" in "the opening of a new play linked to an actual incident" required that the family concerned have the raw nerve of its past trauma reopened to public exhibition against its will and wishes.

A number of commentators[62] have noted that, in the *New York Times* case, the Supreme Court virtually adopted the theory of the first amendment long advocated by Professor Meikeljohn.[63] The *Time, Inc.* case represents still another attempt to apply the Meikeljohn theory. I believe, however, that the Court misapplied the theory. More generally, I believe that the Meikeljohn theory, properly understood, allows ample place for the mass publication privacy tort.

The Meikeljohn theory, briefly stated, is that under the first amendment "the point of ultimate interest is not the words of the speakers, but the minds of the hearers."[64] The interest protected, in other words, is not the private right to speak but the public right to know. "[F]reedom of speech is derived, not from supposed 'Natural Right,' but from the necessities of self-government by universal suffrage . . . ."[65] Speech is protected because the people, "the rulers" in a democratic state, must, "so far as possible, understand the issues which bear upon our common life."[66] The importance of this distinction between the interest of the hearers and that of the speakers is that it affords a new basis for understanding what restrictions, if any, may be placed on free speech.

"What is essential," says Meikeljohn, is "not that everyone shall speak,"[67] not that there be "unregulated talkativeness,"[68] but that "everything worth saying shall be said."[69] It follows that, although "the private right of speech may on occasion be denied or limited"[70] because it is "contrary to the common good,"[71] the public right to know "admits of no exceptions."[72]

Of course, the important question is when and for what purposes

---

[62] Kalven, *The New York Times Case*, 1964 SUP. CT. REV. 191; Comment, *Privacy, Defamation and the First Amendment: The Implications of Time, Inc, v. Hill*, 67 COLUM. L. REV. 926 (1967).

[63] A. MEIKELJOHN, POLITICAL FREEDOM: THE CONSTITUTIONAL POWERS OF THE PEOPLE (1965).

[64] *Id.* at 26.

[65] *Id.* at 79.

[66] *Id.* at 75.

[67] *Id.* at 26.

[68] *Id.*

[69] *Id.*

[70] *Id.* at 36-37.

[71] *Id.* at 57.

[72] *Id.* at 20.

the private right of speech may be limited. Meikeljohn answers this question by drawing upon a most fruitful and suggestive analogy.[73] He asks us to think of our national life as being, in one respect, just like one great big town meeting. He then suggests that just as there are rules of order and propriety that maintain the integrity of a town meeting by limiting the right of speakers at that meeting, there must also be rules of order that maintain the integrity of our national debate by limiting the right of speakers in that debate.

The analogy drives us to ask how speech at a town meeting is limited. Although Meikeljohn does not say so in so many words, he intimates that two major principles of limitation are at issue. The first is that the subject matter be relevant to the purposes of the meeting; the second is that the speaker must not violate the good order of the meeting and thereby defeat its purpose.[74] Translated into terms applicable to our national debate, these principles of limitation are that what is said must be relevant to the purposes of our national debate, namely, self-government,[75] and that it be said in such a way and under such circumstances that it will provide opportunity for full discussion.[76]

Meikeljohn states the principle of relevance—the limitation on speech most important for my present purposes—in this fashion: "[N]o idea, no opinion, no doubt, no belief, no counterbelief, no information [relevant to the issues that bear upon our common life], may be kept from [the people] . . . ."[77] At another point he states the same principle as follows: "The guarantee given by the First Amendment is not then assured to all speaking. It is assured only to speech which bears, directly or indirectly, upon issues with which voters have to deal—only, therefore, to the consideration of matters of public interest."[78]

If I understand Meikeljohn correctly, his basic contention is this: The test for freedom of speech under the first amendment is whether discussion of the given subject matter contributes to the public understanding essential to self-government. If the communication fulfills this purpose, it should not be restricted. If it does not fulfill this purpose, the communication may be subject to reasonable limitation in the public interest just like the exercise of any other private right.

Meikeljohn's distinction between the unlimited right of the public

---

[73] *Id.* at 24.
[74] *Id.*
[75] *Id.* at 79.
[76] *Id.* at 27, 46.
[77] *Id.* at 75.
[78] *Id.* at 79.

to be informed about issues relevant to self-government and the limited right of an individual to communicate sheds new light, I believe, on the concept of "newsworthiness" as a constitutional defense to Warren and Brandeis' mass publication tort. Anything that is "newsworthy" in the sense of contributing to the public understanding of its common purposes should not be subject to limitation or restriction. But the mere fact that a publisher considers something "newsworthy" in the sense of its being interesting or attractive to the public is not sufficient to warrant its constitutional protection. "Newsworthiness" as a form of constitutional protection is identical with the public's right to be informed rather than the publisher's right to communicate.

Understood in these terms, a legal right of action against a publisher who, without malice, makes a public spectacle out of a private life is *not* necessarily unconstitutional; the defense of "newsworthiness" does not "swallow the tort." The constitutional test to be applied is whether what is published concerning a private life is relevant to the public understanding necessary to the purposes of self-government. If this test of relevance is met, there should be no restriction on the publication even though there is malice. If the test of relevance is not met, the publication should be subject to reasonable restriction in the public interest.

The result and the reasoning of the Supreme Court in the *Time, Inc.* case are at odds with this analysis. To be sure, as the Court indicated, publication of a news story about the opening of a new play is relevant to the purposes of self-government; knowledge of what is happening in the theatre is of importance to the decisions of government, and a people aspiring to be self-governing cannot be deprived of that information without impairing its competency to govern.

But was it relevant to the purposes of self-government to publish in a mass medium the name of the family that was linked to the play by something that had happened three years previously? What conceivable governmental decision that the general public could be called upon to make would involve knowledge of the name of the family linked to the play? What real purpose other than titillation of the magazine reader's urge to pry into other people's lives was served by identifying the family involved? It seems to me that the use of the family name in the *Time, Inc.* case did not meet the first amendment test of relevance and that the Supreme Court failed to distinguish the issue of the relevance of the use of the family name from the issue of the relevance of information concerning the opening of the play.

This does not mean, of course, that the use of a name or picture or intimate details of a person's life is never relevant to the purposes of self-government. Nor does it mean that where such use is not relevant, an adjudication of the use as tortious would necessarily be within constitutional bounds. The so-called public-figure exception to the right of privacy[79] rests, I believe, not on the fiction of waiver, but rather on the legitimacy of the character of the public interest in the life of the individual concerned, on the fact that the interest bears a relation to the needs of a self-governing people. But where such a relation is not made out, "public figure" or not, the cause of action lies.[80]

Even in cases where there is no possible relation between mass publication that violates an individual's privacy and a legitimate interest of a self-governing people, the publication may find constitutional protection, if not under the first amendment, then under the due process clause of the fifth amendment.[81] The right of a private person to publish, unlike the public right to know, is subject to limitation; but the limitation may only be exercised where it bears some reasonable relationship to a valid public purpose. In other words, the public right to know those things relevant to the aims of self-government is protected under the first amendment and is absolute and unlimited. There is also, however, a private right to publish that is protected under the due process clause of the fifth amendment and that, like any other private right, is subject to reasonable limitation in the public interest.

If this distinction is applied to the *Time, Inc.* case, we see that the really important question of the case is one that the Court never reached. Granted that use of the plaintiff's name was irrelevant to the public right to know and to the aims of self-government and, therefore, lacked protection under the first amendment, was the New York statute limiting use of the name a reasonable limitation on the right of the defendant publisher to publish whatever he pleased? If the use of the plaintiff-family's name was not vested with an overriding first amendment interest, the critical concern should have been with the character of the limitation on the defendant's right to publish. What was the purpose of the limitation; what interest did it serve; was this interest within the power of the state to pursue? If there was a legitimate state purpose, were the means chosen rationally related

---

79 *See* W. PROSSER, *supra* note 4, at 642-44.
80 *Id.* at 642-43 nn.6-9.
81 A. MEIKELJOHN, *supra* note 63, at 70-71.

to the end sought? These and other established criteria of due process, I believe, should have defined the character of the Supreme Court's inquiry in the *Time, Inc.* case.

In due process terms of reference, that state privacy law takes into account the purpose of the privacy-invading publication, the interval of time between incidents of personal life described and publication, the falsity of the publication, and the actual or constructive malice of the publisher would all seem to be highly relevant. Characteristically, none of these issues comes into play under the first amendment if one accepts, as I do, Meikeljohn's analysis.

This due process regulation of the cause of action for invasion of privacy by mass publication must be worked out in detail through the decisional process. Some considerations immediately suggest themselves, however. Contemporaneous reports of notorious incidents of personal life would seem less subject to restriction than reports of incidents long past because, in many instances, the contemporaneous publication seems hardly capable of further demeaning the individual. The very happening of some events—for example, a divorce involving a charge of adultery—is itself so destructive of the sense of privacy and dignity of the individual that the contemporaneous publication is simply not taken to be further demeaning of privacy, however great its tendency to cause further embarrassment. It can also be argued under some circumstances that an incident is so notorious that contemporaneous publication can hardly cause a further impairment of privacy. In addition to these considerations of the time lapse between the event and publication, it seems obvious that a publisher who published what is false or fictional or both is more reasonably subject to legal action than one who serves the truth; and the same can be said of the publisher who publishes with malice.

These considerations are suggested as the basis for constitutional limitations on the tort right to privacy under the fifth amendment. They also, it seems clear, should function—and, indeed, have already functioned—as policy considerations in the development by the states of the tort cause of action. In this regard, it is important to emphasize the countervailing interest in preserving the economic viability of a free press. It is at least possible that taking the right to privacy seriously and enforcing it stringently might "kill" the free press by limiting its appeal to a public that feeds on lurid gossip and sensation.

To summarize, I believe that the Meikeljohn theory permits the mass publication tort to be applied consistently with the mandate of the first amendment. Although obviously the demarcation must be worked out in detail through the decisional process, its main outlines are clear: The privacy of an individual may only be invaded by mass publication when that publication is relevant to the purposes of self-government. In all other cases the right of the publisher should be subject to reasonable restriction in order to protect the public interest in privacy.

3

THE FIRST AMENDMENT AND PRIVACY: THE SUPREME COURT JUSTICE AND THE PHILOSOPHER

A professor of law, Malcom Sharp, writing a foreword to a book by his former philosophy teacher, Alexander Meiklejohn, said that "[o]n the great questions of law, the lawyer must still go to school to the philosopher."[1] The observation is a graceful obeisance by a modest student to his revered mentor.

But, of course, it is something more as well. It bespeaks the recurring necessity students of the common law feel when faced by a conflict of legal principles. At such times we look to what Justice Cardozo called "logic" and what he and others of us might loosely call "philosophy."[2] We search for conceptual clarity. We investigate the fundamental presuppositions of fact or value which underlie the warring principles with which we are faced. And we hope thereby to reconcile the conflict by some reformulation of our principles, by some new conceptual accommodation.

Such a reformulation is long overdue in respect to the relation of the right of privacy and the first amendment. It may be that "the life of the law has not been logic: it has been experience,"[3] and that "history" or "the felt necessities of the times" are "likely to predominate over logic or pure reason"[4] in the future development of the law affecting privacy and the mass communications media. But even if conceptual clarity and consistency will not help us get to where we want to go—and I believe it may—it will nevertheless serve us well to know where we are going. If logic and philosophy cannot forge the legal terrain, they can at least provide a map of it, a curious kind of map which we draw as we proceed along the road.

---

1. Sharp, Foreword to A. MEIKLEJOHN, POLITICAL FREEDOM (1960) [hereinafter cited as Sharp].
2. See generally B. CARDOZO, THE NATURE OF THE JUDICIAL PROCESS 9-50 (1921) [hereinafter cited as CARDOZO].
3. O.W. HOLMES, JR., THE COMMON LAW 1 (1881).
4. CARDOZO, supra note 2, at 52. See also New York Trust Co. v. Eisner, 256 U.S. 345, 349 (1921) ("a page of history is worth a volume of logic") (Holmes, J.).

I. The Philosopher's Theory of Free Expression

In its 1964 decision in *New York Times Co. v. Sullivan*[5] the Supreme Court of the United States undertook a radical departure in its application of first amendment doctrine. Although the Court did not declare a new governing theory of the amendment—courts rarely make such pronouncements, of course—the cases since *New York Times* appear to have been decided in a new analytical framework,[6] the precise implications of which cannot yet be fully appreciated.

The classical view of freedom of expression under the first amendment is that the right to speak or to publish inheres in the speaker. I believe that in *New York Times* and its progeny the Court has begun to look upon freedom of expression as an interest inhering in the body politic, not the individual speaker: an interest in hearing what is spoken, in being informed, rather than in speaking or communicating.

Obviously the interest in being informed can only be served if there are those who write, speak, and otherwise communicate. Moreover, society cannot insure being fully and freely informed without some reasonable assurance of full and free expression of opinion.

What difference does it make, then, whether the focus is on the interest in individual freedom of speech—the interest of the speaker—or the social necessity to be informed—the interest of a democratic people? In my view, adoption of the latter value as the primary value underlying the first amendment speech provision has extremely important consequences for the conceptual contours of that provision and its relation to other basic values of our society, including privacy. The distinction I have drawn is one which is well—though obliquely—recognized in the cases and the literature. But some of the crucial consequences which flow from it have been expounded by only one writer, the philosopher Alexander Meiklejohn.[7]

Justice Brandeis, in his classic defense of first amendment principles in *Whitney v. California*,[8] extolled free speech as both "an end and a

---

5. 376 U.S. 254 (1964).
6. *See, e.g.,* Garrison v. Louisiana, 379 U.S. 64 (1964); Rosenblatt v. Baer, 383 U.S. 75 (1966); Curtis Publishing Co. v. Butts, 388 U.S. 130 (1966); Rosenbloom v. Metromedia, Inc., 403 U.S. 29 (1971).
See also Kalven, *The New York Times Case: A Note on "The Central Meaning of the First Amendment,"* 1964 Sup. Ct. Rev. 191 [hereinafter cited as Kalven]; T. Emerson, The System of Freedom of Expression 517-43 (1970) [hereinafter cited as Emerson]; Brennan, *The Supreme Court and the Meiklejohn Interpretation of the First Amendment,* 79 Harv. L. Rev. 1 (1965) [hereinafter cited as Brennan].
7. *See* A. Meiklejohn, Political Freedom (1960) [hereinafter cited as Political Freedom]; Meiklejohn, *The First Amendment Is an Absolute,* 1961 Sup. Ct. Rev. 245 (P. Kurland ed.) [hereinafter cited as First Amendment]. *See also* Meiklejohn, *Public Speech and the First Amendment,* 55 Geo. L.J. 234 (1966).
8. 274 U.S. 357, 372 (1927) (concurring opinion).

means." As an end, it is an aspect of that liberty which is "the secret of happiness," enabling individuals to be "free to develop their faculties."

As a means, it is, first, "indispensable to the discovery and spread of truth." Second, it constitutes "a fundamental principle of American government," necessary to a self-governing people if they are to fulfill their "political duty of public discussion." Finally, Brandeis saw freedom of expression as a means to preserve political stability, since "repression breeds hate" which in turn "menaces stable government."[9]

Professor Emerson has recently succinctly restated the four main premises upon which "[t]he system of freedom of expression in a democratic society rests." Free expression provides: (1) "a means of insuring individual self-fulfillment," integral to "the dignity of man"; (2) "an essential process for advancing knowledge and discovering truth"; (3) a means of insuring "participation in decision making by all members of society . . . in forming the common judgment"; and (4) "a method of achieving a more adaptable and hence a more stable community . . . [and] maintaining the precarious balance between healthy cleavage and necessary consensus."[10]

Both Justice Brandeis and Professor Emerson implicitly recognize the distinction between the values of speaking freely and of being fully or freely informed. The one is, in Brandeis' terms, an end in itself; in Emerson's terms, an aspect of individual self-fulfillment, a value to the individual citizen. This personal value is to be contrasted with the social or political values sustained by freedom of expression. These are what Brandeis calls "means," or values instrumental to the success of a democratic state: namely, the value of "the discovery and spread of political truth," the value of "participation in decision making of all members of society" and the value of "stable government" which is menaced by "repression" of individual "thought, hope and imagination."

Professor Meiklejohn holds, more explicitly and precisely than Brandeis and Emerson, to the same distinction between the individual and social values embodied in free expression. He draws important consequences from it, however, which neither they nor the classical view of free expression recognize. He distinguishes the individual "right to speak whenever, wherever [and] however [one] chooses,"[11] from the political "need to hear."[12] The one involves "the words of the speakers," the other, "the minds of the hearers."[13] He concludes, on

---

9. *Id.* at 372-80.
10. EMERSON, *supra* note 6, at 6-7.
11. POLITICAL FREEDOM, *supra* note 7, at 25.
12. *Id.* at 57, 118-19. *See also First Amendment, supra* note 7, at 255.
13. POLITICAL FREEDOM, *supra* note 7, at 26.

the basis of this distinction—and this is most novel in what he says—that "[t]he First Amendment . . . is not the guardian of unregulated talkativeness," and that "[w]hat is essential under [it] is not that everyone shall speak, but that everything worth saying [is] said."[14]

The first amendment, for Meiklejohn, is not concerned with the individual's right to find self-fulfillment in free expression. That individual right, or aspect of individual liberty, like others such as the right to property, is protected by the fifth amendment. But, like other such fifth amendment liberties, it is subject to reasonable limitation within the confines of due process.[15]

By contrast, the social interest in free expression, in "hearing" or being informed, which inheres in the body politic, not the individual, is protected by the first amendment. But, by contrast to the individual's "right to speak," which is subject to reasonable limitation, the "right to hear" is "absolute," not subject to any limitation.[16]   This social "need to hear" is "prior" to the individual "need to speak," in the sense that it "has a constitutional status which no pursuit of an individual purpose can ever claim."[17]

By any account, Professor Meiklejohn's is an extraordinary and radically different theory of the first amendment. (One which has been given too little critical recognition, I might add.)   What supports it? Two things: a view of the character of American government and the American Constitution and a most fertile analogy.

In the 1897 case of *Robertson v. Baldwin*,[18] the Supreme Court expressed the view that "[t]he law is perfectly well settled that the first ten amendments to the Constitution, commonly known as the Bill of Rights, were not intended to lay down any novel principles of government, but simply to embody certain guarantees and immunities which we had inherited from our English ancestors. . . ."[19]   Meiklejohn denounces this doctrine as "the most disastrous judicial pronouncement" he has ever found.[20]   In its stead, relying on the dissenting opinion of the first Justice Harlan in the *Robertson* case,[21] he urges that our Constitution is extremely novel.   "The distinctive feature . . . that marks it off from British political institutions, is that it is established, not by

---

14. *Id.*
15. *Id.* at 55.
16. *Id.* at 26-27, 36-37, 55, 57, 115, 118-19.   *See also First Amendment, supra* note 7, at 254-56.
17. POLITICAL FREEDOM, *supra* note 7, at 55.
18. 165 U.S. 275.
19. *Id.* at 281.   This view was endorsed as "the authentic view of the Bill of Rights" as recently as 1951.   *See* Dennis v. United States, 341 U.S. 494, 524 (1951) (Frankfurter, J., concurring).
20. *First Amendment, supra* note 7, at 264-65.
21. 165 U.S. at 296.

the legislature, but by the people."²² He goes on to say that "[a]ll constitutional authority to govern the people of the United States belongs" not to the legislature as in Britain, but "to the people themselves, acting as members of a corporate body politic."²³

Meiklejohn's analysis treats the Constitution as having provisions of three distinct kinds: those which establish subordinate agencies of government, those which establish the people's constitutional authority, and those which limit the powers of the subordinate agencies.²⁴ The provisions which establish agencies of government subordinate to the sovereign people and delegate powers to them are, of course, found generally in articles I, II, and III. These articles establish the legislature, the executive, and the judiciary as organs of government and prescribe their specific and limited powers.

The tenth amendment is one of the constitutional provisions which bespeaks the ultimate governing power of the people. It does so by reserving powers not otherwise delegated to subordinate agencies of government in articles I, II, and III "to the people" (and "to the states"). Article 1, section 2, reserves to the people an extremely important power, the electoral power, which is vital to the people's sovereignty. Still another in this category of constitutional provisions is the statement in the preamble: "We, the people of the United States . . . do ordain and establish this constitution."

It is at this point that the radical character of Meiklejohn's structural analysis of the Constitution becomes apparent. He agrees with the classical view that the second through the ninth amendments of the Bill of Rights constitute a set of restraints on the powers of the subordinate agencies of government. But for Meiklejohn the first amendment, like the tenth, is distinguished from the other eight as a provision which establishes the people's sovereignty.

"The revolutionary intent of the First Amendment," says Meiklejohn, "is to deny to all subordinate agencies authority to abridge the freedom of the electoral power of the people." And, he goes on to say,

the title "Bill of Rights" is lamentably inaccurate as a designation of the first ten amendments. They are not a "Bill of Rights" but a "Bill of Powers and Rights." The Second through the Ninth Amendments limit the powers of the subordinate agencies in order that due regard shall be paid to the private "rights of the governed." The First and Tenth Amendments protect the governing "powers" of the people from abridgement by the agencies which are established as their servants. In

22. *First Amendment, supra* note 7, at 265.
23. *Id.* at 253.
24. *Id.* at 253-54.

the field of our "rights," each one of us can claim "due process of law" [under the Fifth Amendment]. In the field of our governing "powers," the notion of "due process" is irrelevant.[25]

Although Meiklejohn did not think it necessary to say so, I would add that the notion of due process, in his view, is irrelevant with respect to the governing powers of the people afforded by the first amendment because those are sovereign or absolute powers, not subject to any limitations, even such as may be compatible with due process. And this, of course, is what explains for Meiklejohn the difference between the constitutional protection afforded speaking and that afforded hearing.

The people in a democracy are both the governed and the governors.[26] The people's need to hear or to be informed is absolute as an attribute of their sovereignty. The individual's need to speak or communicate is subject to limitation within reasonable due process limits, like any other private right.

On the one hand, the need to hear and to be informed is inherent in and necessary to the people's power as governors, and is protected by the preamble, article I, section 2, the first amendment, and the tenth amendment. It may not be limited or abridged by any agency of government, since it is integral to the people's sovereignty. In this sense, the first amendment does not protect a freedom to speak. It protects the freedom of those activities of thought and communication by which we govern. It is concerned, not with a private right but with a public power, a governmental responsibility.[27] It "forbids the legislature to limit the political freedom of the people."[28]

The right to speak and to communicate, on the other hand, is a right of the people, not as governors, but as the governed. Such a right is "an individual possession" or "private right" of the governed, rather than a "political right" of the sovereign people.[29] This private right is protected, like other private rights, such as the rights to life, liberty, or property, by the fifth amendment, which, rather than proscribing any regulation by agencies of government, allows limitation subject only to due process.

Besides a constitutional argument to sustain the distinction between the right to hear and the right to speak, Meiklejohn relies on two fecund comparisons, one philosophical and the other from daily life. First, he asks us "to turn back for a few moments to the [Socratic di-

---

25. *Id.* at 254.
26. *Id.* at 253-54.
27. *Id.* at 255.
28. POLITICAL FREEDOM, *supra* note 7, at 115.
29. *Id.* at 37-38.

alogues of] . . . Plato"[30] and to contrast the Socrates of the *Apology* with the Socrates of the *Crito*. In both dialogues, Socrates is faced by a demand placed upon him by the State. In the one case he refuses obedience; in the other he accepts it as a high-order moral obligation.

In the *Apology*, after having been found guilty of the charge that his teaching had corrupted the youth of Athens, Socrates is offered the opportunity to avoid a sentence of death if he will agree to stop teaching philosophy. He refuses, and is ready to face death, because he believes it is beyond the power of the State to determine what men shall teach, think, or believe.[31]

In the *Crito*, Socrates is in prison awaiting his execution and is approached by his friends, who urge him to flee to safety. He refuses on the ground that, although it is unjust for the state to determine what men should believe, it is within the just exercise of the power of the state to imprison and, if need be, execute its citizens for violations of its laws. Even though Socrates believes that the law he has broken is unjust, it is nevertheless his duty to drink the hemlock and suffer death in obedience to the law.[32]

Meiklejohn draws a lesson from these dialogues which is somewhat mistaken, but nevertheless suggestive. He says Plato is laying down this principle: "If the government attempts to limit the freedom of a man's opinions, . . . that man, and his fellows with him, has both the right and duty of disobedience. But if, on the other hand, by regular legal procedure, his life or his property is required of him, he must submit . . . ."[33]

I believe Meiklejohn's Platonic lesson involved a sleight of mind in respect to the difference between the right to speak and the right to hear. Unless I misunderstand these dialogues, Plato is urging that the right to speak, Socrates' right to teach, is an absolute, *not* subject, in other words, to the authority of the State. Plato nowhere distinguishes—as does Meiklejohn—between the right to speak, which is subject to limitation, and the right to hear, which is absolute. In fact, the *Apology* urges, contrary to Meiklejohn's position, that the right to speak or teach is beyond the authority of the State to limit.

It is only if one reads the *Apology* to be defending the right to hear, the right of public inquiry and the right to be fully and freely informed, (a liberal reading, to be sure, but a possible one), that the Meiklejohn thesis emerges. Read in this way, the *Crito* and *Apology* teach the lesson that a State may justly, and consistently with

---

30. *Id.* at 21.
31. *See* Plato, *Socrates' Defense (Apology)*, in THE COLLECTED DIALOGUES 15-21 (E. Hamilton & H. Cairns eds. 1961).
32. *See* Plato, *Crito*, in *id.* at 33-39.
33. POLITICAL FREEDOM, *supra* note 7, at 23.

government by consent, take a person's life, if done according to due process of law. But the State may not limit the public understanding or restrict the capacity of the public to be informed without violating the democratic principle of government by consent.

Only the informed consent of a sovereign people sustains the obligations imposed by a democratic government. Any limitation on informed consent is a limitation on the people's sovereignty, on their capacity to exercise their governing role knowledgeably and intelligently.

Meiklejohn's second analogy makes his point more directly and effectively than his excursion into the philosophic literature. If you want to understand the difference between the right to hear and the right to speak, he says, "examine the procedure of the traditional town meeting."[34] In such a meeting people gather to discuss and decide upon matters of importance to them: roads, schools, local police, health, etc.

Everyone would agree that all the people at the meeting (put aside, if you will, the problems of the child and the visitor) have a right to speak to the issues at hand. But everyone would also agree, I would assume, that the right to speak at the meeting is subject to certain limitations; for instance, that only one person speak at a time, that people speak only when recognized, and that they follow the order of the agenda.

These limitations flow from and are justified by the purpose of the meeting. The best and most expeditious decisions about roads, schools, etc., will be made (leave aside "the benevolent dictator" problem) if all possible information and all possible points of view are presented at the meeting. These desiderata dictate, in turn, that rules be adopted for the conduct of the discussion.

The rules may attempt to insure that as many people as possible speak so as to provide maximum information and diversity of viewpoint. To this end, a time limit may be set. Intelligent decision is served by orderly and coherent discussion. To this end, within reasonable limits, those who speak are required by the chairperson to confine themselves to the issues before the meeting, in the order those issues are to be decided. Rabble rousers and hecklers who go so far as to threaten the capacity of the meeting to do its business may be subject to ejection.[35] And, of course, many other more technical rules (such

---

34. *Id.* at 24.
35. It is difficult to determine the point at which heckling becomes so destructive of the purpose of a meeting as to threaten that purpose. However, in the context of some disruptions at university gatherings in recent years it is important to recognize this justified limitation on "free speech" and to quote Meiklejohn in this regard:

as what motions lie, and when), each constituting a limitation on the right to speak at the meeting, may also be established.   In each instance, the justification for a particular limit on free speech is the interest in a rational and well-informed meeting which proceeds expeditiously to decision.

Thus, in the town meeting we see exhibited both a need to speak and a need to hear.   These, of course, are the analogues of Meiklejohn's fifth amendment right to speak and his first amendment "right to hear."   The former is an interest held by each individual at the meeting, an interest of those governed or ruled by the meeting.   The latter is an interest of all the individuals at the meeting taken as a group, an interest of the meeting's sovereign governors or rulers.

The right to speak at the meeting is subject to limitation.   The right to be fully and freely informed at the meeting knows no limitation, since it is the very purpose of the meeting and any restriction on it would destroy the democratic or consensual character of the meeting. The very essence of the town meeting as a form of "self-government in its simplest, most obvious form" is that, to quote Meiklejohn again, "[t]he meeting was assembled, not primarily to talk, but primarily by means of talking to get business done.   And the talking must be regulated and abridged as the doing of the business under actual conditions may require."[36]

"But," says the Justice to the Philosopher, "what difference does all this philosophic and constitutional theory make to the decision of the individual cases which come before me?   The sovereign people never appear before me as litigants in first amendment cases claiming their right to hear.   I only decide cases between individuals who seek to sustain their individual right to speak against one or another agency of government which seeks to limit that right in one way or another. How, then, can my legal judgment ever vindicate the right of the people to hear as an aspect of their sovereign power of self-governance?   When does the first amendment apply, in Meiklejohn's terms, absolutely to bar a limitation of speech, and when does the fifth amendment apply authorizing a limitation subject to due process standards of reasonableness?"

When self-governing men demand freedom of speech they are not saying that every individual has an unalienable right to speak whenever, wherever, however he chooses. . . .   The common sense of any reasonable society would deny the existence of that unqualified right. . . .   To you who now listen to my words [Meiklejohn was delivering a lecture], it is allowable to differ with me, but it is not allowable for you to state that difference in words until I have finished my reading.   Anyone who would thus irresponsibly interrupt the activities of a lecture, a hospital, a concert hall, a church, a machine shop, a classroom, a football field, or a home, does not thereby exhibit his freedom.   Rather, he shows himself to be a boor, a public nuisance, who must be abated, by force if necessary.
Id. at 25.
  36. *Id.* at 24.

Think of the nation as one large, continuing town meeting, having as its purpose the best informed electorate possible, and think of the judiciary as the ultimate moderator of that meeting. As at a town meeting, at the nation's meeting under the first amendment any opinion or view may be expressed on any subject. In other words, the truth or falsity of what is said may never serve as a basis for limitation. But unlike the town meeting, in the nation's meeting there is no agenda, and any subject may come up for discussion at any time. Order must be maintained at the nation's meeting, as at the town meeting, however, to insure the success of its purposes. The rules of order fall into three categories.

First, if the very possibility of continuing discussion is subject to an immediate and substantial threat as the result of the expression of an opinion, if the system of government by informed consent is itself in immediate peril as a result of open debate, the debate may be postponed. (Not terminated, it should be noted.) "When the roof falls in, a moderator may, without violating the First Amendment, declare the meeting adjourned."[37]

Second, the good order of the nation's meeting also requires that whatever is said be said at such time and place and in such a manner as to serve the public interest in what is said without unreasonably interfering in the conduct of government or other social institutions or the life of any individual. This means that, if the interference arising out of the circumstances, place, or time in which something is said is not absolutely necessary to serve the public purpose of being informed, a reasonable regulation of what is said may be undertaken to prevent harm to another individual or to the conduct of governmental or other business.

Finally, a rule of relevance applies in the nation's meeting as it does at a town meeting. Not every subject is fit for discussion at a town meeting which must decide upon, for instance, what roads to build. Although any opinion about roads, or schools and shopping centers which need roads, is appropriate, and although the chairperson is expected to allow reasonable leeway for those who wander from the subject, at some point a citizen discussing the color of the bed sheets used by a neighbor may legitimately be declared out of order.

Likewise, in the nation's public meeting under the first amendment, there are some subjects of discussion which bear no logical relationship to the need of a sovereign, self-governing people to be informed. Where a subject is irrelevant to maintaining the informed consent which sustains a democracy, reasonable due process limitations may be applied under the fifth amendment.

---

37. *Id.* at 49. Compare text accompanying note 36.

The nation's meeting analogy teaches that the truth or falsity of what is said may *never* serve as a basis of limitation, or abridgement. In this sense, the first amendment is absolute. However, speech may be reasonably limited or regulated under the due process clause of the fifth amendment if (1) it is irrelevant to maintaining the informed consent of a self-governing people, or (2) it is uttered at such a time or place as substantially and immediately to threaten the system of government by informed consent, or (3) it is uttered at such a time or place or in such a manner as to interfere in the ordinary conduct of any public or private institution or the life of any individual, when such interference is unnecessary to the fulfillment of the interest of a self-governing people in being informed.

The first amendment protects the people's sovereignty by protecting the right of the people to be fully informed about their responsibility to govern. This protection is afforded by denying to any subordinate agency the right to decide what the people shall hear. Any abridgement of this right to hear and consider some view relevant to the purposes of self-government, any attempt by a delegated agent of governance to act as sovereign censor of truth or falsity, limits the sovereign right of the people. It constitutues an abandonment of the democratic principle of consent of the governed, a consent which is only operative if it is fully informed.

II.   THE PHILOSOPHER'S THEORY AND THE RIGHT TO PRIVACY

I turn now to consider what consequences the Meiklejohn theory entails for the right to privacy.[38]   To begin with, however, I want to make it clear that I intend to deal with only one aspect of this burgeoning legal right. I shall consider only that limited aspect of privacy having to do with the interest of an individual in being free of undue and unreasonable publicity.

A.   *The Mass Publication Right of Privacy*

I shall not attempt to review here the extensive scholarly literature and the numerous statutes and cases on privacy.[39]   It is enough for my

---

38. I have dealt with this issue sketchily elsewhere. *See* Bloustein, *Privacy, Tort Law, and the Constitution: Is Warren and Brandeis' Tort Petty and Unconstitutional as Well?*, 46 TEXAS L. REV. 611, 624-29 (1968). Meiklejohn himself never spoke to the question, since the right to privacy had not really come to the fore, outside the relatively narrow reaches of legal scholarship, during his lifetime.

39. It seems invidious to suggest bibliographic sources. However, see A. MILLER, THE ASSAULT ON PRIVACY: COMPUTERS, DATA BANKS, AND DOSSIERS (1971); A. WESTIN, PRIVACY AND FREEDOM (1967) [hereinafter cited as WESTIN]; PRIVACY (J.R. Pennock & J. Chapman eds. 1971); Bloustein, *Privacy As an Aspect of Human Dignity: An Answer to Dean Prosser*, 39 N.Y.U.L. REV. 962 (1964) [hereinafter cited as Bloustein]; Prosser, *Privacy*, 48 CALIF. L. REV. 383 (1960); *Symposium—Comments on*

purposes to indicate that the general concept of privacy has still not
had a definitive analysis[40] and that what began at the turn of the century as a limited private right to prevent undue and unreasonable publicity concerning private lives[41] has now developed into an extraordi-
narily broad constitutional right, the limits of which are still not clear.[42]

In some respects, the general conceptual dimensions of the right to
privacy are still best described in the terms used by Warren and Brandeis, the fathers of the right, in 1890. Privacy is "the right to be let
alone," a right which is one aspect of the broad principle of "inviolate
personality." It serves to protect "man's spiritual nature, . . . his feelings and . . . his intellect," and it is one of "the most comprehensive
of rights and the right most valued by civilized men."[43]

My own view of the principle of privacy is a mere derivative of that
of Warren and Brandeis. I state it here solely to make clear the as-
sumptions I bring to the discussion of the first amendment and privacy.
My view, developed in a 1964 study of the literature and cases, is
that our law of privacy attempts to preserve individuality, our liberty
as individuals to do as we will, our human dignity, by placing sanctions upon outrageous or unreasonable violations of the conditions of
its sustenance.[44]

---

the *Griswold Case and the Right of Privacy*, 64 MICH. L. REV. 197-307 (1965); *Sym-
posium—Privacy*, 31 LAW & CONTEMP. PROB. 251-341 (1966); Note, *On Privacy:
Constitutional Protection for Personal Liberty*, 48 N.Y.U.L. REV. 670 (1973). For a
discussion of privacy outside the United States by the Committee on Privacy of the
International Commission of Jurists see COMMITTEE ON PRIVACY, JUSTICE, PRIVACY AND
THE LAW (M. Littman & P. Carter-Ruck, joint chairmen, 1970) [hereinafter cited as
PRIVACY AND THE LAW].

40. *See* PRIVACY AND THE LAW, *supra* note 39, at 5. "In the course of our work,
we have become increasingly aware of the difficulties which seem to beset any attempt
to find a precise or logical formula which could either circumscribe the meaning of the
word 'privacy' or define it exhaustively." For the most recent attempt at a definition
and a good survey of past attempts see Parker, *A Definition of Privacy*, 27 RUTGERS
L. REV. 275 (1974) [hereinafter cited as Parker].

41. As is well known, the right of privacy owes its origin to what is regarded as
one of the most influential articles in the legal literature, Warren & Brandeis, *The Right
to Privacy*, 4 HARV. L. REV. 193 (1890) [hereinafter cited as Warren & Brandeis].

42. *See, e.g.*, Roe v. Wade, 410 U.S. 113 (1973); Griswold v. Connecticut, 381 U.S.
479 (1965); *Symposium—Comments on the Griswold Case and the Right of Privacy*,
64 MICH. L. REV. 197-307 (1965); Note, *On Privacy: Constitutional Protection for
Personal Liberty*, 48 N.Y.U.L. REV. 670 (1973).

43. *See* Warren & Brandeis, *supra* note 41, at 193, 195, 205.

44. Bloustein, *supra* note 39, at 1002-03. Although many writers define privacy
more narrowly (*see, e.g.*, WESTIN, *supra* note 39; Parker, *supra* note 40) a number of
other recent definitions of the concept are as broad as that of Warren & Brandeis. *See*
Konvitz, *Privacy and the Law: A Philosophical Prelude*, 31 LAW & CONTEMP. PROB. 272,
279-80 (1966) ("Its essence is the claim that there is a sphere of space that has not
been dedicated to public use or control . . . . [As] Locke would say, [it is] the kind of
'property' with respect to which its owner has delegated no power to the state.")
See also PRIVACY AND THE LAW, *supra* note 39, at 4:
  To preserve his sense of identity and the integrity of his personality, to work out
  his personal relationships and find his way to his own salvation, each human being

The specialized aspect of privacy here considered is the threat to our individuality posed by the exploitation of private lives by the mass media. Just as the intimacy and inner space necessary to individuality and human dignity may be impaired by a peeping Tom, a wiretapper, or an eavesdropper, so too may it be impaired by the sensational exposure of the intimate details of a private life in the mass media.[45]

needs to limit the area of his intercourse with others. . . . [W]e need to be able to keep to ourselves, if we want to, those thoughts and feelings, beliefs and doubts, hopes, plans, fears and fantasies, which we call 'private' precisely because we wish to be able to choose freely with whom, and to what extent, we are willing to share them.

For a very broad historic-philosophical treatment of the concept see H. ARENDT, THE HUMAN CONDITION 22-78 (1958).

The first articulate explorer and to an extent even theorist of intimacy was Jean-Jacques Rousseau . . . . He arrived at his discovery through a rebellion not against the oppression of the state but against society's unbearable perversion of the human heart, its intrusion upon an innermost region in man which until then had needed no special protection.

Id. at 38-39.

Finally, for insight into the psychological function served by a sense of individual privacy or dignity see E. GOFFMAN, ASYLUMS (1961) [hereinafter cited as GOFFMAN].

The practice of reserving something of oneself from the clutch of an institution is very visible in mental hospitals and prisons but can be found in more benign and less totalistic institutions, too. . . . [T]his recalcitrance is not an incidental mechanism of defense but rather an essential constituent of the self.

. . . [I]n any . . . unit of social organization . . . [w]e always find the individual employing methods to keep some distance, some elbow room, between himself and that with which others assume he should be identified.

. . . . Our sense of being a person can come from being drawn into a wider social unit; our sense of selfhood can arise through the little ways in which we resist the pull.

Id. at 319-20.

45. In passing I suggest that the reason there is no fully agreed-upon definition of privacy, with some writers espousing a narrow view and some a broad view (*see* note 44 *supra*), is that the relationships between, on the one hand, intimacy or inner space and individuality and, on the other hand, wiretapping, eavesdropping, etc., and intimacy or inner space have been neglected. A wiretap is one means of destroying inner space or intimacy, and intimacy or inner space represents the psychological condition for the sustenance of individuality and human dignity.

These relationships are nowhere better explored as psycho-social phenomena than by Goffman. He writes about asylums and their inmates, but uses the former term broadly to include any "total institution," including convents as well as mental hospitals. GOFFMAN, *supra* note 44, at 4-5. He describes how such total institutions begin, immediately upon an inmate's entry, a series of "abasements, degradations, humiliations, and profanations of self," a process which results in the "mortification of the self." *Id.* at 14. Inmates in turn exercise "recalcitrance," try to reserve "something of [themselves] from the clutch of [the] institution" and devise expedients "to keep some distance, some elbow room between" themselves and what the institution wants them to be. *Id.* at 319-20. Goffman gives some extraordinary examples of means of degradation and debasement, examples which help me immensely, it seems to me, to explain the psycho-social impact of wiretapping and mass media sensationalism, and to explain the relationship between the means used and the result achieved. ("Whatever the form or the source of these various indignities, the individual has to engage in activity whose symbolic implications are incompatible with his conception of self." *Id.* at 23.) They include: forcing all mental patients to eat with a spoon (*id.* at 22); having religious initiates kiss the feet of religious superiors (*id.*), remain prostrate in silence before them (*id.*), or receive food by begging for it and receiving it from their plates and eating from their

A newspaper publishes a picture of a deformed newborn child and the parents are mortified and insulted that the world should be a witness to their private tragedy.[46]   An author undertakes a sympathetic but intimately detailed sketch of someone, who up to that time had only been a face in the crowd, and the subject complains that their[47] anonymity has been replaced by notoriety.[48]   In such cases the individual has been profaned by laying a private life open to public view.   The intimacy and private space necessary to sustain individuality and human dignity has been impaired by turning a private life into a public spectacle.   The innermost region of being—the soul, if you will—has been bruised by exposure to the world.[49]

B.   *The Newsworthiness Defense*

The relationship between a claimed violation of privacy by means of mass media publication and the first amendment is readily apparent. The amendment protects speech and publication against abridgement and, therefore, putatively prohibits a court from granting recovery of damages against a publisher for the publication of intimate details of a private life.

Although in their germinal article Warren and Brandeis do not expressly mention the first amendment, they recognize clearly the potential conflict between the individual's "right to be let alone" and the "legitimate interest to their fellow citizens" of *some* of the personal facts of the lives of *some* people.[50]   "The design of the law [of privacy]," they said, "must be to protect those persons *with whose affairs the community has no legitimate concern*, from being dragged into an undesirable and undesired publicity."[51]   Conversely, they urged that

---

utensils (*id.* at 31); being subject to having all conversations with "outside visitors" overheard (*id.* at 32); having access to personal records of mental patients available to all hospital personnel even though there is information in them the patients are trying to keep to themselves (*id.* at 158-59); taking away patients' false teeth and eyeglasses (*id.* at 250).

46. Bazemore v. Savannah Hosp., 171 Ga. 257, 155 S.E. 194 (1930); Douglas v. Stokes, 149 Ky. 506, 149 S.W. 849 (1912).

47. In referring to a person who may be of either sex, and following a suggestion in a recent letter to the *Harvard Crimson*, I use the pronoun "they" ("their," "them") with a singular meaning. As the letter-writer points out:

> The stellar advantage of using *they* in the singular is that in many forms this construction is already widely used. Indeed, English teachers exert themselves to *stop* students from saying "everyone should hang up *their* coat. . . ." Because "their," in this sense, is already common, this construction would be far more readily accepted than a strange new word, and it is simpler than *him or her*.

Harvard Crimson, Apr. 15, 1974, at 2, col. 2.

48. Cason v. Baskin, 155 Fla. 198, 20 So. 2d 243 (1944); *cf.* Sidis v. F-R Publishing Corp., 113 F.2d 806 (2d Cir. 1940).

49. I have dealt at greater length with these so-called public disclosure cases elsewhere. *See* Bloustein, *supra* note 39, at 977-84.

50. *See* Warren & Brandeis, *supra* note 41, at 214-15.

51. *Id.* at 214 (emphasis added).

"[t]he right to privacy does not prohibit any publication of matter which is *of public or general interest*"[52] and "to whatever degree and in whatever connection a man's life has ceased to be private, . . . to that extent the protection [of privacy] is to be withdrawn."[53]

Although its precise dimensions are still not clear, this so-called "newsworthiness" limitation on the right of privacy has since been well established. The case which firmly embodied it in the law was *Sidis v. F-R Publishing Corp.*,[54] which involved the portrayal of a child-prod-igy of mathematics in a *New Yorker* magazine profile.[55] It was a friendly piece, but it was "merciless in its dissection of intimate details of the life of young Sidis, who loathed public attention and wanted more than anything else in life to remain obscure and anonymous."[56] Recovery of damages for an impairment of privacy was denied in an opinion written by Judge Charles E. Clark, who concluded that "at some point the public interest in obtaining information becomes domi-nant over the individual's desire for privacy." Although he expressed "no comment" on whether or not "news worthiness of the matter printed will always constitute a complete defense," he was of the opin-ion that news stories "focused upon public characters" could not be the subject of legal complaint.[57] Ever since *Sidis*, courts faced with a simi-lar conflict between the claim of privacy and the claims of newsworthi-ness have come down irregularly, some on one side, some on the other, of the uncertain line defined first by Warren and Brandeis and then by Judge Clark.[58]

The line between privacy and newsworthiness is an uncertain one for at least three reasons. First, it has not yet been clearly established

---

52. *Id.* (emphasis added).
53. *Id.* at 215.
54. 113 F.2d 806 (2d Cir. 1940).
55. The profile was edited by James Thurber. J. THURBER, THE YEARS WITH ROSS 210-12 (1959) [hereinafter cited as THURBER]. I am indebted to Shapo, *Media Injuries to Personality: An Essay on Legal Regulation of Public Communication*, 46 TEXAS L. REV. 650, 660 (1968) for this reference. Shapo characterizes Thurber as a "rewrite man" on the article (*accord*, C. GREGORY & H. KALVEN, TORTS 888 (1959)), and this is what Thurber himself implies. *See* THURBER, *supra* at 210-12. At another point in his book, however, he indicates that he was the author and that he used a pseudonym. This adds another element of irony to the Sidis story. A young man looking for ano-nymity is "done in" by an author who uses anonymity to protect himself. It also casts some extra doubt on Thurber's explanation and justification of the piece. He says he thought it might teach the parents of prodigies a lesson. *Id.* at 210-12. It might indeed; but in the *New Yorker* magazine? And at this much unnecessary cost? My guess is that Thurber was feeling some guilt about having done the piece and was not as forthright about his role with respect to it as he might have been.
56. Sidis v. F-R Publishing Corp., 113 F.2d 806, 807 (2d Cir. 1940).
57. *Id.* at 809.
58. For cases upholding the newsworthiness value see Time, Inc. v. Hill, 385 U.S. 374 (1967) and cases cited therein at 383-84 n.7. For citations of cases upholding the privacy value see *id.* at 383-84 n.7; Briscoe v. Reader's Digest Ass'n, 4 Cal. 3d 529, 529, 483 P.2d 34, 37, 93 Cal. Rptr. 866, 869 (1971).

whether newsworthiness is a first amendment constitutional defense to be vindicated at the cost of any right other than a superior constitutional right, or merely a common law defense to be weighed against the common law right of privacy. Second, we lack a clear understanding of what publication is "of public or general interest," in Warren and Brandeis' terms[59]—that is, of what is newsworthy. The third reason is that we have not yet fully determined who is a "public character" or a "public figure," in Judge Clark's terms.[60]

C.   *The Meiklejohn Analysis and Newsworthiness*

In my judgment, these three questions are all of a piece. Moreover, they can be satisfactorily resolved by an application of the Meiklejohn first amendment analysis. "Newsworthiness" is ambiguously used in the cases and literature to denote three very different things: the public right to hear or be informed, the private publisher's right to speak or publish, and the insatiable appetite of the public for gossip about private lives. A "public figure" is someone the public has an unlimited right to hear about, protected by the first amendment as a necessity of their informed consent as governors. The private publisher's right to speak or publish may be limited, however,—subject to the fifth amendment due process clause—by the creation of a state right of common law recovery for the invasion of privacy. Neither the private right of the publisher, protected, to be sure, under the fifth amendment, nor mere public curiosity unrelated to a governing purpose should necessarily deprive the private person who is the object of public curiosity of the protection of the right to privacy if a legislature or a common law court has reasonably determined that the right to privacy shall prevail.

The critical distinctions are those which must be made with respect to newsworthiness.[61] No one would deny Judge Clark's postulate that "at some point the public interest in obtaining information becomes dominant over the individual desire for privacy."[62] But the weight to be given "the public interest in obtaining information" should depend on whether or not the information is relevant to the public's governing purposes.

"Public interest," taken to mean curiosity, must be distinguished from "public interest," taken to mean value to the public of receiving

---

59. Warren & Brandeis, *supra* note 41, at 214.
60. 113 F.2d at 809.
61. Although the term of art used is "newsworthiness" and the discussion which follows is about "news," it should be observed that the issue at hand and the conclusion reached is much broader: it covers all mass media.
62. 113 F.2d at 809.

information of governing importance.[63]   There is, to be sure, a constitutionally protected right to satisfy public curiosity and publish lurid gossip about private lives.   But this, in Meiklejohn's terms, is a limited or qualified fifth amendment right, to be distinguished from the absolute or unqualified first amendment right of the public to learn about those aspects of private lives which are relevant to the necessities of self-government.

The confusion between the public's constitutional right to be informed about the lives of public figures, the publisher's constitutional right to publish private gossip, and the public's thirst for lurid details of any private life, is illustrated in a recent article by Professor Kalven.[64]   He expresses the view that the newsworthiness defense might "be so overpowering as virtually to swallow [the mass publication] tort [of privacy]."[65]   He means, of course, that newsworthiness as a defense is so broad in its coverage that it will be difficult to find a case where it will not prevail over privacy.

Kalven reaches this dire conclusion because he uses the term "newsworthiness" ambiguously; he fails to distinguish the public right, the public curiosity, and the publisher's right.   His conclusion rests on the observation that "whatever is in the news media is by definition newsworthy, that the press must in the nature of things be the final arbiter of newsworthiness."[66]

Whatever is published may indeed be newsworthy, in the sense of satisfying the public interest or curiosity.   It is also certainly the case that the press should be the final arbiter of newsworthiness, of what is worth reporting, in the sense of exercising the right to publish subject to the limitations of the fifth amendment.   But neither of these statements is the same as saying that the press is the final arbiter of newsworthiness in the sense of determining what the public must be informed of for the purposes of fulfilling its self-governing functions.

The press may well known what will "sell" in the way of news about people.   And it surely should determine what it wants to say about them, subject to the due process limitations of the fifth amendment.   But the press should not determine the extent of the people's right to know about the lives of their leaders in the interest of exercising their governing control over them.   This is a first amendment right reserved

---

63. *See* Note, *The Right of Privacy: Normative-Descriptive Confusion in the Defense of Newsworthiness*, 30 U. CHI. L. REV. 722 (1963).

64. Kalven, *Privacy in Tort Law—Were Warren and Brandeis Wrong?*, 31 LAW & CONTEMP. PROB. 326 (1966).

65. *Id.* at 336.

66. *Id.*   A similar ambiguity is to be found in Warren & Brandeis, *supra* note 41, and in Judge Clark's *Sidis* opinion.

unto the people themselves and exercised in their interest by the courts.

D. *The Use of Name or Likeness in the News*

It helps understanding of the concept of newsworthiness and its relation to privacy to ask what function the identification of individuals by the use of a name or likeness plays in news. Again, the threefold distinction between the public right to be informed, the public yearning for gossip about private lives, and the publisher's right to publish, proves instructive.

Gossip and scandal lose their bite without the use of names or likenesses. People tend to read and enjoy news which is about "real people," more than they tend to read and enjoy historical or social generalizations, social statistics, or news about anonymous figures. A news story about a love triangle murder is more satisfying to the public's prying and prurient instincts—more "newsworthy" or of more "public interest"—if the individuals concerned are named and identified. This is true, curiously enough, even when the people concerned are not well-known or known at all to the reader, as long as the identification rings true.

Publishers tend to capitalize on this weakness for gossip,[67] on the need to identify with "real live" participants in the drama of life. They want to print what people want to read, because they want what they publish to be read. Even where publishers' sense of good taste and propriety might otherwise lead them to avoid identifying participants in the news, they may use a scandalous or personalized treatment as a lever to "sell" the substantive information conveyed by what is published. Sometimes their interest, however, is solely or predominantly in selling their publications and in making a profit. That interest is best served by catering to the public propensity to read about the intimate affairs of identifiable people.

But the public's desire to read about "real live" people and the publisher's tendency to satisfy that desire are to be distinguished from the contribution made to the public understanding of issues of governing importance by identifying the participants in news events. The *New York Times* recently ran a story with the headline, "5 Teen-Agers Hunted in Rape of Visiting Nurse."[68] The name of the victim had been withheld by the police, but her age was given, as was every detail of the rape except those which would have identified the victim.[69]

---

67. *See, e.g.,* Nizer, *The Right of Privacy*, 39 MICH. L. REV. 526, 540 (1941).

68. N.Y. Times, June 27, 1974, at 32, col. 4 (N.J. ed.).

69. Although New York State lacks such a statute, many states prohibit the publication of the name of rape victims. New York and many other states prohibit the publication of the names of certain juvenile offenders. For a collection of statutes of both kinds see Briscoe v. Reader's Digest Ass'n, 4 Cal. 3d 529, 537 n.10, 483 P.2d 34, 39

I contend that this story tells the public all they need to know about the victim of the rape to satisfy their governing obligations under the first amendment. To be sure, the name of the victim would have added spice to the story, and a picture of her on the front page might have helped sell more newspapers and induced more people to read the story. But the story without the name served the public's governing purposes in relation to rape as well as a more lurid personalized account might have.

This is not to say that identifying the participants in news events is never relevant to the people's governing purposes. Suppose another news story in which it is reported that a rape suspect has been beaten up while being held in jail, and suppose that the rape victim was the jailer's daughter. Obviously, the identification of the victim in such a case will serve a governing purpose by enabling the local community to assess the jailer's fitness for office, or, indeed, whether he committed a crime.[70]

More generally, there are people whose identification in news and commentary serves the public's governing purposes. This may be so either because they occupy official positions in our political or social life or because, even without official position, they serve roles and undertake functions which affect the public interest. Thus, a story about Senator Kennedy's alleged failure to report accurately upon his involvement in the Chappaquiddick incident is clearly one in which name or likeness are appropriate to the people's governing purposes. So is a story about the conviction for drunken driving of a volunteer leader of a youth organization.

The test in each instance is whether the personal identification is relevant to any possible governing purpose of the reader, whether such use informs the consent upon which self-government is founded. If the name or likeness might serve such an informative purpose, it may be used without regard to the injury to privacy—the right to publish is not subject to restriction, because of first amendment protection. If, however, the use of name or likeness is not relevant to the needs of an informed democratic people, the use is still constitutionally protected, but the protection is qualified in the sense of being subject to the due process test of reasonableness under the fifth amendment.

Look at the matter from the other side. Suppose a state or federal statute, or a common law rule, prohibits the mass publication of name or likeness in reporting rape cases. Is such a statute or common law rule constitutional? Under the Meiklejohn theory, the first amend-

---

n.10, 93 Cal. Rptr. 866, 871 n.10 (1971). Such statutes are discussed at length in Franklin, *A Constitutional Problem in Privacy Protection: Legal Inhibitions on Reporting of Fact*, 16 STAN. L. REV. 107 (1963) [hereinafter cited as Franklin].
    70. *See* Franklin, *supra* note 69, at 34-35.

ment forbids any limitation on publication of information relevant to governing purposes, and the fifth amendment forbids any limitation on publication without due process of law. This means that a statute or common law rule which forbids use of name or likeness in those cases in which publication of name or likeness is relevant to a governing purpose would be unconstitutional. In all other cases, under the due process requirement, the rule would be sustained as long as the prohibition bore some reasonable relationship to a constitutionally permissible governmental purpose.[71] As the Supreme Court defined the due process principle in the classic case of *Nebbia v. New York*, "[i]f the laws passed are seen to have a reasonable relation to a proper legislative purpose, and are neither arbitrary nor discriminatory, the requirements of due process are satisfied . . . ."[72]

Applying this due process test to our hypothetical rule against the publisher's use of name or likeness, we ask first, is there a valid legislative purpose? The answer is clear: protecting the public against impairment of their privacy is certainly a constitutionally permissible purpose. Our next question must be, does the means chosen bear "a rational relation"[73] to this valid purpose? Is a prohibition against the mass publication of name or likeness a reasonable means to protect against the impairment of privacy?

The answer to this question cannot, of course, be given in the abstract, in relation to any and every statutory prohibition of the mass publication of name or likeness. The prohibition found in some states against the use of name or likeness in reports of rape is thought to serve the public purpose of having rape victims come forward to prosecute their assaulters without fear of humiliation, as well as the interest in sparing the victim public witness of her humiliation.[74] Surely, these purposes may be seen to be rationally served by the name or likeness prohibition.

But suppose a statute or common law rule which made *every* use of name and likeness subject to one or another civil or criminal penalty. Besides running afoul of the first amendment in cases in which such use serves to inform self-governing consent—a question we have put to the side for the moment—such statute might also run afoul of the fifth amendment on the ground that privacy is not impaired, the soul not bruised, by every publication of name or likeness, however minimal, innocent, and free of personal humiliation and degradation. Such a rule might well be found to constitute a failure of due process on the

---

71. *See* Nebbia v. New York, 291 U.S. 502 (1934). *See also* Ferguson v. Skrupa, 372 U.S. 726 (1963); Williamson v. Lee Optical, Inc., 348 U.S. 483 (1955); note 263 *infra.*
72. 291 U.S. 502, 537 (1934).
73. *See, e.g.,* Williamson v. Lee Optical, Inc., 348 U.S. 483, 491 (1955).
74. Franklin, *supra* note 69, at 123-24, 128.

ground that the prohibition bore no rational relation to the valid state purpose of protecting privacy.

We see, then, that Meiklejohn's theory of the first amendment as applied to the mass publication privacy cases is a peculiar variant of a "two-level analysis"[75] of the first amendment. At the first level, we decide whether the particular publication of name and likeness is relevant to any possible governing purpose. If it is, it is newsworthy in the constitutional sense and it is protected unqualifiedly under the first amendment as part of the people's right to know. If the particular publication of name and likeness is not protected under the first amendment, it may yet gain constitutional protection under the fifth, as a private right to decide what is worth publishing. The test then becomes whether the particular rule or statute prohibiting the publication of name or likeness bears a reasonable relation to the valid constitutional purpose of protecting privacy.

E. *The Advantages of the Meiklejohn Mass Publication Privacy Analysis*

The virtues of the Meiklejohn analysis of the mass publication privacy issue are numerous. Analyzing the issue in terms of relevance to the public's governing interest in being informed allows a relatively value-free judgment in any case of conflict between first amendment and privacy rights. The judgment is also less subjective and unpredictable than one in which the court approaches the problem of the conflict by balancing the values of publication, in the individual case or as a general social good, against the values of privacy in the individual case or as a general social good.[76] Finally, the judgment is not only more value-free and less subjective, it is also capable of being more flexibly adapted to changing circumstances.

A court facing such a privacy-first amendment conflict, or an individual publisher anticipating it, has solely to ask whether publication of name or likeness is logically relevant to keeping the public informed for its governing purposes. The issue is one of logic rather than of fact or value. And it is one which is rooted in the first amendment itself. Is the first amendment purpose being served by this publication of name or likeness? Can use of name or likeness in this instance serve any possible basis for any possible governing purpose?

Compare these questions with those which must be asked under the balancing of interests approach: Does the value of this publication with

---

75. *See, e.g.*, Kalven, *The Concept of the Public Forum: Cox v. Louisiana,* 1965 SUP. CT. REV. 1, 12-21.

76. For a description of the "balancing" form of first amendment analysis see Brennan, *supra* note 6, at 9. See also EMERSON, *supra* note 6, at 717-18.

name or likeness outweigh the impairment of the individual's privacy as a result of this publication?   Or is preserving the right to publication of name and likeness under any and all circumstances to be preferred to preserving the right to prevent such publication under any and all circumstances?   These latter two questions are fraught with difficulty in the determination of facts and values.   Moreover, since they must be answered in the context of constitutional adjudication, without the Constitution itself providing any guidelines, they would necessarily import into the constitutional framework relatively subjective judgments concerning what might turn out to be detailed issues of fact and value, the stuff of statutes and common law adjudication rather than of constitutions.

This conclusion points up a second benefit of the Meiklejohn approach.   If the publication of name or likeness is not sustained at the first level—not protected by the first amendment—we look to second-level protection under the fifth amendment.   At this level, the constitutional adjudicative process respects and relies upon the weighing of interests and values undertaken by legislatures or common law courts, rather than imposing on the litigants its own evaluation of the relative importance of the interests.

This is so because the criterion under the fifth amendment due process clause is whether the limitation imposed on an individual's liberty is reasonably related to a constitutionally valid purpose.[77]   The purpose is determined by the legislature or the common law courts.   The constitutional court need only decide whether it is a constitutionally valid purpose.   Likewise, the means used to achieve the purpose are determined by the legislature or common law courts.   The constitutional court is required solely to determine whether the means used are reasonably related to the ends sought.   And this is a way of asking whether reasonable legislators might choose such means, *not* whether the constitutional court agrees that the means chosen are the best available or the right or appropriate ones.[78]

In using this second-stage process, we avoid freighting down the Constitution with detailed judgments of fact or value which are likely to express—and should indeed express—local or state sensibilities that vary over time.   The weighing process used to resolve conflicting social values under the fifth amendment is done in a local legislature or common law court.   It is subject to greater change and variation to reflect changing times and circumstances than if undertaken in constitutional adjudication.   Moreover, local legislatures and common law courts are more capable of hearing and assessing evidence on the issue than a constitutional court, because they are physically and culturally

---

77. *See* text accompanying note 71 *supra.*
78. *Accord*, Williamson v. Lee Optical, Inc., 348 U.S. 483, 487-88 (1955).

closer to the people whose interests are at stake and are, therefore, more likely to reflect those interests fairly and appropriately.

Shall *every* use of name or likeness[79] be subject to limitation or only those which substantially or outrageously impair privacy? Should serving the public curiosity and lust for scandal be more important than having rape victims come forward? What about the names of children involved in crime? Questions of this character require for resolution a sensitivity to community morals, mores, and sensibilities which should vary in some instances to reflect varying times and circumstances. They are, therefore, more appropriately dealt with by the processes of legislation and common law adjudication than by the Constitution.

Justice Holmes, in arguing against an older interpretation of the due process clause in which courts were called upon to make substantive judgments on the soundness of legislative attempts at economic regulation—the so-called "substantive due process" interpretation—said that the due process clause "does not enact Mr. Herbert Spencer's Social Statics."[80] More generally, he observed that "[s]ome . . . laws embody convictions or prejudices which judges are likely to share. Some may not." And he concluded that

a constitution is not intended to embody a particular economic theory, whether of paternalism and the organic relation of the citizen to the State or of *laissez faire*. It is made for people of fundamentally differing views, and the accident of our finding certain opinions natural and familiar or novel and even shocking ought not to conclude our judgment upon the question whether statutes embodying them conflict with the Constitution of the United States.[81]

A similar argument may be urged in respect to privacy generally, and the mass publication problem in particular. We know that "man is a social animal and that no human being can exist for long in total isolation from others." And yet we also know that in order to "preserve his sense of identity and the integrity of his personality, to work out his personal relationships and find his way to his own salvation, each human being needs to be able to limit the area of his intercourse with others."[82] An appropriate balance between these two fundamental human impulses is liable to vary in its details from time to time, person to person, and place to place. We should no more enact any particular balance of these interests—whether it be that of the prudish and restrained Victorian era or that of the "swinging sixties"—into our consti-

---

79. I remind the reader that at the second stage of the Meiklejohn analysis we are dealing only with uses of name or likeness which have met the first stage test—uses which are not related to being informed for governing purposes.
80. Cochner v. New York, 198 U.S. 46, 75 (1905) (dissenting opinion).
81. *Id.* at 75-76.
82. PRIVACY AND THE LAW, *supra* note 39, at 4.

tutional framework than we should "enact Mr. Herbert Spencer's Social Statics."

A third virtue of the Meiklejohn analysis of the mass publication privacy problem is that it respects the distinction between the different senses of newsworthiness, a distinction which has been sorely neglected heretofore.[83] Newsworthiness, as a constitutional value protecting the public right to be informed, receives its due under the first amendment, in the first stage. Publishers' freedom to publish, their individual right to do what they will, to determine what is newsworthy or worth reporting, is also separately protected as a distinct but different value in the second stage, under the fifth amendment.

The private right to speak, or to publish what is worth reporting, is sometimes the beneficiary, so to speak, of the public's first amendment right to hear. This results from the fact that what a publisher considers worth reporting sometimes also serves the public's need to be informed for governing purposes. Where this is not the case, the private right to publish what is worth reporting is still given constitutional protection. But it is a lesser right, in the sense that, under the fifth amendment's due process clause, it must compete, like any other private interest, with other values.

The third of the three senses of newsworthiness is also accommodated in the Meiklejohn theory, but at a distinctly lower level of constitutional valuation. Some of what is published is considered newsworthy in the sense that the public is very interested in it, curious about it, or hungry for it. Again, of course, if—as is often the case—there is public curiosity (or interest) about what at the same time serves the public (interest) or need to know for governing purposes, there is a full constitutional vindication of that curiosity. But where the two do not coincide, the only protection that public curiosity receives is not constitutional at all, but rather that which a legislature or common law court might judge appropriate in weighing it against other social or individual values, vindicating it or not at the expense of those other values.

A fourth virtue of the Meiklejohn theory is that it provides a reasonable resolution of other nettlesome problems which have arisen in this area. Should a public officer receive less privacy protection than a private citizen? What is the difference between a public officer and a "public figure" with respect to privacy rights? If a lower level of privacy protection is found appropriate for a public officer or "public figure" than for a private person, as most writers suggest,[84] is some modicum to be preserved or is there no privacy left whatsoever for them?

---

83. *See* text accompanying notes 66, 67 *supra*.
84. Warren and Brandeis originally suggested this possibility and Judge Clark seems to accept their view. *See* Warren & Brandeis, *supra* note 41, at 214-16; Sidis v. F-R Publishing Corp., 113 F.2d 806, 808-09 (1940).

Each of these questions is subject to a relatively simple and systematically consistent answer under the Meiklejohn analysis. It may be important to distinguish between private figures and public figures or officials for other purposes, but, for the purpose of deciding privacy rights under the first amendment, the only relevant question is whether the impairment of their privacy serves the public need to be informed for governing purposes. What matters is the substance of what is reported and whether it serves a first amendment public purpose. It is not status as a public figure that creates a right for the public to be informed about a person. Rather, it is the public's need to be informed about a person in order to fulfill its governing functions which makes that person a public figure.

The distinction between especially intimate facts concerning a public figure which may be private even for that person, and those which, though private for everyone else, are not private for public figures, may be treated similarly. This distinction is unnecessary in terms of the Meiklejohn analysis since the degree of intimacy of what is reported is logically irrelevant to the question of whether the informed consent necessary to a self-governing people requires knowledge of the matter. Instead of allowing considerations of what is private to determine the limits of what the public needs to know about its public figures, the public's right to know should determine what may be maintained in privacy for public figures no less than for private individuals.

The final advantage of the Meiklejohn theory of the application of the first amendment to mass publication privacy problems is the most important one: it maximizes first amendment values while giving due recognition to the protection of privacy from impairment by mass publication. And these purposes are met consistent with constitutional due process being afforded the publisher and with the public's curiosity receiving whatever support a legislature or common law court believes it deserves.

F.   A Case in Point: What Would Have Happened to Sidis Under the Meiklejohn Analysis?

William Sidis, it will be recalled, was the mathematical prodigy who was the subject of a profile in the *New Yorker* magazine in 1937. The profile "was merciless in its dissection of the intimate details of the life of young Sidis,"[85] but Sidis was denied recovery of damages for the heartache and sense of degradation the article caused him because, said Judge Clark, his was the "life of an unusual personality, and it possessed considerable popular news interest."[86]

---

85. Sidis v. F-R Publishing Corp., 113 F.2d 806, 807 (1940).
86. *Id.* at 809.

Reading the profile itself recently for the first time, although I had long known the case, I was struck with the poignancy and pain of Sidis' situation as never before. He had entered Harvard College at ten years of age as a special student. The next year he matriculated and was asked to lecture to the assembled faculty on "Four-Dimensional Bodies." After a nervous breakdown which kept him out of college for a time, he was able to graduate at 16. At graduation he told newsmen that he wanted "to lead a perfect life" and the "only way" to do that was "to live in seclusion."

After attending law school for a while, he left to teach mathematics in Texas. He stayed there only a short time, returning with bitterness to Boston because he had not been able to avoid curiosity about himself and to find anonymity in teaching. Thereafter, he drifted from city to city; generally working as a low-paid unskilled operator of adding machines (he wanted the machine to do the work without the intervention of his genius); collecting streetcar transfers and publishing a 300 page learned treatise on them; drifting from place to place in an attempt to lose himself in the crowd. Every seven or eight years a reporter would discover him and expose to public glare his attempts to preserve his obscurity. And then came the *New Yorker* profile of 1937 and the lawsuit which followed.

There is pathetic irony to the Sidis story and the lawsuit. The young man seeking seclusion begins a lawsuit to vindicate his right to be left alone and the law suit itself immortalizes him, bringing him to the rapt attention of generations of law students and scholars. But there is an important lesson to be derived from this ironic aftermath. Would any scholar or student of law who reads and studies the opinion of Judge Clark in the case learn any less had a pseudonym been used for Sidis' name in the opinion, or had the opinion designated him as Mr. X?

Pseudonyms are often used in legal opinions and case names where children, unwed mothers, or victims of rape, for instance, are involved.[87] Why not follow the same practice in legal opinions involving claimants to privacy? This question leads to a more important one: Was any first amendment purpose served by identifying Sidis in the *New Yorker* profile? The profile is clearly intended to show off a freak; with compassion, to be sure, but it nevertheless puts a freak on public display to amuse, delight, and titillate the reader. The fact is that the profile also educates readers to the diversity, eccentricity, and pathos of life and provokes them to curiosity and wonder.

The question is, however, whether the knowledge and insight we derive from the profile—Meiklejohn's need to inform the public for governing purposes—could not have been served just as well had the pro-

---

87. *See, e.g.*, Roe v. Wade, 410 U.S. 113 (1973).

file used a fictitious name. Was it really necessary to profane and humiliate Sidis to teach the lesson of his life to the reading public? (Who among those who have not heard of the Sidis case before reading of it here can be certain that I have not substituted a fictitious name in this account of it? Would it matter in the least?) There is no doubt that it is important for the Sidis story to be known to an informed people. But do we need to know Sidis' name and identity to learn all the lessons about his life which are relevant to the people's self-governing purposes?

Compare the need for personal identification in the Sidis profile to serve the public's governing purposes with the same need in a profile of Robert Moses which appeared in the *New Yorker* recently.[88] Robert Moses was the former Chairman of the Tri-Borough Bridge and Tunnel Authority of New York City, former Chairman of the New York State and New York City Park Commissions, and former Chairman or an important member of a dozen different other such authorities and commissions. It would have been almost impossible to write the profile without identifying him, if not explicitly, then indirectly as a result of describing all his associations and positions of responsibility.

More important, the value of being informed of how a man in Moses' position gained vast authority over the development of New York City while never having been elected to office or even having been, in practice, accountable to those who had, could not have been achieved without identifying Moses as the person who wielded that authority. He was known, admired, respected, scorned, feared, and revered by thousands upon thousands of people, and this knowledge of him *gained outside the context of the profile* is important to what the profile accomplishes as a tool of political education. The reader literally compares what he knows and feels about Moses independently of the profile with what the writer says. The public learns more from the profile because it identifies a man otherwise known to the public.

As important as the public's capacity to identify the subject of the Moses profile in order to associate and compare previously gained knowledge of him with that in the profile, is the fact that Moses as an individual had been a prior object of the public's governing choices. All the people who had known Moses as a public figure, and had either admired him or scorned him, had reflected that feeling in voting for or against mayors and other elected officials because they had applauded or opposed him, in approving or disapproving legislation which had affected his projects, and in countless other ways. The profile of Moses asks the reader implicitly to review those governing choices in

---

88. *E.g.*, Caro, *Annals of Politics—The Power Broker—III-How to Get Things Done*, New Yorker, Aug. 12, 1974, at 40.

the light of new information.   Therefore, its very value, in these terms, depends upon the reader's being able to identify the subject of the profile and associate him with the reader's own past actions, attitudes, and governing choices.

The Sidis profile is "a pig of different odor."   Unlike the Moses profile, the Sidis story could easily have avoided a direct or indirect identification by use of a pseudonym.   Moreover, although there may have been some public recollection in 1937 of Sidis having been in the news before, the prior public exposure was hardly such as to create a public attitude towards him.   In fact, in the 1937 profile, the author was able to recapitulate all that had been known to the public about him prior to that time.   Finally, and most importantly, the reading public had not committed itself in the past in relation to Sidis as an individual. Readers had not made any governing choices which reflected what they knew and felt about him.   Therefore, the profile was not the occasion for a review or study of those choices; all that could be learned from it could be learned without identifying Sidis at all.

I conclude that the identification of Sidis was not relevant to the public's governing purposes and, as a consequence, was not protected by the first amendment.

But what of the fact that Sidis was, in Judge Clark's words, "an unusual personality," and that his life "possessed considerable popular news interest?"[89]   Must we accept Judge Clark's conclusion that "regrettably or not, the misfortunes and frailties of neighbors and 'public figures' are subjects of considerable interest . . . [a]nd when such are the mores of the community, it would be unwise for a court to bar their expression in the newspapers, books, and magazines of the day?"[90]

I believe we must indeed accept Judge Clark's conclusion, but we must ask what we are to accept it as.   In the perspective of Meiklejohn's analysis of the constitutional protection of free expression, Judge Clark is making a second stage judgment.[91]   He seems to be assessing the publisher's right (although he does not expressly mention it) and the public curiosity as values of more significance than the right of Sidis, or any other such public figure to avoid undue publicity.

This assessment is surely within a common law judge's discretion.[92]

---

89. Sidis v. F-R Publishing Corp., 113 F.2d 806, 809 (1940).
90. *Id.*
91. See text accompanying note 75 *supra.*
Judge Clark seems to have reached a different conclusion about the first stage than I did.   Clark says, Sidis' "subsequent history, containing as it did the answer to the question of whether or not he had filled his early promise, was still a matter of public concern." *Id.* at 809.   I maintain this "public concern" could have been satisfied without identifying Sidis to the public gaze. *Id.*
92. The common law right to privacy was at issue in the case as the first of three causes of action. *Id.* at 807.

But such weighing of interests and establishment of a common law rule which reflects the results of the process is to be sharply distinguished from a judgment that the right of the publisher and the public curiosity command constitutional protection under the first amendment. Moreover, another common law court, or a legislature, facing the same conflicting values today, some 35 years after Judge Clark wrote, is free, on this view, to reflect contemporary mores and sensibilities. A contemporary court might well—and I believe it should—afford the individual more protection of his privacy against unreasonable invasion by mass media publicity than Judge Clark did in *Sidis* case.

III. THE JUSTICES AND THE PHILOSOPHER: FROM *"TIMES"* to "TIME"[93]

A. *Background*

There are at least four important issues which must be addressed in order to understand the United States Supreme Court's doctrinal attitude towards the Meiklejohn thesis. Each of these issues is itself a subject of considerable complexity and a full exposition of the four is beyond the purview of this article. I shall, however, attempt a brief sketch of them.

1. The First Amendment and the "Right to Hear"

The Supreme Court has often recognized not only the right to speak, but also the right to hear as a fundamental first amendment right. Thus, in *Stanley v. Georgia*[94] the Court reversed a conviction for possession of obscene films in a private home on the ground, among others, that it is "well established that the Constitution protects the right to receive information and ideas" and that "[t]his right . . . is fundamental to our free society."[95]   And in *Griswold v. Connecticut*[96] and numerous other cases,[97] the Court has held that "the State may not, consistently with the spirit of the First Amendment, contract the spectrum of available knowledge" and that "[t]he right of freedom of speech and press includes not only the right to utter or to print, but the right to distribute, the right to receive, [and] the right to read

93. This title is inspired by Nimmer, *The Right to Speak from* Times *to* Time: *First Amendment Theory Applied to Libel and Misapplied to Privacy*, 56 CAL. L. REV. 935 (1968) [hereinafter cited as Nimmer].
94. 394 U.S. 557 (1969).
95. *Id.* at 564.
96. 381 U.S. 479 (1965).
97. *See, e.g.*, Kleindienst v. Mandel, 408 U.S. 753, 762 (1972); Martin v. City of Struthers, 319 U.S. 141, 143 (1943); Thornhill v. Alabama, 310 U.S. 88, 101 (1940).

. . . ."[98]   These right to hear cases offer implicitly or explicitly the same political justification as Meiklejohn's theory—that a democratic people must be informed to govern effectively.   Nowhere, however, do the cases distinguish, as Meiklejohn does, the constitutional basis of the right to hear as distinct from that of the right to speak.

2.   The Theory of the First Amendment

The disarray in the Supreme Court's first amendment free expression theory is nowhere better illustrated than in *Dennis v. United States*,[99] where five of the justices wrote five opinions with five different theories.   Almost every student of the Court recognizes that "the Supreme Court has failed to develop a comprehensive, coherent theory of the First Amendment."[100]   Instead, members of the Court, sometimes making up a majority, sometimes not, have expounded a series of different theories, more or less appropriate to one or another fact situation.   Among them is a "two-level theory," a "clear and present danger theory," a "balancing or weighing theory," and a theory of the first amendment as "absolute."[101]   There are also special rules for cases involving "fighting words,"[102] those involving "personal abuse,"[103] those in which speech is described as "inciting or producing imminent lawless action,"[104] and those involving "prurient, patently offensive depiction or description of sexual conduct."[105]   Which of these theories, if any, is particularly appropriate to the problem of mass publication privacy is difficult to say.   It is clear, however, that any theory which deals effectively with the privacy problem and promises—as Meiklejohn's does—to bring greater theoretical coherence into the rest of the first amendment cases must be assessed most carefully.

3.   The Constitution and the Right to Privacy

The Supreme Court has long recognized a right of privacy in the traditional fourth amendment search and seizure context, but it has only recently expanded that right to include electronic searches and seizures.[106]   More significant than this form of expansion into new areas

---

98. Griswold v. Connecticut, 381 U.S. 479, 482 (1965).
99. 341 U.S. 494 (1951).
100. EMERSON, *supra* note 6, at 15-16, 717.
101. *See* Kalven, *supra* note 6, at 213-18; Brennan, *supra* note 6, at 4-9; Nimmer, *supra* note 93, at 935-41; EMERSON, *supra* note 6, at 16, 151-52, 313-34, 487.
102. Lewis v. New Orleans, 415 U.S. 130, 132 (1974); Chaplinsky v. New Hampshire, 315 U.S. 568, 572 (1942).
103. Cantwell v. Connecticut, 310 U.S. 296, 309 (1940).
104. Communist Party v. Whitcomb, 414 U.S. 441, 448 (1974); Brandenburg v. Ohio, 395 U.S. 444, 447 (1969).
105. Miller v. California, 413 U.S. 15, 26 (1973).
106. For one of the earliest statements see Boyd v. United States, 116 U.S. 616

of technological intrusion into the home is an expansion in the constitutional concept of privacy itself.   In the *Griswold* case,[107] and later in the case of *Roe v. Wade*,[108] the Court extended the constitutional protection of privacy "to encompass a woman's decision whether or not to prevent or to terminate her pregnancy."[109]   It went on to say, in passing, that "the right has some extension to activities relating to marriage, . . . procreation, . . . contraception, . . . family relationships, . . . and child rearing and education,"[110] citing decisions to support each of these extensions.   As with the theory of the first amendment, the theory of privacy espoused by the Court seems to lack clear contours, with the opinions in both *Griswold* and *Roe* suggesting that the right, in one or another sense, arises out of the first amendment, the third amendment, the fourth, the fifth, the ninth, and the fourteenth.   However, until the case of *Time, Inc. v. Hill*[111] (which I shall discuss below), the Supreme Court had never addressed the question of mass publication privacy and its relation to the first amendment.

4.   The Constitution and the Law of Libel

The law of libel seems, on its face, to be fraught with first amendment difficulty.   For how can anyone recover damages for words someone else has spoken about him without impairing that other person's right to free speech?   Although the problem seems theoretically to be a grave one, it turns out, in practice, not to be very significant.   In the first place, the common law defenses to a libel action are exceedingly strong.[112]   In the second place, until the Court decided *New York Times Co. v. Sullivan*[113] (which I shall discuss below), it had been well-established constitutional law that libelous words "are no essential part of any exposition of ideas, and are of such slight social value as a step to truth that any benefit that may be derived from them is clearly outweighed by the social interest in order and morality."[114]   In effect, then, for different reasons in each instance, mass publication privacy and libel had, until very recently, not been subject to Supreme Court

---

(1886).   A good review of the legal history until 1967 is to be found in WESTIN, *supra* note 39, at 330-65.

107.   381 U.S. 479 (1965).

108.   410 U.S. 113 (1973).

109.   *Id.* at 153.

110.   *Id.* at 152-53.   For speculation as to further extension of the constitutional right see Note, *On Privacy: Constitutional Protection for Personal Liberty*, 48 N.Y.U.L. REV. 670 (1973).

111.   385 U.S. 374 (1967).

112.   *See generally* 1 F. HARPER & F. JAMES, LAW OF TORTS §§ 5.20-.23 (1956).

113.   376 U.S. 254 (1969).

114.   Chaplinsky v. New Hampshire, 315 U.S. 568, 571-72 (1942).   *See also* Roth v. United States, 354 U.S. 476, 482-83 (1957); Beauharnais v. Illinois, 343 U.S. 250, 256-57 (1952).

review as first amendment problems. What is quite extraordinary is that in a series of recent cases involving mass publication privacy and libel, not only has new Supreme Court doctrine on these subjects been developed, but it is doctrine which may rework the entire fabric of first amendment free expression theory.

B. The Justices "Go to School to the Philosopher"[115]

One of the qualities of the Supreme Court of the United States which substantially contributes to its extraordinary statute and its unique role as an instrument of democratic government is that by inveterate institutional practice and deep personal inclination its Justices "go to school to the philosopher." I know of no other instance of individuals holding such high government office who maintain so close and fruitful a working relationship with scholars and scholarship.[116]

As one might suppose, there are fads, trends, and styles in the reigning scholars whose views influence the Court on legal issues. For a time, Professor Zachariah Chafee[117] influenced the views of the Court profoundly on free speech issues. Professor Thomas Emerson[118] has also exerted and continues to exert a strong influence on these issues. Recently, the views of Professor Alexander Meiklejohn[119] have seemed to play an extremely important role in determining the dramatic turn in Supreme Court free expression theory, signaled by the *New York Times* case. Although other Justices have cited and relied upon Meiklejohn with approval,[120] Justices Douglas and Brennan have felt his influence most strongly.

1. Justice Douglas and Professor Meiklejohn

In his dissent in *Branzburg v. Hayes*, Justice Douglas states: "my view [on the first amendment] is close to that of the late Alexander Meiklejohn."[121] His opinion then quotes the latter[122] at length on the distinction between " 'the rights' of the governed and 'the powers' of the governors." Later in the same dissent Douglas writes:

The press has a preferred position in our constitutional scheme not

---

115. Sharp, *supra* note 1, at xi.
116. In some measure I attribute this fact to the institution of the judicial clerkship, whereby recent graduates of law schools, fresh from their classrooms and their work on scholarly law journals, spend a year or two "instructing" the Justices in "what's new" in legal scholarship.
117. See Z. CHAFEE, FREE SPEECH IN THE UNITED STATES (1942).
118. See EMERSON, *supra* note 6.
119. See articles cited note 7 *supra*.
120. *See, e.g.*, Gertz v. Robert Welch, Inc., 94 S. Ct. 2997, 3028 (1974) (White, J., dissenting).
121. 408 U.S. 665, 713 (1972).
122. *First Amendment, supra* note 7, at 254.

to enable it to make money, not to set newsmen apart as a favored class, but to bring fulfillment to the public's right to know. *The right to know is crucial to the governing powers of the people, to paraphrase Alexander Meiklejohn.* Knowledge is essential to informed decisions.[123]

Other references in the Justice's opinions demonstrate that he has been attracted to Meiklejohn's theory.[124] I believe, however, that he has not savored it deeply enough. After all, the distinction between the right to speak and the right to know, if not a commonplace of constitutional analysis, is not unique with Meiklejohn.[125] Moreover, the role of the people as "governors," and the importance of informed opinion as guaranteed by the first amendment to that role, is a well-known facet of James Madison's teaching, of which Justice Douglas is well aware.[126] It is difficult to believe that Meiklejohn has taught the Justice anything in this respect.

As a matter of fact, the Justice seems to be missing Meiklejohn's distinctiveness, if not misunderstanding him. Thus, in his dissent in *Branzburg*, Douglas quotes a long passage from Meiklejohn on "the rights of the governed" and "the powers of the governors,"[127] without seeming to appreciate its radical significance in that Meiklejohn means thereby to distinguish between the constitutional foundation of the right to speak in the fifth amendment—a right of the governed— and that of the right to hear in the first amendment—a right of the governors. When he later says in the same dissent that "the press has a preferred position in our constitutional scheme,"[128] and claims in the next sentence to be paraphrasing Meiklejohn, he seems thereby to suggest that the latter was also committed to that view. But, of course, Meiklejohn expressly denies such a preferred position to the press.[129]

2.   Justice Brennan and Professor Meiklejohn

The influence of Meiklejohn on Justice Brennan seems to be of more significance. Since Brennan was the main architect of the revolution in constitutional thinking about the first amendment which was initiated in the *New York Times* case, Meiklejohn's influence on the Court through Brennan has possibly been more profound than his influ-

---

123.   408 U.S. at 721 (emphasis added).
124.   *See, e.g.,* Pell v. Procunier, 94 S. Ct. 2827, 2828 (1974) (dissenting opinion); Miller v. California, 413 U.S. 15, 44 (1973) (dissenting opinion).
125.   *See* text accompanying notes 94-98 *supra.*
126.   *See* W.O. DOUGLAS, THE RIGHTS OF THE PEOPLE 19-20 (1958).
127.   *See* text accompanying notes 121-23 *supra.*
128.   408 U.S. at 721.
129.   *See* text accompanying notes 11-17 *supra.*

ence through Douglas. Unfortunately, however, Justice Brennan, like Justice Douglas, does not seem to have recognized as yet the full import of Meiklejohn on the analysis of the first amendment free expression provision.

Brennan has written an article exclusively devoted to the subject.[130] We can, therefore, see at first hand what he thinks of Meiklejohn's views, rather than reading this through a glass, darkly, in his judicial opinions.

Brennan begins his analysis of Meiklejohn by outlining a variety of views of the first amendment espoused by members of the Supreme Court, including the "absolute" view, and the "redeeming social value," "clear and present danger," and "balancing" tests.[131] He observes that "only the so-far-rejected [by the majority of the Court[132]] 'absolute' view of the amendment embraces a flat denial of all governmental power to regulate speech as such."[133]   And he goes on to say that, in contrast to the "absolute" view, "one or all of the tests may be employed more generally to sustain governmental regulation of speech." Most significantly, he then concludes that "Meiklejohn would have none of them," none of the "tests" or of the "regulation of speech."[134] He clearly implies that Meiklejohn's view is similar in this respect to the "absolute" view held by Justices Black and Douglas.

This represents, I believe, a plain misunderstanding of Meiklejohn's views. As demonstrated,[135] Meiklejohn denies that freedom of speech is unlimited or unqualified. Speech for him is not only subject to governmental regulation in respect of the "how," "when," and "where" of its exercise[136]—a position the "absolutists" on the Supreme Court also accept[137]—it is also subject to regulation in instances where it does not address itself to matters of governing importance.[138]   This indeed explains why Meiklejohn, unlike Justice Black, the "absolutist" in this matter, supports the view that the laws of libel do not represent an unconstitutional abridgement of speech where they allow damages

---

130. Brennan, *supra* note 6.
131. *Id.* at 4-11.
132. This view is attributed only to Justices Black and Douglas. *Id.* at 4-5.
133. *Id.* at 11.
134. *Id.*
135. See text accompanying notes 30-37 *supra.*
136. *See* text accompanying notes 30-37 *supra.*
137. *See, e.g.*, Adderly v. Florida, 385 U.S. 39, 47-48 (1966) (Black, J.): "[We reject] the assumption that people who want to propagandize protests or views have a constitutional right to do so whenever and however and wherever they please." Justice Douglas, although he dissented in the case, agreed with the principle at issue: "There may be some public places which are so clearly committed to other purposes that their use for the airing of grievances is anomalous." *Id.* at 54. *See also* Cox v. Louisiana, 379 U.S. 559 (1964); Poulos v. New Hampshire, 345 U.S. 395 (1953); Kovacs v. Cooper, 336 U.S. 77 (1949).
138. *See* text accompanying notes 61-66 *supra.*

for private defamation.[139]

Although Justice Brennan recognizes that Meiklejohn's views differ from Justice Black's and the absolutists in respect of private libel,[140] he does not see the respect in which Meiklejohn remains, nevertheless, an absolutist. What is absolute about Meiklejohn's view is not that it proscribes any and all regulation of speech, but rather that it proscribes any and all regulation of speech which is relevant to the public's governing purposes.[141]

Indeed, although Brennan asserts the contrary,[142] Meiklejohn can be read to accept a form of the clear and present danger test, a form of the redeeming social value test, and a form of the weighing test, all tests which limit or qualify the right to speech. Thus, Meiklejohn argues that

> when such a civil or military emergency comes upon us . . . no advocate of the freedom of speech, however ardent, could deny the right and the duty of the government to declare that public discussion must be . . . stopped until the order necessary for fruitful discussion has been restored.[143]

This is at least a close cousin to the clear and present danger rule.

Moreover, the requirement under Meiklejohn's analysis that speech have a "relation to the business of governing" before it receives the protection of the first amendment[144] is a species of the redeeming social value test. And, finally, for Meiklejohn, speech which fails of first amendment protection because it is not of governing importance is given protection at a second level under the due process clause of weighing or balancing by the constitutional court itself, but rather review by that court of the weighing or balancing done by legislatures and common law courts.[145]

Thus, Meiklejohn is an absolutist, though not an absolutist like Justice Black. But, even as an absolutist, he accepts governmental regulation of speech for purposes very much like those asserted in the clear and present danger, the redeeming social importance, and the balancing tests.

The point at which Justice Brennan comes closest to the essence of the Meiklejohn theory is in his recognition of the importance to Meiklejohn of the first amendment as a protector of the people's sovereign power. Brennan quotes at length from Meiklejohn's structural analysis

---

139. *First Amendment, supra* note 7, at 259.
140. Brennan, *supra* note 6, at 14.
141. *See* text accompanying note 16 *supra*.
142. Brennan, *supra* note 6, at 11.
143. POLITICAL FREEDOM, *supra* note 7, at 49. *See also First Amendment, supra* note 7, at 259-60.
144. *See* POLITICAL FREEDOM, *supra* note 7, at 25-27.
145. *See* text surrounding note 78 *supra*.

of the Constitution, including the statement "over [the people's] governing, [the government and the courts] have no power. Over their governing we have sovereign power."[146]   He correctly concludes that the heart of the Meiklejohn theory is stated in the proposition that—in Brennan's words—"freedom of expression in areas of public affairs is an absolute."[147]   And he then goes on to note that in two of the recent critical cases in the Supreme Court in which he had written the opinion for the majority—the *New York Times* case[148] and the *Garrison* case[149]—this concept was central to the decision of the case.[150]

Apparently it was because the *New York Times* and *Garrison* cases reflected the Meiklejohn analysis of the first amendment as embodying an element of the people's sovereign power that Professor Kalven wrote that "if the Court [follows the logic of the situation], it will slowly work out for itself the theory of free speech that Alexander Meiklejohn has been offering us for some fifteen years now."[151]   Brennan quotes this observation from Kalven in his article on Meiklejohn and also notes what is almost a paraphrase of Meiklejohn in the *Garrison* opinion,[152] intimating by both of these references how close his own and, perhaps, the Court's views are to Meiklejohn's.   This same intimation is also to be found in the fact that he quotes Kalven as reporting that Meiklejohn had told him that the *New York Times* case "is an occasion for dancing in the streets."[153]   I cannot agree with Justice Brennan's implied assessment (or Professor Kalven's either) of how close the Supreme Court has come to Meiklejohn's theory.

After all, the idea attributed in the *New York Times* case to James Madison "that the censorial power is in the people over the Government, and not in the Government over the people,"[154] is, although central to Meiklejohn, as Justice Brennan recognizes, obviously not unique to him.   Indeed, it would seem that Justice Brennan and the Court (and, perhaps, Professor Kalven) have really not yet seen what is so very extraordinary and distinctive about Meiklejohn's theory.   It is that speech has two different forms of protection under the Constitution, depending upon whether it is of governing importance or not. Where it is, speech is absolutely protected; where it is not, it is subject to the qualified protection of the due process clause.   The adoption of this view goes much further than the recognition "that the censorial

---

146. Brennan, *supra* note 6, at 12.
147. *Id.*
148. New York Times Co. v. Sullivan, 376 U.S. 254 (1964).
149. Garrison v. Louisiana, 379 U.S. 64 (1964).
150. Brennan, *supra* note 6, at 14-16, 18-19.
151. Kalven, *supra* note 6, at 221.
152. Brennan, *supra* note 6, at 19.
153. *Id.* at 17.
154. 376 U.S. at 275.

power is in the people over the government" and would lead, as will be shown, to different solutions of the first amendment problems which have recently come before the Court than either Justice Brennan or the majority of the Court reached.

C. *From* "Times" *to* "Time" *and Beyond*

As I have already indicated, the *New York Times* case[155] is a turning point in constitutional development. Any theory of the first amendment must therefore be tested against it and its progeny, and it is to such a task that I now turn.

1. The Cases

a. *New York Times Co. v. Sullivan.* In 1960 the *New York Times* ran an advertisement signed by dozens of prominent civil rights leaders, including Martin Luther King. It was entitled "Heed Their Rising Voices" and was designed to win moral and financial support for "thousands of Southern Negro students . . . engaged in widespread non-violent demonstrations in positive affirmation of the right to live in human dignity." In the course of the advertisement, the assertion was made that the students "are being met by an unprecedented wave of terror by those who would deny and negate the Bill of Rights," and the advertisement then proceeded to give illustrations of the "wave of terror."[156]

Sullivan, the Commissioner responsible for public safety in the City of Montgomery, Alabama, brought suit charging that the advertisement was filled with falsehoods and traduced his reputation. He also charged that it had been negligently and willfully published with intent to injure him. A jury returned a verdict against the *Times* for $500,000 which was upheld by the Supreme Court of Alabama.[157]

The Supreme Court of the United States, with Justice Brennan writing an opinion representing the views of six Justices, reversed and dismissed the action. The Court agreed that statements in the advertisement could reasonably be considered false and defamatory, and that, moreover, the *Times* had been negligent in not checking their accuracy. The Court found, however, that there had been no knowing falsehood or reckless disregard of the truth on the part of the *Times*. It, therefore, denied recovery on the principle that

> [t]he constitutional guarantees of a free press and free speech require . . . a federal rule that prohibits a public official from recovering damages for a defamatory falsehood relating to his official conduct

---

155. New York Times Co. v. Sullivan, 376 U.S. 254 (1964).
156. *Id.* at app. (following p. 292).
157. *Id.* at 256-65.

unless he proves that the statement was made with "actual malice"—
that is, with knowledge that it was false or with reckless disregard of
whether it was false or not.[158]

b. *Garrison v. Louisiana.*[159]   Garrison, the District Attorney of New
Orleans, had held a press conference and charged some judges of that
city with inefficiency, laziness, overlong vacations, and sympathies towards racketeers.   He was thereupon charged and convicted of criminal libel and the conviction was upheld in the Louisiana courts.[160]
The Supreme Court, with Justice Brennan again expressing the views
of six members of the Court, reversed the conviction and dismissed the
prosecution, declaring that "the *New York Times* rule also limits state
power to impose criminal sanctions for criticism of the official conduct
of public officials."[161]   Thus, in *Garrison*, the *New York Times* rule
was extended so as to require a showing of "actual malice" in criminal
prosecutions for defamation in cases involving "public officials" and
official conduct.

c. *Rosenblatt v. Baer.*[162]   Baer had been employed (whether as a
contractor, a simple employee, or an official is not clear from the
record of the case) as the operator of a New Hampshire ski resort run
by county government, but there had been a change in management
and he was dismissed.   Rosenblatt, a reporter on a local newspaper,
reflecting on the change in management and the results achieved as
a result of the change, wrote: "the difference in cash income [is]
simply fantastic, almost unbelievable."   He then asked, "what happened to all the money last year? and every other year?"[163]   Baer succeeded in a civil suit for defamation in the New Hampshire courts
against Rosenblatt, but the recovery was reversed by the Supreme
Court on the basis of the *New York Times* rule, and it was sent back
for a new trial under new jury instructions.[164]

This time Justice Brennan wrote the opinion expressing the views
of five members of the Court.   The Court clearly regarded Baer as
a public official, saying that the term "applies at the very least to
those among the hierarchy of government employees who have, or appear to the public to have, substantial responsibility for or control
over the conduct of governmental affairs."[165]   Justice Douglas suggested in a separate opinion that even a "file clerk," "anyone on the
public payroll," a "public contractor," or a "dollar a year man" might

158. *Id.* at 279-80.
159. 379 U.S. 64 (1964).
160. *Id.* at 64-67.
161. *Id.* at 67.
162. 383 U.S. 75 (1966).
163. *Id.* at 78.
164. *Id.* at 77-83.
165. *Id.* at 85.

be considered an "official" from the point of view of the *New York Times* rule. He raised the question of whether industrialists and labor leaders should not fall within the same rule and he concluded with the observation that "the question is whether a public *issue,* not a public official is involved."[166]

    d. *Curtis Publishing Co. v. Butts.*[167] The next in this series of cases raised the issue Justice Douglas and Justice Black had foreshadowed in the *Baer* case: Would the *New York Times* rule apply even if a public official were not involved? And on this issue the Court began to split badly.

    Actually, two cases were resolved by the *Butts* opinion. In one, the *Saturday Evening Post* had written an exposé of Wally Butts, the Athletic Director of the University of Georgia, stating that, just before a football game, Butts had given to Paul Bryant, the Alabama coach, "Georgia's plays, defensive patterns, all the significant secrets Georgia's football team possessed."[168] In the other case, the Associated Press had written of a well-known retired Army General, Edwin A. Walker, that, during a riot at the University of Mississippi over the admission of its first black student, he "had taken command of the violent crowd and had personally led a charge against federal marshals."[169] Both Butts and Walker had recovered huge money verdicts in libel actions in the lower courts.[170]

    The Supreme Court unanimously reversed the judgment in favor of Walker,[171] but sustained that in favor of Butts[172] by a five to four vote.[173] All the members of the Court agreed that Butts and Walker were not public officials and that they were rather "public figures," men "involved in issues in which the public has a justified and important interest."[174] Justice Harlan, joined by three others, was of the opinion, however, that even though the article concerned a public issue, it was not about a public official, and hence recovery in defamation could be allowed simply on a clear and convincing "showing of highly unreasonable conduct" by the publishers, without a showing of malice as required by the *New York Times* case.[175] Justice Brennan and two

---

166. *Id.* at 91.
167. 388 U.S. 130 (1967).
168. *Id.* at 136.
169. *Id.* at 140.
170. *Id.* at 138, 141-42.
171. Those Justices who applied the actual malice standard did not think it had been met and those who applied the "highly unreasonable conduct" standard did not think it had been met.
172. Those Justices who applied the "highly unreasonable conduct" standard thought it had been met and Justice Warren, who applied the "actual malice" test, thought it had been met.
173. *Id.* at 161-62.
174. *Id.* at 134.
175. *Id.* at 155.

others thought the same "actual malice" rule should apply to public figures as applied to public officials.[176]   Justices Black and Douglas were of the opinion which they had expressed in the *New York Times, Garrison,* and *Baer* cases, that there should be no liability even with a showing of actual malice.[177]

e. *Time, Inc. v. Hill.*[178]   In 1952 James Hill and his wife and two children were held hostage in their house for 19 hours by three escaped convicts.   The incident was the subject of considerable news coverage at the time.   The following year a fictionalized version of the incident, which did not identify the Hills, was published.   In 1955 a play depicting the incident was published; it also did not identify the Hills.   But a notice of the play in *Life* magazine, appearing shortly after the play opened, identified the play as being about the Hills.   James Hill sued in the New York courts on a theory of invasion of privacy, alleging that the *Life* story had revived a painful incident causing much mental distress, and also that it had depicted him and his family in a false light. (The family had never been molested or threatened.   The *Life* article depicted them as having been "roughed up," subjected to physical assault.)[179]   A New York jury awarded Hill $50,000 compensatory damages and $25,000 punitive damages,[180] but the Supreme Court reversed and returned the case for a new trial on the ground that recovery could only be had upon a showing that the false facts in the story were the product of actual malice.   In effect, the Court applied the *New York Times* libel rule to the privacy action.[181]

There were five opinions on the application of the first amendment to the right of privacy.   Justice Brennan and two others thought the *New York Times* actual malice rule should apply and voted for reversal because the trial jury had not been so instructed.[182] Justice Fortas and two others agreed that the actual malice rule should apply, but were of the opinion that the jury instruction which had been given could be so interpreted.[183]   Justices Black and Douglas voted with the majority to reverse, but they insisted upon absolute freedom of liability for a publisher of matter in the public interest.[184] Justice Douglas wrote to express the view that the *Hill* case did not really involve privacy since Hill was "catapulted into the news by events

176. *Id.* at 163, 172.
177. *Id.* at 170-72.
178. 385 U.S. 374 (1967).
179. *Id.* at 376-80.   Under the New York privacy statute no recovery could be had for a true news story, the only basis of recovery being a story which falsified the privacy-invading facts.   *See id.* at 376 n.1, 384.
180. *Id.* at 379.
181. *Id.* at 390.
182. *Id.* at 394-97.
183. *Id.* at 411.
184. *Id.* at 398-401.

over which he had no control."[185]   Finally, Justice Harlan dissented
on the ground that he believed that a publisher should be held liable
in such cases without malice if there is a failure to make "a reasonable
investigation of the underlying facts."[186]

f. *Rosenbloom v. Metromedia, Inc.*[187]   Seven years after *New York
Times* we reach a case involving the libel of a private person involved
in an event of public interest.   Rosenbloom was a distributor of "girlie"
magazines who had been arrested, but subsequently acquitted in state
court, on an obscenity charge.   While the criminal prosecution was still
pending a radio station owned by Metromedia broadcast several reports
of Rosenbloom's arrest, in the course of which they described him as
a "smut merchant" and a "girlie-book peddler," and characterized the
books he sold as "obscene."   He sued for libel and won a substantial
jury verdict which was reversed on appeal by the Court of Appeals for
the Third Circuit.   The reversal was sustained in the Supreme Court.[188]

Again the Court was badly split.   Justice Brennan and two others
sustained the reversal on the ground that the "robust debate" required
by the first amendment is to be honored "by extending constitutional
protection [under the *New York Times* rule of actual malice] to all
discussion and communication involving matters of public or general
concern, without regard to whether the persons involved are famous
or anonymous."[189]   Justice Black concurred, but urged once more his
absolute view.[190]   Justice White also concurred, but on the narrow
ground that the reports concerned were about a public official, the prosecutor, and only incidentally about whom he had arrested and, therefore,
the *New York Times* rule applied directly.[191]   Justice Harlan and Justices Marshall and Stewart dissented and urged that in such cases the
states may allow recovery under any standard but one of absolute liability;[192] they disagreed about the appropriate rule of damages.[193]

g. *Gertz v. Robert Welch, Inc.*[194]   The most recent in this series
of first amendment publication cases involved Nelson, a black youth
who had been shot and killed in Chicago by a white police officer.   The
police officer, Nuccio, had been convicted of second degree murder as
a result of the shooting.   Gertz, the plaintiff in this libel case, was retained by the Nelson family to sue Nuccio.   Robert Welch, the defend-

185. *Id.* at 401.
186. *Id.* at 409.
187. 403 U.S. 29 (1971).
188. *Id.* at 57.
189. *Id.* at 43-44.
190. *Id.* at 57.
191. *Id.* at 62.
192. *Id.* at 64, 84-85.
193. *Id.* at 72-77, 85-87.
194. 94 S. Ct. 2997 (1974). See also note 263 *infra.*

ant, was the publisher of *American Opinion*, a monthly journal of opinion of the John Birch Society, in which there had appeared an article entitled *FRAME-UP: Richard Nuccio And The War On Police*. In the course of the article it was suggested that the Nelson lawsuit was part of a communist plot and that Gertz, an instigator of the plot, had a long history of past communist associations. Gertz instituted suit and proved the falsity of many of the charges and also that they had been published without any effort on the part of the managing editor to verify the facts. The jury returned a verdict in his favor, but the trial judge set it aside and was sustained in the Court of Appeals for the Seventh Circuit. The Supreme Court ordered a new trial on the ground of a faulty instruction on damages, but indicated that the legal basis for the trial judge's and circuit's objection to the original jury verdict could not be sustained.[195]

Again there were multiple opinions; six this time. Justice Powell, writing for himself and four others, expressed the view that the *New York Times* rule does not apply to private persons and that in such cases a state could apply any rule of liability other than liability without fault.[196] He also urged a more restricted rule of damages.[197] Justice Blackmun concurred, but indicated that he still preferred the application of the *New York Times* rule for which he had voted in the *Rosenbloom* case.[198] Chief Justice Burger dissented out of concern that a new rule of negligence liability for publishers might be too unsettling.[199] Justice Douglas and Justice Brennan restated views they had expressed consistently since the *New York Times* case, the former espousing an absolute immunity for the press on public issues, the latter the *New York Times* actual malice rule.[200] Finally, Justice White dissented on the ground that allowing private persons libel actions is no abridgement of the first amendment where a person enjoys no "general fame or notoriety," is not "pervasively involved in the affairs of society" and has not "thrust [themself] into the vortex of [a given] public issue . . . in an attempt to influence its outcome."[201]

2. The Newly Emerging Supreme Court First Amendment Theory

Two preliminary observations may be made concerning the theoretical foundations of the *New York Times* case and its progeny. The first

---

195. *Id.* at 3013.
196. *See id.* at 3010-13.
197. *Id.* at 3012.
198. *Id.* at 3013-14.
199. *Id.* at 3014.
200. *See id.* at 3015-18.
201. *Id.* at 3036, *quoting id.* at 3013 (Powell, J.).

is that, although the opinions in the cases speak to the nature of the first amendment in general terms, as a matter of fact, what the Court has been concerned with during the last decade is a theory of the first amendment as it affects libel.   No serious attempt has been made to see the problem of libel in the context of other first amendment issues such as obscenity and sedition.   Thus, in effect, the Court has added another patch to its patchwork first amendment approach, without making significant progress on a unified theory of the first amendment along the lines suggested by Professor Meiklejohn and Professor Emerson.[202]

The second observation is obvious: Even within the area of first amendment libel, the Court is sharply divided.   The judicial "score card"[203] shows that one of the Justices (Douglas) is committed to absolute immunity for the publisher in any defamation action involving issues of public or general interest.   One of the Justices (White) is committed to immunity for the publisher except where there is a showing of actual malice, for defamation affecting issues of "public or general interest when recovery is sought by a public official or public figure, but absolute liability for such utterances when recovery is sought by a private person.   Four Justices (Powell, Rehnquist, Marshall, and Stewart) favor immunity for the publisher for defamation actions brought by public figures and public officials, except where there is a showing of actual malice, but liability upon a showing of negligence, and a requirement of proof of actual damages, where a private party brings the suit.   One Justice (Brennan) accepts the *New York Times* actual malice rule for all defamation actions which involve issues relating to the public or general interest.   One Justice (Blackmun) accepts this same position but will vote with the plurality in cases where a private person is involved.   And Chief Justice Burger seems not to be quite sure of where the law is to go in this area, except that he would "prefer to allow this area of law to continue to evolve [as it had under the *New York Times* rule] . . . with respect to private citizens rather than to embark on a new doctrinal theory which has no jurisprudential ancestry."[204]

Obviously, in the face of these disparate legal postures, a consistent theoretical framework of the first amendment cannot be said to have emerged.   However, some extremely hopeful first steps may be discerned.   First among these is that all the Justices are now committed to the proposition that "libel can claim no talismanic immunity from constitutional limitations."[205]   This represents a sharp break with the past.   I believe

---

202. See notes 6, 7 *supra.*
203. Kalven, *The Reasonable Man and the First Amendment,* 1967 Sup. Ct. Rev. 267, 275, is the source of this irreverence.
204. 94 S. Ct. at 3014 (dissenting opinion).
205. New York Times Co. v. Sullivan, 376 U.S. 254, 269 (1964).

this, in itself, has great significance for the eventual development of a unified first amendment theory. What it means is that the Court will no longer as readily pass off, without serious attention, whole classes of utterances as outside the purview of the first amendment. There will no longer be talismanic or magic immunity. Any exception will be a reasoned exception, and like any other exception from a general rule, it should tell as much about the rule as do confirming instances. Over time, the necessity to avoid talismanic exceptions and provide reasoned ones to the coverage of the first amendment should assist greatly in creating a unified theory.

The next important step taken in *New York Times* and its progeny is the general recognition that the "central meaning of the First Amendment"—to use Justice Brennan's pregnant term—is to be found in the controversy over the Alien and Sedition Acts.[206] By condemning these Acts as unconstitutional under the first amendment, the Court clearly characterizes the amendment as designed to protect the sovereign right of the people, rather than individual liberty. Instead of invoking the clear and present danger test, or any of the other traditional tests of free expression, the Court asks what function free expression performs in our political system. The first amendment, it concludes, was intended to eliminate seditious libel as a crime and thereby to preserve political democracy by insuring that the sovereign people would not be silenced by those to whom they had temporarily delegated the power to govern. The amendment protects the sovereign power of the people. It insures that—to use Madison's formula—"the censorial power is in the people over the Government and not in the Government over the people."[207] It is, I believe, this identification of the purpose of the first amendment which explains why all the Justices sitting on the Court today, however they may disagree on other aspects of these issues, are at least able to agree on the rule of the publisher's immunity, absent actual malice, from defamation actions founded on utterances relevant to the general or public interest and brought by public officials and public figures.

It is Meiklejohn's espousal of the first amendment as a bulwark of the people's sovereignty, rather than of individual liberty—the right to hear, rather than the right to speak—which led Professor Kalven and Justice Brennan to see his influence so strongly in the *New York Times* case.[208] Kalven underscores this impression, it will be recalled, by going so far as to quote Meiklejohn (who in turn is quoted by Bren-

---

206. *Id.* at 273. *See also* Brennan, *supra* note 6, at 16; Kalven, *supra* note 6, at 208.
207. 4 ANNALS OF CONG. 934 (1794) [1789-1824], *quoted in* New York Times Co. v. Sullivan, 376 U.S. 254, 275 (1964).
208. *See* text accompanying notes 151-53 *supra*.

nan[209]) as saying that the decision in the *New York Times* case was "the occasion for dancing in the streets."[210] I wonder whether Meiklejohn had been informed by Kalven of the actual malice exception to the immunity of a publisher when he responded so joyfully.

My guess is that he had not, because the exception to the coverage of the *New York Times* case for actual malice is incompatible with Meiklejohn's theory and represents one of the disappointing aspects of the *New York Times* generation of cases. Meiklejohn, it will be recalled, believes that the first amendment is an absolute in respect of all utterances of governing importance, all utterances of general or public interest. The majority opinion in *New York Times* is obviously contrary to Meiklejohn's position, while that of Justice Douglas (and Justices Black and Goldberg) is consistent with it.

Justice Brennan appears not even to attempt to justify the exception for actual malice in his *New York Times* majority opinion; he merely states it. However, in his opinion in the *Garrison* case,[211] he attempts a form of justification by quoting from the *Chaplinsky* case. He says, "[c]alculated falsehood falls into that class of utterances which 'are no essential part of any exposition of ideas, and are of such slight social value as a step to truth that any benefit that may be derived from them is clearly outweighed by the social interest in order and morality. . . .' "[212]

In Meiklejohn's terms, it is precisely any test of what is or is not of "slight social value as a step to truth" which must and should be avoided under the first amendment. To be forced to establish the social value of what are alleged to be lies or intentional falsehoods is but one step removed from being called upon to establish the social value of allegedly false ideas. It bespeaks the same proscribed censorial power of the government over the sovereign people.

Moreover, if account is taken of the fact that any falsehood may serve a valuable function in inviting the search for truth—as Justice Brennan himself recognizes[213]—why should it make a difference whether the falsehood concerned is willfully and knowingly uttered or innocently and carelessly asserted? Restricting speech on account of malice has the identical effect on the search for truth and the assurance of the people's sovereign right to be informed as does suppression of a false idea put forward in good faith.

Viewing the matter in terms of the town meeting analogy,[214] would

209. Brennan, *supra* note 6, at 17.
210. Kalven, *supra* note 6, at 221 n.125.
211. Garrison v. Louisiana, 379 U.S. 64 (1964).
212. *Id.* at 75, *quoting* Chaplinsky v. New Hampshire, 315 U.S. 568, 572 (1941).
213. New York Times Co. v. Sullivan, 376 U.S. 254, 287 (1964).
214. See text surrounding note 37 *supra*.

the moderator in a town meeting ever declare someone out of order in debate for lying?   The intentional lie violates no rule of relevance or good order in a meeting and must be accorded the same hearing in debate as an innocent falsehood or the truth.   The protection against it in debate is of the same order as our protection against the innocent falsehood, but perhaps slightly stronger.   In "the marketplace of ideas," falsity must be met by truth to be overcome.   Intentional falsehood is often overcome more forcefully and fully by demonstrating the truth, while also unmasking the lie.

Still another basis of judging the actual malice rule is its effect on publishers.   As Justices Douglas, Goldberg, and Black argued so eloquently in their concurring opinions in *New York Times*,[215] the malice exception should be rejected for the same reasons that Justice Brennan rejected, in his majority opinion, founding publishers' defenses to defamation on their establishing the truth of what they say.   "A rule," says Justice Brennan,

> compelling the critic of official conduct to guarantee the truth of all his factual assertions—and to do so on pain of libel judgments virtually unlimited in amount—leads to . . . "self-censorship." . . . Under such a rule, would-be critics of official conduct may be deterred from voicing their criticism, even though it is believed to be true and even though it is in fact true, because of doubt whether it can be proved in court or fear of the expense of having to do so. . . .   The rule thus dampens the vigor and limits the variety of public debate.[216]

In "tough cases," where political or religious passions have been aroused, having to prove freedom from malice will "dampen the vigor and limit the variety of public debate" no less than having to prove the truth of what is said.   This problem is pointedly illustrated in the *New York Times* case by the fact that the Alabama jury had found intentional and willful falsehood on the part of the *New York Times*, as witnessed in its award of punitive damages.   Its finding had to be reviewed and reversed by the Supreme Court which, rather than risk sending the case back to still another Alabama jury inflamed by political passions, declared that the record "is constitutionally insufficient to show the recklessness that is required for a finding of actual malice."[217]

This tendency of a jury to find a willful lie where the publisher's views are detested flows easily from the fact that determining whether someone has intentionally lied frequently depends, in the first instance, upon determining that what has been said is a falsehood.   One who feels passionately that what someone else has said is false, outrageous, and unreasonable tends to consider that the detested opinion cannot

---

215.   376 U.S. at 293-305.
216.   *Id.* at 279.
217.   *Id.* at 288.

honestly be professed.   As Professor Noel has said, "in the case of charges against a popular figure . . . it may be almost impossible to show freedom from ill will."[218]   Thus, consideration of the truth or falsity of an opinion, in cases of emotion-laden beliefs, is inextricably bound up with whether the opinion is honestly held.   The attempt to separate the two as the *New York Times* case does is unrealistic.

Another consideration which militates against the "actual malice" exception arises out of the natural tendency of heated debate to generate shading of the truth, exaggeration, and outright lies.   These are intended, on occasion, to persuade people—sometimes for ultimately "good" reasons—as truth cannot.   Again, Justice Brennan's opinion in the *New York Times* case quotes a most effective statement of the point:

> In the realm of religious faith, and in that of political belief, sharp differences arise.   In both fields the tenets of one man may seem the rankest error to his neighbor.   *To persuade others to his own point of view, the pleader, as we know, at times resorts to exaggeration, to vilification . . . and even to false statement.*   But the people of this nation have ordained in the light of history, that, in spite of the probability of excesses and abuses, these liberties are, in the long view, essential to enlightened opinion and right conduct on the part of the citizens of a democracy.[219]

Exaggeration and even false statement, intentionally made, are so natural to the character of heated debate that we must risk them as the price we pay for unrestrained and vigorous participation.

Finally, I would urge, as Professor Emerson has, that the "actual malice" exception "fails to take into account that false statements, whether intentional or not, perform a significant function in a system of freedom of expression by forcing citizens to defend, justify, and rethink their positions."[220]   *Chaplinsky*[221] to the contrary notwithstanding, calculated falsehood is "an essential part of any exposition of ideas," if by "exposition of ideas," is meant vigorous, full, and open debate.   John Stuart Mill expressed this view most eloquently when he pointed out that, at the canonization of a saint, the Roman Catholic Church "admits, and listens patiently to, a 'devil's advocate.' "[222]   He then goes on to observe that "if opponents of all important truths do not exist, it is indispensable to imagine them, and supply them with the strongest arguments which the most skillful devil's advocate can conjure up."[223]   Only then will

---

218.   Noel, *Defamation of Public Officers and Candidates*, 49 Colum. L. Rev. 875, 893 (1949).
219.   376 U.S. at 271, *quoting* Cantwell v. Connecticut, 310 U.S. 296, 310 (1939) (emphasis added).
220.   Emerson, *supra* note 6, at 530.
221.   315 U.S. 568, 572 (1942).
222.   J. Mill, On Liberty, in Problems and Styles of Communication 314 (W. Howell ed. 1945).
223.   *Id.* at 331.

we have "the opportunity of exchanging error for truth," or, as important, the opportunity of attaining "the clearer impression and livelier impression of truth, produced by its collision with error."[224]

Judicial statesmanship may well have required Justice Brennan to moderate his views to admit the "actual malice' exception so as to achieve as much as he did in the *New York Times* case.[225]   And it may well be that it smacks of "demeaning . . . carping" to criticize "so distinctly liberal an opinion" for its "illiberality."[226]   But it also is the case that "truth is truth," and, after applauding Justice Brennan for striking a new direction in the discussion of first amendment free expression, it is also necessary to say that the *New York Times* case did not go far enough.

As I have indicated, Justice Douglas, unlike Justice Brennan, rejects the actual malice rule and, in this respect, is closer to Meiklejohn. They both agree, however, with respect to another issue, critical to Meiklejohn's theory, an issue on which, unfortunately, they now seem to be in a minority.   Shall the protection afforded a publisher under the *New York Times* rule affect defamation suits involving any utterance of public or general interest, or shall it only affect those which involve utterances of "public or general interest" and are brought by a public official or public figure?

In the most recent offspring of *New York Times*, the *Gertz* case, the plurality expressed the view "the state interest in compensating injury to the reputation of private individuals requires that a [rule other than the *New York Times* rule] should obtain with respect to them."[227] Instead of a publisher being immune to suit except upon a showing of malice, if a private party is defamed, that party may, consistent with the first amendment, recover on a showing of negligence.[228]   The reason for distinguishing the private party from the public official is that the latter, because of their[229] position, has greater opportunity to publicly rebut the libel[230] and because the public official also may be said to have assumed the risk of such injury.[231]

Justice Brennan argues against this view most forcefully.   "Matters

224. *Id.*
225. Kalven, *supra* note 6, at 220.
226. *Id.*
227. 94 S. Ct. at 3009.
   It is not clear from Justice Powell's opinion whether a "public official" or "public figure" would fall under the *New York Times* rule in a case *not* involving an issue of "general or public interest."
228. Actually, any standard other than a standard of absolute liability would be constitutionally acceptable, according to Justice Powell. *Id.* at 3011.
229. See note 47 *supra.*
230. Gertz v. Robert Welch, Inc., 94 S. Ct. 2997, 3010 (1974).
231. *Id.* at 3009.

of public or general interest do not 'suddenly become less so merely because a private individual is involved, or because in some sense the individual did not "voluntarily" choose to become involved.' "[232]   This same view had also been expressed by Justice Douglas in *Rosenblatt*, where he said "the question is whether a public *issue*, not a public official is involved."[233]   As for the power of rebuttal and assumption of the risk arguments, Justice Brennan asserts that there is no effective form of rebuttal even for the public official or public figure,[234] and "social interaction exposes all of us to some degree of public view," "we are all public men to some degree."[235]

The *Gertz* plurality seems to be taking too restricted a view of the first amendment as a bulwark of the people's sovereignty. It is true that Madison said that "the censorial power is in the people over the Government"[236] and that, in the *New York Times* case, Justice Brennan wrote, "[t]he right of free public discussion of the stewardship of public officials was thus, in Madison's view, a fundamental principle of the American form of government."[237]   But these pronouncements stressing public officials and government as sources of the people's concern must be read in the context of the immediate problems to which they were directed, rather than as limitations on the scope of the first amendment.

The people, in order to fulfill their governing function, require the widest possible acquaintanceship with public affairs of every variety. Therefore, the first amendment must be read liberally to protect the sovereign right to be informed by protecting discussion of all public affairs, not solely discussion of public officials involved in public affairs. The Court in *Thornhill v. Alabama*[238] quoted a letter from the Continental Congress to the inhabitants of Quebec: "The importance of the [freedom of the press] consists, besides the advancement of truth, science, morality and arts in general, in its diffusion of liberal sentiments on the administration of Government . . . ."[239]   And the Court then went on to say: "Freedom of discussion, if it would fulfill its historic function in this nation, must embrace all issues about which information is needed or appropriate to enable the members of society to cope with the exigencies of their period."[240]   The restriction of the important

232. *Id.* at 3018 (dissenting opinion).
233. Rosenblatt v. Baer, 383 U.S. 75, 91 (1966).
234. Gertz v. Robert Welch, Inc., 94 S. Ct. 2997, 3018 (dissenting opinion).
235. *Id.* at 3019.
236. 4 ANNALS OF CONG. 934 (1794) [1789-1824], *quoted in* New York Times Co. v. Sullivan, 376 U.S. 254, 275 (1964).
237. 376 U.S. at 275.
238. 310 U.S. 88 (1940).
239. *Id.* at 102.
240. *Id.*

New York Times rule to public officials and public figures hardly seems compatible with the letter and spirit of the *Thornhill* doctrine.

Look at the matter in terms of the facts of the *Gertz* case.[241]   The publisher there believed a private citizen, a lawyer, was involved in a communist plot to undermine confidence in American police departments.   Would the public interest in or need to know about such a communist plot have been any greater—deserving the protection of the *New York Times* rule rather than the *Gertz* rule—had a minor official of government (a local tax assessor or dog catcher, say) been involved, rather than a private attorney?   Hardly, I believe.

The first amendment embraces all issues of governing importance, including "the advancement of truth, science, morality and arts in general."   This high purpose can hardly be achieved if public issues in which private citizens are involved (a scientific discovery, a scheme for utopia, or an artistic creation, say) are subject to less vigorous discussion, because they are provided less stringent protection, than those in which public officials or public figures are involved.   To draw the distinction between forms of first amendment protection on these grounds "has no basis in law or logic," as Chief Justice Warren observed.[242]   It is the *issue*, not the person, which should control under the first amendment.

In a curious way, however, the very distinction, whether mistaken or not, between these two forms of first amendment protection, the *New York Times* rule for public persons and the *Gertz* rule for private persons, brings the Supreme Court closer to Alexander Meiklejohn.   He too, it will be recalled,[243] believed in two forms of protection of speech, that befitting speech which served the public's need to be informed of matters of governing importance—deserving of absolute or unqualified protection—and that befitting speech which fulfilled an individual's right of expression—deserving of the qualified protection of the due process clause.

Interestingly enough, Justices Douglas and Brennan also seem to be committed to, or, at the least, to leave open, the concept of a two-level theory of the protection of speech.   Their theory, however, comes closer to Meiklejohn's than that of the plurality in *Gertz*.   Justice Douglas is not an absolutist in the same sense Justice Black is because he, unlike Black,[244] admits the constitutional validity of private defamation.   Justice Douglas joined Justice Goldberg's concurring opinion in the *New York Times* case in which they said "[p]urely private defa-

241. Gertz v. Robert Welch, Inc., 94 S. Ct. 2997 (1974).
242. Curtis Publishing Co. v. Butts, 388 U.S. 130, 163 (1967) (concurring opinion).
243. See text accompanying note 75 *supra*.
244. *See* New York Times Co. v. Sullivan, 376 U.S. 254, 293 (1964) (Black, J., dissenting).

mation has little to do with the political ends of a self-governing society" and in which they admitted the constitutional validity of a cause of action for libel for "defamatory statements against the private conduct of a public official or a private citizen."[245]

As for Justice Brennan, in his dissent in the *Gertz* case he indicates that he "would leave open the question of what constitutional standard, if any, applies when defamatory falsehoods are published or broadcast concerning either a private or public person's activities not within the scope of the general or public interest."[246]   In the *Garrison* case, he also leaves open the question of "private libels," indicating "different interests may be involved."[247]   A similar reservation is made in his opinions in *Rosenblatt*[248] and *Rosenbloom.*[249]

This recognition by Justices Douglas and Brennan that a different interest may be involved in private libels, than public ones—libels, that is, involving "a private or public person's activities not within the scope of the general or public interest"[250]—brings the Justices almost to the point of agreement with the most distinctive feature of the Meiklejohn first amendment analysis.   They may well be on the verge of recognizing the difference, so critical to Meiklejohn, between the "right to hear" and the "right to speak," one absolute, the other limited or qualified under the due process reasonableness test.[251]

3. The Significance of the *New York Times* Case and Its Progeny for the Mass Publication Right to Privacy.

Among the progeny of the *New York Times* case, the *Hill* case[252] is distinctive in that it alone directly involved privacy, not libel.   Before discussing *Hill,* however, two observations should be made about the impact of the entire line of cases upon the right to privacy.   The first is that in many respects the Court has begun, although not explicitly, to regard libel as being of the same species of wrong as invasion of privacy.   This tendency first appeared in Justice Stewart's concurring opinion in *Rosenblatt,* where he spoke of the right to protection of reputation as an aspect of "private personality" and as one aspect of the "basic concept of the essential dignity and worth of every human be-

---

245. *Id.* at 301-02. *See also* W.O. DOUGLAS, THE RIGHTS OF THE PEOPLE 36 (1958); Gertz v. Robert Welch, Inc., 94 S. Ct. 3016 n.6 (1974) (Douglas, J., dissenting).

246. 94 S. Ct. at 3021 n.3.

247. Garrison v. Louisiana, 379 U.S. 64, 72 n.8 (1964).

248. Rosenblatt v. Baer, 383 U.S. 75, 86 n.12 (1966).

249. Rosenbloom v. Metromedia, Inc., 403 U.S. 29, 48 n.17 (1971).

250. Gertz v. Robert Welch, Inc., 94 S. Ct. 2997, 3021 n.3 (1974) (Brennan, J., dissenting).

251. See text accompanying note 75 *supra.*

252. Time, Inc. v. Hill, 385 U.S. 374 (1967). For discussion of the most recent in this line of cases see note 263 *infra.*

ing,"[253] language almost identical to that of Warren and Brandeis.[254] Justice Stewart's view was then quoted by Justice Brennan in his plurality opinion and by Justice Marshall in his dissenting opinion in *Rosenbloom*.[255] And finally it was reiterated in Justice Powell's opinion for the plurality in *Gertz*.[256] There is a clear suggestion that libel and the invasion of privacy are aspects of the same wrong, both assaults on human dignity or worth.

The second noteworthy point in respect to the impact of this line of cases on privacy is that the identification of libel as bearing a close relationship to invasion of privacy possibly promises more protection for privacy than had been expected by Professor Kalven,[257] among others, after the *Hill* decision. Kalven said, it will be recalled, that the first amendment privilege to publish what is newsworthy may be "so overpowering as virtually to swallow [the mass-publication] tort"[258] of privacy.

The fact is, however, that it was out of deference to the privacy-related rights of those who had been defamed in the *Rosenblatt, Rosenbloom,* and *Gertz* cases that the Justices began to identify libel, explicitly or implicitly, as an assault on private personality. Moreover, Justices Stewart, Marshall, and Powell, each of them having recognized this relationship, and each of them having identified privacy as bearing a constitutional status, carved out an exception to the *New York Times* publisher's immunity rule in favor of affording the private person involved in the *Gertz* case a new privacy-related form of protection.

Thus, what the *New York Times* and *Hill* rules threatened with respect to legal protection against invasion of privacy by mass publication, the *Gertz* decision partially restored. Prior to *New York Times*, any person who was defamed could recover under the usual common law rule of absolute liability; in other words, one could recover even if the publisher acted with the highest standard of care. The *New York Times* case, at least for defamations where an utterance of general or public interest was concerned, made the publisher immune, absent a showing of actual malice. And it seemed after the *Rosenbloom* case[259] that the *New York Times* rule might apply to private persons as well as public persons. The *Gertz* case took a step back from the rule of the *New York Times* and *Rosenbloom* cases and, although con-

253. 383 U.S. at 92.
254. *See* text accompanying note 43 *supra*.
255. 403 U.S. at 48, 78.
256. 94 S. Ct. at 3008.
257. Kalven, *Privacy in Tort Law—Were Warren and Brandeis Wrong?*, 31 LAW & CONTEMP. PROB. 326, 336 (1966).
258. *Id.*
259. Rosenbloom v. Metromedia, Inc., 403 U.S. 29 (1971).

stitutionally forbidding absolute liability for defamations of private persons involved in a matter of general or public interest, invited a rule of due care or any other rule except absolute liability. In some large measure, this result rests on the identification of defamation as bearing a close relationship to the mass publication invasion of privacy. Whether one agrees with the conclusion of the Court in *Gertz* or not, the case displays a climate of sensitivity to privacy-related issues and a vindication of privacy-related rights which is highly significant.

This observation leads one to question whether the *Hill* case, were it to come before the Court today, would be decided as it was in 1967. The changed membership on the Court, and the emergence of what might be a new majority which regards privacy with greater awareness of its constitutional significance, might well dictate another result.

However, aside from any change in the views of the majority of the Court on the specific issues in the *Hill* decision, the general approach taken in *Hill* seems to me mistaken. In fact, in one important sense, it runs contrary to the salutary form of analysis of first amendment problems initiated in *New York Times*. If the "central meaning of the First Amendment" involves a proscription against any legal bar to political defamation,[260] why should it be used to bar the attempt of a private person to recover damages for a use of his name or likeness in a mass publication where that use in no way contributes to the discussion of issues of general or public interest?

Admittedly, the *Life* story on a play which had recently opened and which described the plight of a family held hostage in its home by escaped convicts was an "utterance" which served the sovereign need of the people to be informed of matters of general or public interest. But was that need also served by identifying the people concerned? Could it have been served as well without identifying them? A book and a play were done without identifying the Hills. Did the *Life* article serve a higher general or public interest? In fact, in the first draft of the *Life* article, the name of the family concerned had not even been used. The trial record shows that the family name was inserted into the second draft by a senior editor of the magazine because he found the first draft was not "newsy enough."[261]

The *Hill* case exhibits the same ambiguity in the meaning of "newsworthiness" as discussed above in reference to the *Sidis* case.[262] The second draft was more "newsy," but the need to know about matters of general or public interest would have been as well served by the article without the use of the family's name. To be sure, the publisher

---

260. See text accompanying notes 206-07 *supra*.
261. Record at 220-21, Time, Inc. v. Hill, 385 U.S. 374 (1967).
262. See text accompanying notes 54-62 *supra*.

has a private right to speak the name of the Hill family in his news story, a private right to make it more "newsy." This right deserves the protection of the Constitution under the due process clause. But this is different from the public right to hear the name of the Hill family, which is absolute, and only applies if the identification of the name or likeness serves the public need to know matters of governing importance.

IV. CONCLUSION

The central first amendment question which the mass publication tort raises is whether speech which serves the public's governing purposes and is of general or public concern deserves a higher order of constitutional protection than speech which serves solely as an aspect of individual liberty and a form of self-fulfillment. Meiklejohn believes it does. He accords the public's right to hear speech which informs governing choices absolute protection or freedom from all legal limitation, because being fully and freely informed is a necessary requirement of democracy and popular sovereignty. He accords the individual's right to speak, speech which does not concern matters of general or public interest, the qualified protection of due process, because it deserves no fuller protection than other aspects of personal life, liberty, and property.

For many years the Supreme Court has decided first amendment free expression cases without the benefit of a consistent and systematic theory. There has long existed, to be sure, a strong commitment to free expression and an explicit recognition that it is vital to our constitutional structure. But it has never been quite clear what consequences, if any, should flow from the fact that free expression is both an aspect of liberty of the individual and a necessary attribute of the informed consent basic to democratic government. Moreover, although most, if not all, of the members of the Court have acknowledged the necessity of some form of regulation of speech, attempts to justify such regulation have gone little further than the invention of talismanic or ritual formulas which have sanctified exceptions to free expression rather than explained them. And finally, again and again, when faced with a conflict between constitutional protection of free expression and some other constitutional value the Court has resorted to a weighing process, which has substituted subjective political judgment for constitutional analysis of the function served by the warring principles. As a consequence, rather than a constitutional theory of free expression, we find in the Supreme Court first amendment cases a set of sometimes overlapping, sometimes independent, sometimes contrary, ad hoc decisions applicable to discrete fact situations in which free expression is at issue.

The great virtue of the cases which have followed the *New York*

Times case is that they have begun to place free expression as a constitutional doctrine in an appropriate theoretical perspective. Free expression is beginning to be seen to serve a profound political purpose, the assurance of the informed consent necessary to a democratic people. Once this insight is gained, and political or public libel is recognized to be at the heart of the matter, questions arise concerning the constitutional status of private libel.

Here, Professor Meiklejohn's views should become increasingly important. Not, however, because he distinguishes first and fifth amendment protection of speech; in fact, I regard this identification of the two different constitutional sources of protection of speech as relatively unimportant. Rather, his views are significant because, first, he explains why two forms or two levels of protection of speech are necessary and appropriate. And second, they are significant because this same explanation may readily be extended to the entire range of free expression cases, substituting a single theoretical framework for what has heretofore been a patchwork of ad hoc rules.

This paper has attempted to demonstrate the successful application of the Meiklejohn theory to the mass publication privacy tort. The theory developed enables one to distinguish the public's governing interest from the public's curiosity and the publisher's private right. This, in turn, allows one to ask what constitutional interest is served by the actual identification of name or likeness in a particular instance of its mass publication. The *Hill* case seemed to some students of the first amendment to foreclose any recovery for invasion of privacy by mass publication. As I see it, however, the increasing sensitivity of the Court to the distinction between public and private libels and public and private uses of speech suggests, to the contrary, that the *New York Times* case and its progeny will establish a firm constitutional foundation for the mass publication privacy tort.[263] Meiklejohn's theory, by exposing the private and public uses of speech, enables us, I believe, to assure the robust exposition of public issues without inviting the lurid exploitation of private lives.

---

263. Indeed, as this article goes to press the Supreme Court seems to be moving in that direction. Petitioners in *Cantrell v. Forest City Publishing Co.*, 43 U.S.L.W. 4079 (U.S. Dec. 18, 1974), alleged that respondent's newspaper article discussing the impact of the death of a husband (and father) due to a bridge collapse was an invasion of privacy. The Court held that where there was evidence of knowing falsity or reckless disregard of the truth, and where the judge charged the jury on that standard, compensatory damages could be awarded.

Two other cases, soon to be decided, may further indicate the Court's future direction. *See* Cox Broadcasting Corp. v. Cohn, 231 Ga. 60, 200 S.E.2d 127 (1973), *probable jurisdiction noted*, 415 U.S. 912 (1974) (No. 93-938) (constitutionality of statute prohibiting disclosure of rape victim's name); Doe v. Roe, 42 A.D.2d 559, 345 N.Y.S.2d 560, *aff'd*, 33 N.Y.2d 902, 307 N.E.2d 823, 352 N.Y.S.2d 626 (1973), *cert. granted*, 94 S. Ct. 2601 (1974) (No. 73-1446) (constitutionality of preliminary injunction barring publication of mental patient's case history).

4

GROUP PRIVACY:
THE RIGHT TO HUDDLE

I. INTRODUCTION

People act either alone or in association with one another to achieve their purposes. By nature they require and enjoy both privacy and fraternity. And what nature thus plants, our society—including the system of law—cultivates.

The legal structure of the concept of privacy began to take form only in the late nineteenth century, in an article by Louis Brandeis and Samuel Warren entitled *The Right to Privacy*.[1] Although recognition of specific privacy rights predated Brandeis and Warren's enunciation of the concept, their conceptualization provided a new perspective and stimulated a more structured development of the law of privacy.[2] Brandeis and Warren, however, dealt primarily with the *individual right to privacy*—the "right to be let alone."[3] There is now a need to develop an understanding of *group privacy*—the "right to huddle."

The right of individuals to associate privately with one another has long been legally protected in certain contexts and for limited purposes. Although a few writers have recognized the concept and outlined its scope briefly,[4] there has been no comprehensive treatment of the incipient right. Group privacy rights thus currently lack a theoretical framework relating them to one another and to other classes of rights. This article attempts such a systematic statement.

---

1. Warren & Brandeis, *The Right to Privacy*, 4 HARV. L. REV. 193 (1890).
2. See A. WESTIN, PRIVACY AND FREEDOM ch. 13 (1967), for an historical treatment of the development of the American law of privacy.
3. *See* Warren & Brandeis, *supra* note 1, at 193, 195.
4. Westin discusses the concept of "organizational privacy." A. WESTIN, *supra* note 2, at 42-51. Levi does not use the terminology, but he clearly has the concept in mind. Levi, *Confidentiality and Democratic Government*, RECORD OF N.Y.C.B.A. 323, 324 (1975). *See also* E. SHILS, THE TORMENT OF SECRECY 21-57 (1956).

A. The Concept of Group Privacy: A Preliminary Statement

(1) What Is a Group and in What Sense Can Privacy be Attributed to Groups?

In the history of social theory, there is a longstanding, unresolved —perhaps unresolvable—controversy over whether groups exist independently of the individuals who make them up.[5] On the one hand, the holists and organic theorists assert the independent reality of the group.[6] Opposing them are the nominalists or individualists, who assert that all statements about groups are reducible without loss of meaning to statements about the actions, feelings and relationships of individuals.[7]

Without attempting to resolve this controversy, I can only say that my philosophical view is individualist rather than holist. I believe with Karl Popper that "social phenomena, including collectives, should be analyzed in terms of individuals and their actions and relations."[8] Therefore, when I use the term "group privacy," I mean by it a form of privacy that people seek in their associations with others. "Group privacy" is an attribute of individuals in association with one another within a group, rather than an attribute of the group itself.[9]

(2) The Interest Protected

There are at least two overlapping concepts of individual privacy. Some say privacy protects "man's spiritual nature,"[10] an "innermost

---

5. See Gellner, *Holism versus Individualism in History and Sociology,* in THEORIES OF HISTORY 489-503 (P. Gardiner ed. 1959).

6. Plato is the philosophical precursor of "holism." His theory of "Forms," developed principally in the *Republic,* the *Phaedo* and the *Timaeus,* is central to the argument. Hegel later developed the theory specifically in relation to the state and society. G. HEGEL, THE PHILOSOPHY OF RIGHT (1821). Rousseau's *Social Contract* also embodies this view. A modern proponent of it is Mandelbaum, *Social Facts,* in THEORIES OF HISTORY 476-88 (P. Gardiner ed. 1959).

7. See, e.g., T. HOBBES, LEVIATHAN ch. 16 (1651); R. HORN, GROUPS AND THE CONSTITUTION 8 (1956); H. KELSEN, GENERAL THEORY OF LAW AND STATE 96-109 (1945); K. POPPER, CONJECTURES AND REFUTATIONS 336-46 (1962) [hereinafter cited as CONJECTURES]; K. POPPER, THE OPEN SOCIETY AND ITS ENEMIES 18-34 (5th ed. 1966).

8. CONJECTURES, *supra* note 7, at 341.

9. Eisenstadt v. Baird, 405 U.S. 438 (1972), does not expressly treat the distinction between the reality of the group and the reality of the individuals in the group. It is nevertheless interesting to note this language from the Court's opinion: "[T]he marital couple is not an independent entity with a mind and heart of its own, but an association of two individuals each with a separate intellectual and emotional makeup." *Id.* at 453.

10. Warren & Brandeis, *supra* note 1, at 193, 195, 205.

region in man,"[11] his "inner space."[12] Some define it more narrowly as "the right of the individual to decide for himself how much he will share with others his thoughts, feelings and the facts of his personal life."[13]

Group privacy is an extension of individual privacy. The interest protected by group privacy is the desire and need of people to come together, to exchange information, share feelings, make plans and act in concert to attain their objectives. This requires that people reveal themselves to one another—breach their individual privacy—and rely on those with whom they associate to keep within the group what was revealed. Thus, group privacy protects people's outer space rather than their inner space, their gregarious nature rather than their desire for complete seclusion. People fashion individual privacy by regulating whether, and how much of, the self will be shared; group privacy is fashioned by regulating the sharing or association process.[14]

(3)   The Love Affair and the Football Huddle: Paradigms of Group Privacy

The love affair and the football huddle are paradigmatic of the importance of group privacy to the success of interpersonal associations. Lovers give themselves up to each other. They lay bare their innermost feelings to each other, they are lewd and foolish with each other, they stand naked before each other. Between themselves, there is no individual privacy, nothing is held back. But the premise for giving up individual privacy in love is the feeling that what is shared so intimately will not be broadcast to the world at large. Indeed, this is the very condition for achieving intimacy. If love did not promise, and

---

11. H. ARENDT, THE HUMAN CONDITION 7-78 (1958). Arendt traces the cultural development of the "inner man" concept (*vita contemplativa*) and the concept of man as a social being (*vita activa*).

12. *See* Bloustein, *The First Amendment and Privacy: The Supreme Court Justice and the Philosopher*, 28 RUTGERS L. REV. 41, 52-53 (1974).

13. OFFICE OF SCIENCE AND TECHNOLOGY, EXECUTIVE OFFICE OF THE PRESIDENT, PRIVACY AND BEHAVIORAL RESEARCH 2 (1967). *See also* A. WESTIN, *supra* note 2, at 7; Parker, *A Definition of Privacy*, 27 RUTGERS L. REV. 275 (1974).

14. The two-fold nature of the privacy right was hinted at by Brandeis and Warren:
    The common law secures to each individual the right of determining, ordinarily, to what extent his thoughts, sentiments, and emotions shall be communicated to others. . . . [E]ven if he has chosen to give them expression, he generally retains the power to fix the limits of the publicity which shall be given them.
Warren & Brandeis, *supra* note 1, at 198 (footnote omitted). *See also* Lopez v. United States, 373 U.S. 427, 449 (1963) (Brennan, J., dissenting): "The right of privacy would mean little if it were limited to a person's solitary thoughts . . . . It must embrace a concept of the liberty of one's communications . . . ."

most often provide for, such protected intimacy, falling in love would be rare indeed.

Similarly, the football huddle is an association of people which rests on shared confidences. The essence of the game is the team strategy communicated in the huddle. If players on the same team could not trust one another to maintain the secrets of the huddle, football as we know it simply could not be played.

B. The Analytical Framework

The football huddle illustrates the analytical framework for group privacy: ordinarily only the players in the huddle are party to what is said there. On rare occasions, quarterbacks have worn microphones and broadcast their signals for the enjoyment of television audiences. But this does not destroy the usefulness of the huddle, so long as the opposition does not learn what is said in time to anticipate the next play.

The extent of legal regulation of confidences among associates depends on similar factors. Who are the parties to, and what are the purposes of, the association? What is the subject of the confidence? How long is it intended that the confidence be maintained? Who are the parties seeking access to the group confidence, and for what purpose? What is the legal form by which access to the confidence is sought? Thus, it is impossible to delineate general forms of protection of group privacy which disregard the specific duration, purpose and circumstances of the association.[15]

The term "association" has at least two meanings in the context of group privacy. First, it denotes a relatively stable and structured relationship among a number of people, for one purpose or for a number of purposes. "Association" in this sense is synonymous with "group" or "organization." But "association" also denotes less formal, less stable relationships between as few as two people for single, transitory purposes. In this sense, one associates with a stranger at the scene of an accident for the purpose of directing traffic, or with a businessman or professional who sells a product or renders a service. Group privacy covers the large, formal organization, as well as the relatively informal relationship, and the whole range of intermediate variations in size, duration and formality. Moreover, although the sharing of confidences characterizes many associations, it is not an invariable characteristic.

---

15. The importance of the legal context in which relief is sought has most recently been recognized in United States v. Nixon, 418 U.S. 683, 712 n.19 (1974).

Indeed, many group goals can be achieved without any confidences being shared.

C.   The Nonlegal Factors Which Serve to Protect Confidences Among Associates

Students of the law and, more often, laymen suppose that law plays a much more important role in human events than it does.   A number of areas of law, from the law of contract to constitutional law, govern confidences among associates.   But most confidences are maintained without any reference to law at all.   Among other factors, a sense of good faith, the fear of reprisal or loss of face, traditional practice, religious or ethical compunctions and the intricacies of bureaucratic or organizational structure are important to the support of a system of confidences.   Law acts as only one influence among many.

II.   AN OUTLINE OF THE LAW OF GROUP PRIVACY

A.   Physical Intrusions Upon Confidential Associations

Secure places and means of communication are necessary to many forms and purposes of association.   In recent years, however, the fast-developing technology of surveillance has threatened the security of the places and means of communication which support privacy.[16]   Because the group's effectiveness so often depends on confidential discussion, I believe that the first amendment right of association[17] and freedom of communication[18] should protect against such surreptitious intrusions on the privacy of groups.   Since many confidential communications take place within the automobile, the home and the office, the fourth amendment guarantee of "the right of the people to be secure in their . . . houses . . . against unreasonable searches and seizures"[19] also

---

16. A. WESTIN, *supra* note 2, at 69-85; Donner, *Political Intelligence: Cameras, Informers and Files,* in FINAL REPORT, ANNUAL CHIEF JUSTICE EARL WARREN CONFERENCE ON ADVOCACY IN THE UNITED STATES, PRIVACY IN A FREE SOCIETY 56, 58 (1974).

17. [F]reedom of association [is] a peripheral First Amendment right. . . .
In other words, the First Amendment has a penumbra where privacy is protected from governmental intrusion. . . .

    . . . .

    . . . Various [constitutional] guarantees create zones of privacy.   The right of association contained in the penumbra of the First Amendment is one

. . . .

Griswold v. Connecticut, 381 U.S. 479, 483-84 (1965).

18. "Electronic surveillance strikes deeper than at the ancient feeling that a man's home is his castle; it strikes at freedom of communication, a postulate of our kind of society." Lopez v. United States, 373 U.S. 427, 470 (1963) (Brennan, J., dissenting).

19. U.S. CONST. amend. IV.

protects the right of group privacy against physical intrusion. Although at one time the amendment was held inapplicable to wiretaps[20] and electronic eavesdropping,[21] both means of surveillance are now within its scope.[22]   In addition, a recent federal statute[23] prohibits wiretaps without a valid warrant showing probable cause, and prohibits as well any use of the illegally overheard communication.[24]   As the Senate Report recommending the legislation made clear, it is "intended to protect the privacy of the communication itself."[25]

Maintaining the mails as a means of confidential communication is also a subject of constitutional concern.   In the early case of *Ex parte Jackson*,[26] the United States Supreme Court decided that the "secrecy of letters" was protected under the fourth amendment against intrusion by postal officials.[27]   And the Court recently declared that "[i]t has long been held that first-class mail such as letters . . . is free from inspection by postal authorities, except in the manner provided by the Fourth Amendment."[28]   Although grave abuse has recently been demonstrated in FBI and CIA operations,[29] the mantle of the Constitution and of federal and state[30] legislation shields the home and the office as prime sites of confidential communication, and the telephone and the mails as prime means of confidential communication.

Recently, a very disturbing form of intimidation of political organizations has come to light: the use of both undercover agents and traditional police forces to monitor the operations of radical political groups.[31]   Mail-covers, burglaries, wiretaps and other illegal forms of intelligence gathering outlined in the infamous Houston Plan[32] have

---

20. Olmstead v. United States, 277 U.S. 438 (1928).

21. Goldman v. United States, 316 U.S. 129, 135 (1942).

22. *See* Katz v. United States, 389 U.S. 347 (1967); Berger v. New York, 388 U.S. 41 (1967).   *See also* Note, *From Private Places to Personal Privacy: A Post-Katz Study of Fourth Amendment Protection*, 43 N.Y.U.L. REV. 968 (1968).

23. Title III of the Omnibus Crime Control and Safe Streets Act of 1968, 18 U.S.C. §§ 2510-20 (1970).

24. *Id.* § 2515; *see* Gelbard v. United States, 408 U.S. 41 (1972).

25. S. REP. No. 1097, 90th Cong., 2d Sess. 89-90 (1968).

26. 96 U.S. 727 (1878).

27. *Id.* at 733.

28. United States v. Van Leeuwen, 397 U.S. 249, 251 (1970). *Compare* Rowan v. United States Post Office Dep't, 397 U.S. 728 (1970), *with* Lamont v. Postmaster General, 381 U.S. 301 (1965).

29. *See, e.g.*, N.Y. Times, Oct. 21, 1976, at 15, col. 1.

30. *See, e.g.*, CAL. PENAL CODE §§ 630-637.2 (West 1970); ILL. REV. STAT. ch. 38, § 14 (Cum. Supp. 1975); N.J.S.A. 2A:156A-1 *et seq.* (1971).

31. *See* Donner, *supra* note 16.

32. *See* N.Y. Times, June 2, 1973, at 1, col. 1.

been widely used by the FBI, as have photographic surveillance and the gathering of large numbers of files on organizations and their members.[33]   Most insidious has been the widespread use of informers planted in organizations under surveillance.[34]   As one writer has said, "[i]t is not merely that political surveillance challenges the protected freedom of expression, . . . it destroys the pre-condition, the matrix, for the exercise of such freedoms by inspiring widespread fear and mistrust."[35]   Under these circumstances, surveillance becomes a form of suppression of the association itself; it "tampers with the very process by which political change is brought about."[36]   Yet, no effective legislative or judicial restriction on this form of interference with the freedom of association has been devised.[37]

Thus far, I have been directing attention solely to intrusions by government agents.   However, a threat to associational privacy arises from private surveillance as well.   Forms of industrial espionage, wiretapping and eavesdropping on business and professional associations by private persons are now frequent occurrences.[38]   Although the fourth amendment extends only to governmental action, limited legal protection against private invasions of confidential associations may be found in the statutory and case law of many jurisdictions.[39]

B.   Nongovernmental Associations Between Two People

Unlike the totalitarian ideology,[40] democratic political philosophy favors autonomous or private associations[41] because they constitute in-

---

33. *See* Donner, *supra* note 16, at 58-61, 66-69.

34. *Id.* at 61-66. *See also* N.Y. Times, Sept. 5, 1976, at 24, col. 1.

35. Donner, *supra* note 16, at 57.

36. *Id.*

37. *See* Note, *Judicial Control of Secret Agents*, 76 YALE L.J. 994 (1967). *But see* Anderson v. Sills, 106 N.J. Super. 545, 256 A.2d 298 (App. Div. 1969), *rev'd*, 56 N.J. 210, 265 A.2d 678 (1970). *Compare* Gouled v. United States, 255 U.S. 298 (1921), *with* Hoffa v. United States, 385 U.S. 293 (1966).

38. A. WESTIN, *supra* note 2, at 104-18.

39. *See id.* at 360-64.

40. *See* B. MUSSOLINI, FASCISM, DOCTRINE AND INSTITUTIONS (1935). Mussolini declared: "The Fascist conception of the State is all-embracing; outside of it no human or spiritual values can exist . . . . No individuals or groups (political parties, cultural associations, economic unions, social classes) [exist] outside the state." *Id.* at 10. *See also* H. ARENDT, THE ORIGINS OF TOTALITARIANISM 389-419 (1958); D. FELLMAN, THE CONSTITUTIONAL RIGHT OF ASSOCIATION chs. 1 & 2 (1963); R. HORN, *supra* note 7, at ch. 1; W. McGOVERN, FROM LUTHER TO HITLER 646-58 (1941).

41. If men living in democratic countries had no right and no inclination to associate for political purposes, their independence would be in great jeopardy, but they might long preserve their wealth and their cultivation; whereas if they

dependent sources of power and initiative which act to forestall undue accumulation of state power. Thus, to the extent that confidentiality strengthens autonomous associations, and absent other countervailing interests, the law should favor maintenance of confidences among private associates.

(1) The Marital Relationship

Marriage is an association of two people in which the implicit promise of confidentiality is of the essence of the relationship. Marriage partners give up their privacy in relation to each other in the expectation that their mutual confidences will not be shared with others. The psychological characteristics of intimacy, social convention, literary tradition, emotional reticence and fear of a partner's retaliation, among other nonlegal influences, support this expectation. But there are legal supports as well, arising from the Constitution, the common law and statutes.

Marriage is one of the "basic civil rights" long protected under the Constitution.[42] Legal recognition of a right of privacy within the marriage relationship, however, is of relatively recent origin. Constitutional protection of the intimacy of marriage was first raised in the 1961 case of *Poe v. Ullman*,[43] involving state regulation of the sale and use of contraceptives. The majority of the United States Supreme Court did not reach the constitutional issue in the case, but in dissent Justice Harlan expressed the opinion that "a statute making it a criminal offense for *married couples* to use contraceptives is an intolerable, unjustifiable invasion of privacy . . . ."[44] Justice Harlan would have extended fourth and fourteenth amendment protections against state intrusion to the intimacies of marital relations—the core of family life and of the home.[45]

---

never acquired the habit of forming associations in ordinary life, civilization itself would be endangered.

2 A. DE TOCQUEVILLE, DEMOCRACY IN AMERICA 115 (rev. ed. 1966). *See also* 6 B. DE JOUVENAL, ON POWER 294, 299-300, 332-34 (1949); THE FEDERALIST No. 10 (J. Madison); *id.* No. 15 (A. Hamilton); G. MCCONNELL, PRIVATE POWER AND AMERICAN DEMOCRACY 88-90, 119-54 (1966); E. SHILS, *supra* note 4, at 21-22; A. WESTIN, *supra* note 2, at 23-26.

42. Skinner v. Oklahoma, 316 U.S. 535, 541 (1942); *see* United States v. Orito, 413 U.S. 139, 142 (1973); Paris Adult Theatres v. Slayton, 413 U.S. 49, 65 (1973); Loving v. Virginia, 388 U.S. 1, 12 (1967); Meyer v. Nebraska, 262 U.S. 390, 399 (1923). *See also* Maynard v. Hill, 125 U.S. 190 (1888).

43. 367 U.S. 497 (1961).

44. *Id.* at 539 (Harlan, J., dissenting).

45. *Id.* at 550-53.

It was not until 1965 that the Supreme Court, in *Griswold v. Connecticut,*[46] decided that criminal sanctions against the use of contraceptives by marriage partners were unconstitutional. Writing for the majority, and relying on a "penumbra" of constitutional provisions, Justice Douglas established a constitutional bar to the breach of marital confidences: "Would we allow the police to search the sacred precincts of marital bedrooms for telltale signs of the use of contraceptives? The very idea is repulsive to the notions of privacy surrounding the marriage relationship."[47]

In the more recent case of *Roe v. Wade,*[48] the Court upheld the right of a woman to seek an abortion in the face of a statute that would have imposed criminal sanctions on both her and her physician. In dictum, the Court went further, noting that the constitutional right of privacy extended broadly "to activities relating to marriage, . . . procreation, . . . contraception, family relationships, . . . and child rearing and education."[49] Thus, *Poe, Griswold* and *Roe v. Wade* exhibit the constitutional protection of marriage and its intimacies.

In addition to this constitutional support, the law also affords protection to the confidences of the marital relationship through the eviddentiary privilege. Although the law rarely requires confidences to be broken, there is no general testimonial privilege for confidential communications between two people.[50] With limited exceptions, testimony as to confidential communications must be given to serve the public interest in the prosecution of crime, in civil litigation and in legislative inquiry. Among the limited exceptions to this rule is the prohibition of testimony by one spouse regarding confidential communications with the other.[51] The policy underlying this testimonial privilege was stated by the Commissioners on Common Law Procedure in New York in 1853:

> So much of the happiness of human life may fairly be said to depend on the inviolability of domestic confidence that the alarm

---

46. 381 U.S. 479 (1965).

47. *Id.* at 485-86. See Eisenstadt v. Baird, 405 U.S. 438, 453 (1972), which extended the *Griswold* principle to single individuals.

48. 410 U.S. 113 (1973).

49. *Id.* at 152-53 (citations omitted); *see* Planned Parenthood of Central Missouri v. Danforth, 96 S. Ct. 2831 (1976); United States v. Orito, 413 U.S. 139, 142 (1973).

50. *See generally* 8 J. WIGMORE, EVIDENCE §§ 2285, 2286 (J. McNaughton rev. 1961).

51. *See id.* at §§ 2286, 2290, 2332-41. This limited evidentiary privilege is distinguished from disqualification of a marital partner's testimony as an "interested party" and from a privilege against any testimony, whether of mutually exchanged confidences or not, of a spouse against the other spouse.

and unhappiness occasioned to society by invading its sanctity and compelling the public disclosure of confidential communications between husband and wife would be a far greater evil than the disadvantage which may occasionally arise from the loss of light which such revelations might throw on questions in dispute. . . . [Hence,] all communications between them should be held to be privileged.[52]

The marital privilege thus protects confidences in a relationship in which confidences are of the essence; any adverse effect on finding the truth of the matter at issue in a trial or before a legislative committee is outweighed by the public interest in protecting the institution of marriage. We shall see that this balancing of policy interests is applicable broadly to issues of group privacy.

It should be noted that despite constitutional and testimonial protections of the marital relationship, there is no rule of law in the United States that prevents or lays a penalty upon a spouse "telling all" to a newspaper, or to anyone else for that matter.[53] Moreover, in some circumstances, a spouse is required to provide information to government agencies, even though the information might be subject to a testimonial privilege in a courtroom. For instance, welfare recipients must inform government authorities of the status of their marriages.[54] These observations are intended to emphasize that associational privacy depends upon who asks whom to disclose what, what purposes the confidence serves, over what period of time these purposes continue to be served and what purposes the disclosure would serve.

(2)   The Priest-Penitent and the Lawyer-Client Relationships

The priest-penitent and lawyer-client relationships are also protected by a testimonial privilege in most jurisdictions.[55] Even the English political philosopher, Jeremy Bentham, who generally opposed testimonial privilege, agreed that the "assistance to justice" gained from confessional testimony is far outweighed by the "mischief" which would be produced were the testimony required.[56] Denial of the privilege

---

52. Common Law Commission, Second Report 13 (1853), *quoted in* 8 J. Wigmore, *supra* note 50, § 2332, at 643.

53. Compare the English case, Argyll v. Argyll, [1967] Ch. 302, in which a wife obtained an order to restrain her husband from publishing marital secrets.

54. *See, e.g.*, 42 U.S.C. § 402 (1970); *cf.* Roe v. Norton, 422 U.S. 391, 392-93 (1975) (per curiam).

55. 8 J. Wigmore, *supra* note 50, at §§ 2290-91, 2394-95.

56. 4 J. Bentham, Rationale of Judicial Evidence 586-92 (1827).

would drastically hamper the exercise of the Roman Catholic religion, in which confession is essential.

The argument is of deductive force. The testimonial privilege is justified because confidentiality is necessary to the confession; confession is necessary to the practice of the Roman Catholic religion; and toleration of that religion is of greater value to society than the slight gain for our system of justice were the testimony required.

A similar argument may be made for the attorney-client privilege. People would not confer freely and fully with attorneys were they not assured of the confidentiality of the interchange; attorneys are necessary because of the complexity of law and legal transactions; therefore, if people are to enjoy the full benefits of our system of justice, society must forego the benefits of disclosure by counsel of their clients' confidences. As the high court of New York said in 1864: "[T]he privilege . . . is not founded upon any idea of the sacredness of confidential communications, whether made to an attorney or to any other person;" rather, it rests on "the convenience of the public, as well as the benefit of suitors, of having the business of the courts conducted by professional men."[57]

(3)   The Physician-Patient Privilege

Despite its widespread acceptance,[58] the doubt that Wigmore[59] and others[60] have voiced about the physician-patient privilege tells a great deal about testimonial privileges and about the law's protection of confidentiality among associates. Wigmore sets out the following four criteria for a testimonial privilege: (1) the communication must originate in a confidence; (2) the sharing of confidences must be of the essence of the relationship; (3) the relationship must be favored by public policy; and (4) the injury which flows from the breach of confidence must be more significant to society than the loss of the testimony.[61]

Although Wigmore was satisfied that the spousal, the priest-penitent and the lawyer-client privileges met these four tests,[62] he

---

57. Whiting v. Barney, 30 N.Y. 330, 341-42 (1864) (per curiam).
58. 8 J. WIGMORE, *supra* note 50, at §§ 2380-91.
59. *Id.* at § 2380a.
60. *See* Maine v. Maryland Cas. Co., 172 Wis. 350, 357-62, 178 N.W. 749, 752-53 (1920) (dissenting opinion).
61. 8 J. WIGMORE, *supra* note 50, at § 2285.
62. *See* notes 50 & 55 *supra* and accompanying text.

believed that the physician-patient relationship satisfies only the third.[63] He argued that physicians are not normally told or expected to keep secrets in the way that spouses, lawyers and priests are. Moreover, unlike spouses, penitents and legal clients, patients would continue to seek medical care even if they were not assured of the secrecy of their communications. Thus, even though the third of Wigmore's criteria is met—medical care is favored by social policy—the physician-patient relationship fails Wigmore's fourth criterion.

Finally, it should be noted that in those jurisdictions in which the physician-patient testimonial privilege has been adopted, an exception is made in respect of physicians reporting venereal disease and the use of narcotic drugs.[64] This is another illustration of the principle that a confidence may be protected in one legal context, but not in another. Although a physician is required to report cases of venereal disease to health authorities in order to prevent contagion,[65] the patient's identity is generally kept confidential and is not admissible in court if the patient is a criminal defendant.[66]

(4)   Contractual Forms of Protection

Contractual provisions protecting confidential relationships are frequently used, but rarely enforced. Thus, contracts may bind employees to confidence after termination of their employment,[67] and lawyers or physicians may be sued for breach of either express or implied promises of confidentiality.[68] Such suits are rare, probably because breaches are rare and damages would be difficult to prove. Injunctive relief, however, may sometimes be provided.[69]

---

63. 8 J. WIGMORE, *supra* note 50, at § 2380a.

64. *Id.* at § 2220.

65. *See, e.g.,* N.Y. PUB. HEALTH LAW § 2306 (McKinney 1971).

66. *See, e.g.,* ILL. REV. STAT. ch. 126, § 21 (Supp. 1976); Taylor v. United States, 222 F.2d 398 (D.C. Cir. 1955). *But see* CAL. HEALTH & SAFETY CODE § 3197 (West 1970).

67. *See* Totten v. United States, 92 U.S. 105 (1875); United States v. Marchetti, 466 F.2d 1309 (4th Cir. 1972); RESTATEMENT (SECOND) OF AGENCY §§ 395-96 (1958); W. PROSSER, THE LAW OF TORTS § 123 (4th ed. 1971). *See also* Blake, *Preventing Competition by a Former Employee*, 15 ABA ANTITRUST SECTION 235, 259-64 (1959); McClain, *Injunctive Relief Against Employees Using Confidential Information*, 23 KY. L.J. 249 (1935).

68. *See, e.g.,* Hammonds v. Aetna Cas. & Sur. Co., 243 F. Supp. 793 (N.D. Ohio 1965); Stockton Theatres, Inc. v. Palermo, 121 Cal. App. 2d 616, 624-25, 264 P.2d 74, 80-81 (1953); Schaffer v. Spicer, — S.D. —, 215 N.W.2d 134 (1974).

69. *See, e.g.,* Roe v. Doe, 34 N.Y.2d 562, 310 N.E.2d 539, 354 N.Y.S.2d 941 (1974), *petition for cert. dismissed*, 420 U.S. 307 (1975). *See also* Karst, *"The Files":*

(5)   The Journalist's Privilege

The newsman's privilege of refusing to testify about confidential communications with informers is recognized in many jurisdictions.[70] Recently, however, the United States Supreme Court decided in *Branzburg v. Hayes*[71] that the privilege is not an incident of the freedom of the press under the first amendment.[72]

In *Branzburg*, reporters had refused to testify before grand juries about their confidential sources of information concerning the Black Panthers. The reporters urged that they should be compelled to testify only if it could be shown: (1) that they had evidence relevant to a grand jury inquiry into the commission of a crime; (2) that the information was unavailable from other sources; and (3) that the need for the information was sufficiently compelling to overcome the inevitable impingement on first amendment rights.[73]

The majority of the Court, in a 5 to 4 decision, rejected the privilege as an incident of the first amendment on the grounds— echoing Wigmore—that

> [n]othing before us indicates that a large number or percentage of *all* confidential news sources . . . would in any way be deterred by our holding that the Constitution does not, as it never has, exempt the newsman from performing the citizen's normal duty of appearing and furnishing information relevant to the grand jury's task.[74]

The Court later added:

> Accepting the fact . . . that an undetermined number of informants . . . will . . . , for whatever reason, refuse to talk to newsmen if they fear identification . . . , we cannot accept the argument that the public interest in possible future news about crime from undisclosed, unverified sources must take precedence over the public interest in pursuing and prosecuting those crimes reported to the press by informants and in thus deterring the commission of such crimes in the future.[75]

Legal Controls over the Accuracy and Accessibility of Stored Personal Data, 31 LAW & CONTEMP. PROB. 342, 350-53 (1966).

70. *See* Note, *The Journalistic Privilege: Newsgathering Versus the Public's Need to Know*, 10 IDAHO L. REV. 235, 236 (1974); Note, *Reporter's Privilege—Guardian of the People's Right to Know?*, 11 N. ENG. L. REV. 405, 427-57 (1976).

71. 408 U.S. 665 (1972).

72. *Id.* at 689-91.

73. *Id.* at 680.

74. *Id.* at 691.

75. *Id.* at 695.

A distinguished group of scholars, newsmen and lawyers concluded in 1973 that "[a] journalist should be accorded a legally-protected privilege [,] to include confidential information and sources [,] against compelled testimony."[76] But "the facts concerning journalists' reliance on confidential information and the adverse impact of actual or threatened subpoena are to a large degree speculative."[77] I, therefore, agree with the *Branzburg* majority, and with many other commentators, that neither a common-law privilege nor the first amendment should unqualifiedly protect a reporter against testifying about what was learned from a confidential informant.[78] I note, however, as did Justice Powell in his concurrence, that because of first amendment considerations, a newsman should be sustained on a motion to quash if "called upon to give information bearing only a remote and tenuous relationship to the subject of the investigation, or if he has some other reason to believe that his testimony implicates confidential source relationships without a legitimate need of law enforcement . . . ."[79] Moreover, in light of the recent incident involving reporter Daniel Schorr,[80] and in light of the extraordinary and unique role that confidential source information plays in ferreting out political corruption, I urge that courts and legislatures consider adopting the privilege for any bona fide claim that the testimony sought would uncover the identity of a confidential governmental informant of government corruption.

(6)   A Summary Concerning Testimonial Privilege

The conclusion to be drawn from the *Branzburg* case reinforces that drawn from our discussion of the other testimonial privileges. The law rarely requires people to break their confidences with one another; indeed, the law protects and favors confidences in most circumstances.[81] Subpoenas to appear before a grand jury or a legislative com-

---

76. FINAL REPORT, ANNUAL CHIEF JUSTICE EARL WARREN CONFERENCE ON ADVOCACY IN THE UNITED STATES, THE FIRST AMENDMENT AND THE NEWS MEDIA 11 (1973) [hereinafter cited as 1973 FINAL REPORT].

77. Schmidt, *Journalists' Privilege: One Year After* Branzburg, in 1973 FINAL REPORT, *supra* note 76, at 45.

78. 408 U.S. at 690.

79. *Id.* at 710 (Powell, J., concurring).

80. *See* N.Y. Times, Feb. 14, 1976, at 26, col. 1. *See generally* Lewis, *Making Leaks a Crime: Not a Simple Matter*, N.Y. Times, Feb. 22, 1976, at 26, col. 1.

81. For a novel application of the rule of confidentiality see *In re* J.P.B., 143 N.J. Super. 96, 362 A.2d 1183 (App. Div. 1976) (information adduced in group rehabilitation session for juveniles held inadmissible at criminal trial).

mittee or at trial are among the few instances in which the law compels testimony about confidential communications.[82]

Exceptions to the rare cases of testimonial compulsion are themselves rare. Testimonial privileges are sanctioned only when confidential communications are normally induced by, and are a regular incident of, an association—only if, indeed, the association would not take place without them. Even here, however, the law weighs the harm to the association from compelled testimony against the benefit afforded to our system of justice.

I must also add that even when a testimonial privilege is available, full disclosure by a party to the confidence outside the courtroom may frequently take place without legal penalty or impediment. And, under certain circumstances, there may be a statutory requirement of disclosure to government agencies for some limited purpose. Finally, it should be reiterated that confidences between two people may be the subject of contractual protection and enforced like any other contract provision.

C. Other Nongovernmental Associations

Thus far we have dealt with confidences between two people. But, as de Tocqueville and many others have noted,[83] we are a nation of joiners; associations of one kind or another in which confidences are shared abound in American life. Although the general character of such associations is often subject to legal regulation—general corporate, banking and credit statutes, for instance—protection of the confidences of the parties to them has only recently become the subject of the law's concern.

(1)   Political and Social Organizations

Groups like the Masons and the Ku Klux Klan often maintain secret rituals designed to provide a "bond of acceptance and cohesiveness" as well as to establish the group's "exclusiveness and identity."[84]

82. As Wigmore noted: "No pledge of privacy nor oath of secrecy can avail against demand for the truth in a court of justice." 8 J. WIGMORE, supra note 50, § 2286, at 528.
83. 2 A. DE TOCQUEVILLE, supra note 41, at 114-18; see J. BRYCE, THE AMERICAN COMMONWEALTH 278-79 (1899); Douglas, The Right of Association, 63 COLUM. L. REV. 1361, 1362-64 (1963); Rice, The Constitutional Right of Association, 16 HASTINGS L.J. 491, 492-93 (1965); Robison, Protection of Associations from Compulsory Disclosure of Membership, 58 COLUM. L. REV. 614, 622 (1958); Schlesinger, Biography of a Nation of Joiners, 50 AM. HIST. REV. 1 (1944).
84. A. WESTIN, supra note 2, at 43-44.

There is no impediment in law to such secretiveness unless the ritual employed involves dangerous[85] or seditious acts,[86] such as the use of poisonous snakes or flag burning. In those circumstances the normal criminal penalty for such acts is enforceable.

Sometimes political or social associations prefer to keep confidential the identities of their members. In most jurisdictions the registration of social, political or charitable organizations, when necessary at all, will require only that the names of incorporators and officers be made public.[87] However, in some states with a primary election system, and for political parties that choose their candidates through primary elections, members of the political party must declare their affiliation publicly.[88]

Under some circumstances the confidentiality of group membership is assured by the first amendment. Thus, in *NAACP v. Alabama*,[89] the Supreme Court of the United States declared an Alabama statute requiring the NAACP to provide the state with its membership list an unconstitutional impairment of the right of association.[90] The Court noted that past disclosure under the statute had subjected members to "economic reprisal, loss of employment, threat of physical coercion and other manifestations of public hostility."[91] In these circumstances, absent an overriding and compelling state interest, the disclosure requirement was held an unconstitutional price to pay for

85. *See, e.g.,* United States v. Kuch, 288 F. Supp. 439 (D.D.C. 1968) (defendant failed to demonstrate necessity of use of psychedelic drugs for religious purposes); State v. Massey, 229 N.C. 734, 51 S.E.2d 179 (1949) (city ordinance prohibiting handling of poisonous snakes in religious ritual does not impinge on religious freedom). Some bona fide religious groups, however, are exempt from certain drug regulations. *See* People v. Woody, 61 Cal. 2d 716, 394 P.2d 813, 40 Cal. Rptr. 69 (1964).

86. *See, e.g.,* 18 U.S.C. § 700 (1970); N.Y. GEN. BUS. LAW § 136 (McKinney 1968). *See also* Street v. New York, 394 U.S. 576 (1969); United States v. Crosson, 462 F.2d 96 (9th Cir.), *cert. denied,* 409 U.S. 1064 (1972).

87. *See, e.g.,* CAL. CORP. CODE § 10201 (West 1955); ILL. REV. STAT. ch. 32, § 163a28 (1970); N.Y. SOC. SERV. LAW § 482 (McKinney 1972). Fraternal organizations typically are required or permitted to register only the name or symbol of the organization as a protection against infringement by another group. *See, e.g.,* CAL. BUS. & PROF. CODE § 14492.5 (West 1964); 54 PA. CON. STAT. §§ 41-42 (Purdon 1964).

88. *See, e.g.,* N.J.S.A. 19:23-45 (Cum. Supp. 1976).

89. 357 U.S. 449 (1958).

90. *Id.* at 466; *see* Gibson v. Florida Legislative Investigation Comm., 372 U.S. 539, 542 (1963); Shelton v. Tucker, 364 U.S. 479, 490 (1960); Bates v. Little Rock, 361 U.S. 516, 524 (1960); American Communications Ass'n v. Douds, 339 U.S. 382, 402 (1949). *See also* Runyon v. McCrary, 96 S. Ct. 2586 (1976); T. EMERSON, THE SYSTEM OF FREEDOM OF EXPRESSION 431-32 (1970). *But see* Communist Party v. S.A.C. Board, 367 U.S. 1, 88-94 (1961); Bryant v. Zimmerman, 278 U.S. 63 (1928).

91. 357 U.S. at 462.

group association.[92]   More recently, although the Court upheld the reporting disclosure requirements of the Federal Election Campaign Act, it declared in dictum that "compelled disclosure . . . [of membership] can seriously infringe on privacy of association and belief guaranteed by the First Amendment."[93]

This same rationale has been applied in cases involving more clearly political associations. Thus, in *Sweezy v. New Hampshire*[94] and *DeGregory v. Attorney General*,[95] in which the validity of inquiries into subversive political ties was at issue, the Court held that constitutional protections extend to confidentiality of membership in subversive groups as well. The *Sweezy* Court said that "[m]erely to summon a witness and compel him, against his will, to disclose the nature of his past expressions and associations is a measure of governmental interference"[96] with the constitutionally protected right to associate with others. In a concurring opinion, Justices Frankfurter and Harlan referred to a right of "political privacy."[97]   And in *DeGregory*, the Court found constitutionally indefensible the compelled "exposure of one's associational and political past—exposure which is objectionable and damaging in the extreme to one whose associations and political views do not command majority approval."[98]   Only a valid state interest, not present in *DeGregory*, will justify overriding the first amendment guarantees in such circumstances.[99]

A similar sensitivity to the confidentiality of associations is manifest in *Lamont v. Postmaster General*.[100]   There the Supreme Court struck down a Post Office requirement that addressees of "communist political propaganda" had to request the literature before it could be delivered.[101]   The theory of the case was that the requirement unreasonably inhibited free political ideas and associations and was, therefore, an unconstitutional limitation of first amendment rights.[102]

---

92. *Id.* at 466.
93. Buckley v. Valeo, 424 U.S. 1, 64 (1976).
94. 354 U.S. 234 (1957).
95. 383 U.S. 825 (1966).
96. 354 U.S. at 250.
97. *Id.* at 267 (Frankfurter, J., concurring).
98. 383 U.S. at 829.
99. *Id.* at 830; *cf.* Eastland v. United States Servicemen's Fund, 421 U.S. 491 (1975).
100. 381 U.S. 301 (1965).
101. *Id.* at 302; *see* Talley v. California, 362 U.S. 60, 64-65 (1960); United States v. Rumely, 345 U.S. 41 (1953).
102. 381 U.S. at 307.

Under most circumstances, the proceedings of social and political organizations are kept confidential. Although the organization may decide to open its meetings and publish its minutes, and although the minutes may be subject to subpoena, there is no general requirement of law which would open meetings or make minutes available to the public, as there is with governmental bodies.[103] An exception is made in some jurisdictions, however, for charitable organizations, which are required by statute to make their financial records and annual reports available for public inspection.[104]

Thus, the membership, relationships and communications of individuals in private social and political organizations may be kept confidential under most circumstances. But there are specialized, compelling governmental purposes which may justify disclosure of one facet or another of organizational life. Disclosure may also be compelled by subpoena in the trial of law suits, and for certain legislative and investigative purposes. Nevertheless, such disclosure is subject to limitation under the provisions of the first amendment as interpreted in *NAACP v. Alabama* and similar cases.[105]

(2)   Business Organizations

Business organizations began to be subject to state regulation in Anglo-Saxon law sometime in the fourteenth century.[106]   It was then

103. *See* text accompanying notes 230-34 *infra*.

104. *See, e.g.*, CAL. GOV'T CODE § 12590 (West 1963) (registration instruments and reports filed with Attorney General made open to public inspection); ILL. REV. STAT. ch. 23, § 5102 (1968) (mandatory registration and annual reports of charitable organizations made open to public inspection); N.Y. SOC. SERV. LAW § 482 (McKinney Supp. 1976) (variety of financial reports and other documents made open to public inspection). *But see* N.J.S.A. 15:1-1 *et seq.* (1939) (no obligation to publicly disclose information, and no requirement for registration of charitable organizations).

Charitable organizations seeking to qualify for exempt status under the federal income tax laws are also required to make certain organizational data available to the Internal Revenue Service. *See, e.g.*, INT. REV. CODE OF 1954, §§ 6033, 6034, 6056. Likewise, political organizations and candidates must report certain financial contributors' names under the laws of some states and under federal statute. *See, e.g.*, Federal Election Campaign Act of 1971, 2 U.S.C. § 434 (Supp. V, 1975), *amending* 2 U.S.C. § 434 (Supp. II, 1972) (requiring reports of receipts and expenditures by treasurers of political committees and by political candidates); Federal Election Campaign Act of 1971, 2 U.S.C. § 438(a)(4) (Supp. V, 1975), *amending* 2 U.S.C. § 438 (Supp. II, 1972) (requiring reports filed with Commission be made available to the public for inspection and duplication); N.J.S.A. 19:44A-1 *et seq.* (Cum. Supp. 1976). *See also* Robison, *supra* note 83, at 637-41; Note, *State Control over Political Organizations: First Amendment Checks on Powers of Regulation*, 66 YALE L.J. 545 (1957).

105. *See* text accompanying notes 89-93 *supra*.

106. 1 F. POLLACK & F. MAITLAND, THE HISTORY OF ENGLISH LAW 669 (2d ed. 1898).

that the English king asserted the doctrine that corporations were not consensual relationships among individuals, but rather "artificial persons" and, as such, creatures of sovereign power.[107]   The doctrine became more fully developed in the early seventeenth century, under the Tudors, with the formulation of the "concession theory"—the view that corporations are formed as concessions from the state.[108]   This theory of the artificial personality of the corporation is generally regarded as a political expedient:[109] on his part, the king exercised a new form of regulation over the corporate structure; in return, he gave it perpetual life and limited the personal liability of its stockholders, thereby making the corporation a more attractive vehicle of commerce.

Originally, the privileges of group association "had been claimed by the burghers without offense and exercised without restriction.   But the day came when the kingly prerogative was asserted in order to uphold the kingly dignity and fill the kingly pocket."[110]   As another commentator put it: "[T]hat the sovereign alone could create a corporation was originally asserted as a means of bridling and subduing group units which had already grown to statures that threatened the power of the state."[111]   Once established, the state prerogative of incorporation was used "to confer monopolies, to encourage the expansion of trade through combined wealth and to regulate and restrain several 'extravagant and unwarrantable practices . . . .' "[112]

The American states adopted the English theory of the corporation.   In Chief Justice Marshall's words, a corporation is "an artificial being, . . . existing only in contemplation of law.   Being the mere creature of law, it possesses only those properties which the charter of its creation confers upon it . . . ."[113]   Two important consequences follow from this theory.   First, the fifth amendment privilege against

107. Maitland, *Introduction* to D. GIERKE, POLITICAL THEORIES OF THE MIDDLE AGES xxx (1900).
108. H. HENN, HANDBOOK OF THE LAW OF CORPORATIONS AND OTHER BUSINESS ENTERPRISES 13-14 (2d ed. 1970).
109. *See, e.g.,* Carr, *Early Forms of Corporateness,* in 3 SELECT ESSAYS IN ANGLO-AMERICAN LEGAL HISTORY 161 (E. Freund, W. Mikell & J. Wigmore eds. 1909).
110. *Id.* at 171.
111. R. STEVENS, CORPORATIONS 2 (2d ed. 1949). *See also* P. FREUND, STANDARDS OF AMERICAN LEGISLATION 39-42 (1965); 3 W. HOLDSWORTH, HISTORY OF THE ENGLISH LAW 475-79 (5th ed. 1942).
112. R. STEVENS, *supra* note 111, at 3, *quoting* The Bubble Act, 6 Geo. I, c. 18 (1719).
113. Trustees of Dartmouth College v. Woodward, 17 U.S. (4 Wheat.) 518, 636 (1819). *See also* H. KELSEN, *supra* note 7, at 96-109.

self-incrimination does not apply to corporate bodies;[114] and secondly, because the state breathed legal life into corporations, it has the right to "subject [them] to broad visitorial power."[115]

The fifth amendment privilege against self-incrimination may be broadly characterized as providing the individual the right to a "private enclave where he may lead a private life."[116] But the privilege is "essentially a personal one, applying only to natural individuals," because only they—and not artificial persons like corporations—can be subject to "physical torture and other less violent but equally reprehensible modes of compelling the production of incriminating evidence . . . ."[117] Another reason the privilege against self-incrimination does not apply to corporations is that their records

> are not the private records of the individual members or officers of the organization. Usually, if not always, they are open to inspection by the members [of the organization] . . . . They therefore embody no element of personal privacy and carry with them no claim of personal privilege.[118]

The difference between compelling people's testimony and searching their homes or offices for evidence of crime is clear. But there is no such distinction in the case of groups or corporations. They can only be "compelled to speak," as it were, by searching for and seizing their records. In this sense, then, there is no distinction between the application of the fourth and the fifth amendments to corporations. I believe this is the significance of what is largely a figure of speech involved in the judicial pronouncements that the fifth amendment only applies to natural, and not to artificial, persons.

The issue of the application of the fourth amendment to corporations turns on the assumption that their creation by the state gives the state powers over corporations that it does not have over natural persons. A natural person "owes nothing to the public so long as he does not trespass upon their rights. [But] . . . the corporation is a creature of the state. . . . There is a reserved right in the legislature to investigate its contracts and find out whether it has exceeded its

114. See Bellis v. United States, 417 U.S. 85, 88 (1974); Wilson v. United States, 221 U.S. 361, 384 (1911); Hale v. Henkel, 201 U.S. 43, 74-75 (1906).
115. Oklahoma Press Publishing Co. v. Walling, 327 U.S. 186, 204 (1946); see Bellis v. United States, 417 U.S. 85, 89 (1974); United States v. Morton Salt Co., 338 U.S. 632, 652-53 (1950).
116. Bellis v. United States, 417 U.S. 85, 91 (1974) (citations omitted).
117. United States v. White, 322 U.S. 694, 698 (1944).
118. Id. at 699-700.

powers."[119]   This does not mean, however, that the fourth amendment prohibition against unreasonable searches and seizures does not apply to the corporation; to the contrary, it *has* been applied in this context.[120] It means only that "corporations can claim no equality with individuals in the enjoyment of a right to privacy."[121]   "The gist of the protection [afforded the corporation] is in the requirement that the disclosure sought shall not be unreasonable."[122]

But how does the test of reasonableness differ in respect of an individual and a corporation?   In the case of an individual, no search warrant may issue unless "a specific charge or complaint of violation of law be pending . . . [or] 'probable cause supported by oath or affirmation' " be shown.[123]   In the case of a corporation, however, "[i]t is enough that the investigation be for a lawfully authorized purpose, within the power of Congress to command."[124]   Again, putting aside the argument that simply flows from the artificial person metaphor, one reason for the difference in the treatment of persons and corporations is that the latter "are endowed with public attributes . . . [and] have a collective impact upon society."[125]   As a result, "law-enforcing agencies have a legitimate right to satisfy themselves that corporate behavior is consistent with the law and the public interest."[126] Another reason for treating individuals and corporations differently under the fourth amendment is that corporations derive certain privileges from the state—limited liability and perpetual existence, among others—and "favors from government often carry with them enhanced regulation."[127]

(a)   The Privacy of Business Affairs

Corporate officers and directors are required to disclose to corporate stockholders, and frequently to the public generally, a wide range of information concerning their corporate ownership interest, their financial affairs and their salaries.[128]   The Securities and Ex-

119. Hale v. Henkel, 201 U.S. 43, 74-75 (1906).
120. *See* Oklahoma Press Publishing Co. v. Walling, 327 U.S. 186, 205-06 (1946).
121. United States v. Morton Salt Co., 338 U.S. 632, 652 (1950).
122. Oklahoma Press Publishing Co. v. Walling, 327 U.S. 186, 208 (1946); *see* United States v. Morton Salt Co., 338 U.S. 632, 652 (1950).
123. Oklahoma Press Publishing Co. v. Walling, 327 U.S. 186, 209 (1946).
124. *Id.*
125. United States v. Morton Salt Co., 338 U.S. 632, 652 (1950).
126. *Id.*
127. *Id.*
128. *See, e.g.,* 15 U.S.C. § 80a-44 (1970) (information, including that in registration

change Commission, the Comptroller of the Currency, the Federal Reserve Board and individual state departments of banking and commerce require vast amounts of data from business corporations.[129]   In many instances, information concerning the business is also required to be made available routinely to stockholders, while other information, especially bank regulatory agency audits and the like, is specifically maintained in confidence.[130]   Earnings of the corporation must be reported for tax purposes, of course, and these same purposes require the corporation to inform the Internal Revenue Service of the dividend earnings of stockholders as well as the salaries of employees.[131]

Significantly, numerous federal and state agencies require extensive reporting of the day-to-day operations of a variety of business organizations, but maintain that information in confidence.   Thus, for example, the Department of Agriculture, the Civil Aeronautics Board and the Food and Drug Administration each require detailed reports of operations and business activity from a great variety of business organizations.[132]   In the hands of competitors, such information would

---

statements, open to public inspection); N.J.S.A. 14A:5-28 (Cum. Supp. 1976) (shareholders' right to inspect certain corporate records); *id.* 14A:4-5 (corporation required to file annual report, open to public inspection); N.Y. Bus. Corp. Law § 624 (McKinney Supp. 1975) (certain shareholders allowed to inspect corporate records). *See also* Corporate "News" Dissemination (R. Haft ed. 1974); Disclosure Requirements of Public Companies and Insiders (J. Flom, B. Garfinkel & J. Freund eds. 1967).

129. *See, e.g.,* 12 U.S.C. § 334 (1970) (requiring submission of triannual reports by affiliate banks to Federal Deposit Insurance Corporation by insured state nonmember banks); 15 U.S.C. § 78o (Supp. V, 1975) (requiring registration by brokers, dealers and issuers of securities); *id.* § 78m(a) (requiring filing of periodic reports by issuers of registered securities); *id.* § 80a-8 (requiring registration by investment companies); 15 U.S.C. § 80a-29 (1970) (requiring filing of annual reports by investment companies); N.J.S.A. 17:9A-256 (1963) (requiring all banks to file at least two reports annually with Commissioner of Banking and Insurance); N.Y. Bank. Law § 37 (McKinney Supp. 1975) (requiring biannual banking reports to Superintendent of Banking). *See also* United States v. Miller, 425 U.S. 435 (1976) (bank depositor's personal records relating to his accounts not protected under fourth amendment).

130. *See, e.g.,* 15 U.S.C. § 78x (Supp. V, 1975) (making unlawful the disclosure, other than to member, officer or employee of the SEC, or use for personal benefit, of any information obtained by the Commission when the Commission has determined such information should be accorded confidential treatment); 15 U.S.C. § 80b-10 (1970) (making available to public information in any registration application report); N.J.S.A. 17:9A-264 (1963) (providing for confidentiality and qualified immunity from subpoena of information acquired by Commissioner of Banking and Insurance under state law); N.Y. Bank. Law § 36 (McKinney 1971) (providing for qualified immunity from subpoena of information arising out of authorized bank inspections).

131. *See, e.g.,* Int. Rev. Code of 1954, §§ 3402, 6038, 6046.

132. *See, e.g.,* 7 C.F.R. § 20.1 (1976) (requiring weekly reports of transactions by wheat, grain and cotton exporters); 14 C.F.R. § 242.2 (1976) (requiring reports by air

be the subject of unfair use. As a result, first by agency practice and statutes governing individual agencies,[133] and now by general statutory requirement,[134] the information is kept confidential.

Such statutes and practices embody, in part, the common-law doctrine of trade secrets, whereby—via a testimonial privilege or under tort law or by the terms of an employment contract—certain persons may be prevented from using or divulging business secrets.[135] The Supreme Court described the doctrine in *Dr. Miles Medical Co. v. John D. Park & Sons Co.*:[136] "Anyone may use [a trade secret] who fairly, by analysis and experiment, discovers it. But [the holder of the trade secret] is entitled to be protected against invasion of its right in the process by fraud or by breach of trust or contract."[137]

It is the old story of "Macy's not telling Gimbels"—department stores could not compete successfully without a degree of privacy in their affairs, nor could industrial corporations, nor news organizations.[138] Ironically, the *New York Times* required great secrecy, although for a short period of time, to produce its Pentagon Papers story;[139] the federal government then sought to enjoin publication of the story because it disclosed government secrets.[140] As the Supreme

---

carriers of scheduled all-cargo services); 21 C.F.R. § 207.20 (1976) (requiring registration and listing of all drugs in commercial distribution by owners and operators of all drug establishments); 27 C.F.R. § 194.231 (1976) (requiring semiannual reports by wholesale liquor dealers of quantities and dispositions of distilled spirits received).

133. A list of such statutes appears in *Hearings on H.R. 4938, H.R. 5983, H.R. 6438 Before a Subcomm. of the House Comm. on Gov't Operations*, 93d Cong., 1st Sess. 99-101 (1973).

134. The Freedom of Information Act, 5 U.S.C. § 552(b)(4) (1970), provides an exemption for "trade secrets." *See* note 292 *infra* and accompanying text. See also 18 U.S.C. § 1905 (1970), which forbids generally the release by the government of trade secrets and competitive financial information.

135. *See, e.g.*, Dr. Miles Medical Co. v. John D. Park & Sons Co., 220 U.S. 373, 402 (1911); Board of Trade v. Christie Grain & Stock Co., 198 U.S. 236, 250-51 (1904); Saltman Eng'r Co. v. Campbell Eng'r Co., [1948] 65 Pat. Cas. 203, [1963] 3 All E.R. 413; Prince Albert v. Strange, 64 Eng. Rep. 293 (Ch. 1849).

136. 220 U.S. 373 (1911).

137. *Id.* at 402; *see* Kewanee Oil Co. v. Bicron Corp., 416 U.S. 470, 475-76 (1974).

138. *Cf.* International News Serv. v. Associated Press, 248 U.S. 215, 248-67 (1918) (Brandeis, J., dissenting). It is interesting to note that the Freedom of Information Act is being widely used, according to the Food and Drug Commissioner, to support what he calls "industrial espionage." The Washington Post, July 27, 1976, § A, at 4, col. 1.

139. This special irony was suggested by Bennis, *Open Covenants Not So Openly Arrived At*, The Washington Post, Oct. 26, 1975, § D, at 2, col. 2. For a report of FBI efforts to discover the New York Times' confidential sources see N.Y. Times, June 18, 1971, at 15, col. 3.

140. New York Times v. United States, 403 U.S. 713 (1971).

Court recently said, the doctrine of trade secrets guards "the very life and spirit of the commercial world."[141] Any unauthorized disclosure of such secrets threatens "a most fundamental human right"[142] (*i.e.,* the right to group privacy) and is condoned and made profitable only at a "cost to the basic decency of society."[143]

(b) The Privacy of Records Involving Customers and Employees

Increasingly, business customers and employees are seeking legal protection to insure the confidentiality of their personal data held in business files.[144]   They are concerned about the content of the files, the purposes of those who have access to them and their own right of inspection and correction.   Despite indications that the emergence of computer technology has not radically changed the character of the privacy problems posed by massive filing systems,[145] it has undoubtedly enhanced the possibility of abuse and heightened public concern over the issues.

There is no estimate of the total number of files of a personal nature held by business.   However, the number of credit files alone was estimated at one hundred million in 1969.[146]   These records ordinarily contain information which, in theory, is given voluntarily; in this respect they pose a somewhat different problem from that posed by government files, for which much of the information is elicited under legal compulsion.   Yet, because the person seeking credit, or insurance, or a job, is often under economic pressure, it is doubtful that the information in business files is truly given voluntarily.

Beyond the question of voluntariness is the question whether all

---

141. Kewanee Oil Co. v. Bicron Corp., 416 U.S. 470, 481-82 (1974).

142. *Id.* at 487.

143. *Id.*

144. The problem of the privacy of business files is similar in many respects to that of government files.   For a brief discussion of the latter see text accompanying notes 171-78 *infra.*   The files of nonprofit corporations and associations present similar problems.   For extensive discussion of files in these three contexts see A. MILLER, THE ASSAULT ON PRIVACY: COMPUTERS, DATA BANKS AND DOSSIERS (1972); A. WESTIN & M. BAKER, DATA BANKS IN A FREE SOCIETY (1972); S. WHEELER, ON RECORD: FILES AND DOSSIERS IN AMERICAN LIFE (1969); Countryman, *The Diminishing Right to Privacy: The Personal Dossier and the Computer,* 49 TEXAS L. REV. 837 (1971); Karst, *supra* note 69.   *See also* Creech, *The Privacy of Government Employees,* 31 LAW & CONTEMP. PROB. 413 (1966); Mirel, *The Limits of Government Inquiry Into the Private Lives of Government Employees,* 46 B.U.L. REV. 1 (1966).

145. A. WESTIN & M. BAKER, *supra* note 144, at 341.

146. S. WHEELER, *supra* note 144, at 143; *see* A. WESTIN & M. BAKER, *supra* note 144, at 135.

of the information compiled is necessary to the purposes for which the file has been established. For instance, is knowledge of a divorced woman's sexual life necessary to a decision to grant her credit? Is knowledge of an employee's marital life a necessary and appropriate part of a personnel file?[147]

Additionally, there are questions relating to the means by which information on the file subject gets into the file and the extent of the subject's knowledge of its existence. Is a polygraph test a fair means of gathering information?[148] What about surveillance of employees in washrooms?[149] Are credit agency practices involving the use of relatively untrained personnel to investigate a credit applicant's background fair and reasonable?[150] Many subjects, particularly when the information was gleaned from third parties, are actually unaware that the files exist and that they have a right to challenge them. Many insurers do regularly inform insurance applicants of the nature of information which led them to deny an application and offer an opportunity to correct erroneous information.[151] Yet, businesses which deny credit on the basis of a credit report rarely made such disclosures before corrective legislation was enacted.[152] Employees, too, have often been totally uninformed regarding the nature of their personnel files and rarely were afforded an opportunity to correct them.[153]

Finally, there is a series of questions relating to the care with which files are kept and the uses to which they are put. Is there a limit on what information about an employee may be shared and with whom? Are files kept under conditions that protect against illicit and improper use?[154] Are businesses free to share with one another, and

---

147. *Unions Act on Threats to Privacy*, Business Week, Mar. 13, 1965, at 87-88.

148. *Id.* at 87; *see* Note, *Lie Detectors in Private Employment: A Proposal For Balancing Interests*, 33 Geo. Wash. L. Rev. 932, 939-40 (1965). *See also Hearings Before the Subcomm. on Constitutional Rights of the Senate Comm. on the Judiciary, Psychological Tests and Constitutional Rights*, 89th Cong., 1st Sess. (1965) (dealing with the unfairness of questionnaires); Creech, *supra* note 144, at 419; Mirel, *supra* note 144, at 18-22.

149. *See generally Hearings before the Subcomm. on Administrative Practice and Procedure of the Senate Comm. on the Judiciary, Invasions of Privacy*, 89th Cong., 1st Sess. (1965).

150. S. Wheeler, *supra* note 144, at 156.

151. *Id.* at 214.

152. *See* text accompanying notes 161 & 162 *infra*.

153. S. Wheeler, *supra* note 144, at 196-97.

154. *See* N.Y. Times, Sept. 3, 1976, § A, at 1, col. 6 (grand jury indictment of six persons for misuse of the records of a credit information company which stores information on the borrowing habits of more than 50 million Americans).

under what conditions may they share,[155] their knowledge of the credit-worthiness of customers? May businesses exchange lists of customers?[156]

Although the whole range of these questions predated the computer, modern technology apparently poses new problems.[157] More data can now be collected, and it can be stored more easily. The stored information is controlled by technicians who lack the personal accountability of the more traditional record storage keepers. And the unauthorized sharing of personal data in vast computer networks, beyond anyone's power to control, becomes a significant possibility.

Until very recently the business file was rarely the subject of legal concern. Except for the very limited doctrine that confidentiality was sometimes owed to a client or patient on a contract or trust theory,[158] there was no protection afforded to the subject of a business file. To the contrary, when an employee or a subject of a credit report did sue—generally on the theory of defamation but sometimes on the theory of privacy—the law provided a strong defense. Absent malice, information shared for a bona fide business purpose could not be the basis for recovery, even if it was mistaken and even if inadequate care was taken in gathering or sharing the information.[159]

Heightened awareness of privacy matters, however, especially the concern associated with modern data processing technology, has recently prompted considerable legislative concern. Some states have limited the use of the polygraph.[160] In 1970, the federal Fair Credit Reporting Act[161] was enacted to provide a broad range of protection

155. *See* Peterson v. Idaho First Nat'l Bank, 83 Idaho 578, 587-88, 367 P.2d 284, 290 (1961). *But see* California Bankers Ass'n v. Schultz, 416 U.S. 21, 54, 78 (1974).

156. To date, there is apparently no legal impediment to the exchange of customer lists, although individuals may request that their names be deleted from these lists. Compliance with the request is voluntary, however.

157. *See* A. MILLER, *supra* note 144; Countryman, *supra* note 144.

158. *See* cases cited notes 67-69 *supra*.

159. 1 F. HARPER & F. JAMES, JR., THE LAW OF TORTS ch. 5 (1956); W. PROSSER, THE LAW OF TORTS ch. 21 (4th ed. 1971); *see* McNamara, *The Fair Credit Reporting Act: A Legislative Overview*, 22 J. PUB. LAW 67, 69-71 (1973). The defense to a suit sounding in privacy was established in Voneye v. Turner, 240 S.W.2d 588 (Ky. 1951). Some cases impose liability on a showing of lack of due care. *See, e.g.*, Altoona Clay Prods., Inc. v. Dun & Bradstreet, Inc., 367 F.2d 625 (3d Cir. 1966); Dun & Bradstreet, Inc. v. Robinson, 233 Ark. 168, 345 S.W.2d 34 (1961).

160. *See, e.g.*, CAL. LABOR CODE § 432.2 (West 1969); N.J.S.A. 2A:170-90.1 (1971); ORE. REV. STAT. § 659.225 (1975). *See also Hearings Before a Subcomm. of the House Comm. on Government Operations, The Use of Polygraphs as "Lie Detectors" by Federal Government*, 88th Cong., 2d Sess. (1964).

161. 15 U.S.C. § 1601 (1970).

of confidentiality in the credit field.   And there is continued legislative interest, on the state and federal level, in further regulation of credit bureaus, mailing list companies and the data banks of private businesses.[162]

This review of the law regulating the privacy of business associations is obviously far from exhaustive.   My point, however, is not to provide a detailed analysis of this body of law, but rather to search for underlying principles.   What we see is a number of intersecting public policies.   There is, in the first place, a desire to protect the private character of business associations, not only because autonomous organizations constitute a barrier to statism, but because businesses cannot compete with one another if they cannot maintain their trade secrets.[163]

Secondly, many statutes invade group privacy by requiring a variety of disclosures to stockholders, the public and government agencies.   This is done in the interest of protecting the investing public as well as the consuming public.   Interestingly enough, sometimes group privacy intersects with the public right of access to government records. In such cases, the Freedom of Information Act[164] (FOIA) and other more specialized statutes,[165] in an attempt to balance the two competing values, still maintain the confidentiality of certain categories of information, including trade secrets and information which, if disclosed, would violate individual privacy.

The third public policy at work here is the protection of individual privacy as against the private business organization.   This is evidenced, for instance, in the protection of employees' records under the Freedom of Information Act[166] and in the Fair Credit Reporting Act.[167]   Finally, it must be noted that, as with almost all other confidences, business confidences are normally respected in the courtroom.

---

162. A good sense of the legislative interest in this area is provided in *Joint Hearings on S. 3418, S. 3633, S. 3116, S. 2810, S. 2542 Before the Ad Hoc Subcomm. on Privacy and Information Systems of the Senate Comm. on the Judiciary*, 93d Cong., 2d Sess. (1974).   Control of files in schools and universities is regulated by 20 U.S.C. § 1232 (Supp. V, 1975).   The operative legislation covering federal employees' records is 5 U.S.C. § 552(a) (1970), *as amended*, 5 U.S.C. § 552(a) (Supp. V, 1975).   *See also* H.R. 15657, 94th Cong., 2d Sess. (1976).
163. Moore & Tumin, *Some Social Functions of Ignorance*, 14 Am. Soc. Rev. 787, 792 (1949).
164. 5 U.S.C. § 552 (1970).
165. See *Hearings, supra* note 33.
166. *See* 5 U.S.C. § 552(b)(6) (1970).
167. 15 U.S.C. § 1601 (1970).

D.   Governmental Organizations

In the modern state, the difference between governmental and private agencies is a matter of degree. A governmental organization is one whose entire existence is dictated by law.[168] State agencies can only come into being by operation of law, and they can only operate in the manner prescribed by law. In contrast, although private associations are most often formed within a framework of law, and although much of their activity may be subject to legal regulation, there are large areas of initiative and discretion left undirected by law.[169]

As we shall see, a further difference between public and private organizations turns on the degree to which they are subject to public scrutiny. In fact, a good explanation for the distinction between public and private agencies in a democracy is precisely that the former organizations are subject to much more public scrutiny than the latter.

(1)   The Individual Citizen

The extent of protection afforded to the individual citizen in association with other citizens and with state officials is determined by the character of the individual's role within the association. On one level, the citizen, as the "governed," is subject to the penal law, to the motor vehicle and welfare laws and to a whole body of similar criminal and regulatory statutes. On another level, the citizen, as "governor," is a creator, rather than a subject, of law.[170]

(a)   The Citizen as One of the Governed

As "subjects," individuals are required to provide a great deal of information about themselves under, for instance, the census and the income tax laws, the motor vehicle laws and statutes regulating the licensing of certain businesses and professions.[171] The privacy issue

---

168. *See generally* H. KELSEN, THE GENERAL THEORY OF THE LAW OF THE STATE (1949).

169. *See* E. SHILS, *supra* note 4, at 22.

170. *See* A. MEIKLEJOHN, POLITICAL FREEDOM 98-100 (1960). Meiklejohn sees citizens and government as coexisting within three relationships: (1) the people as "governor," delegating authority to a body of agencies known as the "government;" (2) the people as the "governed;" and (3) the people as the "government," governing themselves. To Meiklejohn, it is this concept of the citizen-government relationship that is the essence of American political freedom. *Id.* at 101-06.

171. *See, e.g.,* 13 U.S.C. § 5 (1970) (empowering Secretary of Commerce to specify inquiries to be made in the census); *id.* § 141 (providing for decennial population, unemployment and housing census); CAL. VEHICLE CODE §§ 4451, 4453 (West 1971); N.J.S.A. 39:3-4 (1973); N.J.S.A. 33:1-25 (Cum. Supp. 1976) (applicant for liquor

involved in this aspect of the citizen-government relationship is the individual's "right to be let alone"—individual, rather than group privacy. An extraordinary body of literature exists on this subject, including, besides the important works on privacy already mentioned,[172] two governmental studies of great value: a United States Senate study, *Federal Data Banks and Constitutional Rights*,[173] and an HEW report on *Records, Computers, and the Rights of Citizens*.[174]

Under these circumstances, I would make only the following observations concerning the citizen's privacy as one of "the governed," rather than as one of "the governors": (1) the problems of individual privacy in this context are of extraordinary importance, as even a cursory examination of the studies mentioned will show; (2) individual privacy is currently protected in this respect by constitutional provisions, by numerous specialized statutes[175] and by a new general statute, The Privacy Act of 1974;[176] and (3) protection of the individual's privacy in relation to government is not only required as an individual right, but is sometimes necessary to assure a group purpose.

To amplify this last point, the Freedom of Information Act was designed with a promise of confidentiality of business data so that individuals who are required to provide information to government agencies would not be restrained by the prospect of public disclosure under the Act.[177] A successful price support program for crops, for example, depends on the Secretary of Agriculture having available the best data on farmers' production. Farmers, however, concerned about the possibility of an IRS audit of income, will provide data only on the

license must not have been convicted of a crime involving moral turpitude); N.Y. ALCO-HOLIC BEVERAGE CONTROL LAW § 110 (McKinney 1970) (applicant for liquor license must state that he has not been convicted of a felony); N.Y. BUS. CORP. LAW § 402 (McKinney Supp. 1975) (requiring registration of names and addresses of incorporators); N.Y. VEHICLE TRAFFIC LAW § 401 (McKinney Supp. 1975) (listing requirements for motor vehicle registration application).

172. *See* A. MILLER, *supra* note 144; A. WESTIN, *supra* note 2; Countryman, *supra* note 144.

173. SUBCOMM. ON CONSTITUTIONAL RIGHTS OF THE SENATE COMM. ON THE JUDI-CIARY, 93D CONG., 2D SESS., FEDERAL DATA BANKS AND CONSTITUTIONAL RIGHTS (Comm. Print 1974).

174. REPORT OF THE SECRETARY'S ADVISORY COMMITTEE ON AUTOMATED PERSONAL DATA SYSTEMS, DEP'T OF H.E.W., RECORDS, COMPUTERS AND THE RIGHTS OF CITIZENS (1973).

175. *See, e.g.*, INT. REV. CODE OF 1954, § 6103; 15 U.S.C. § 46(f) (1970) (trade secrets).

176. 5 U.S.C. § 552a (Supp. V, 1975).

177. *See* Soucie v. David, 448 F.2d 1067, 1075-80 (D.C. Cir. 1971), and the legislative history sources cited at note 46 therein.

condition that it is kept confidential. It follows that the reporting system must provide confidentiality if the purposes of the program are to be achieved.[178] In this sense, the farmer is a participant in the price support program, rather than being merely subject to it. The confidentiality promised to the farmer is as necessary to the system of price supports—to the group purpose—as it is to the farmer's own sense of well being.

This is true, I believe, of numerous other such occasions in which the individual provides the government with information necessary to govern effectively. In such cases privacy or confidentiality is functionally necessary to governmental purpose, in very much the same sense that the marital privilege serves marriage, the lawyer-client privilege serves the system of justice and the priest-penitent privilege serves the needs of religion.

(b) The Individual as a Governor

This situation represents a purer case of group privacy than the individual functioning as among the governed. There are three sets of circumstances under which legally fostered confidentiality of communication is of significance: (1) the citizen as voter; (2) the citizen as informer to law enforcement agencies; and (3) the citizen as juror.

The principle of the secret ballot is one of the important supports of democracy. Justice Frankfurter, concurring in *Sweezy v. New Hampshire*,[179] stated: "It cannot require argument that inquiry would be barred to ascertain whether a citizen had voted for one or the other [party]."[180] And he characterized the secret ballot as an attribute of constitutionally protected "political privacy."[181]

We are now so accustomed to this form of confidential communication that we tend to neglect its significance. The rule that no one may be compelled to reveal how he voted avoids unreasonable and coercive forms of pressure and helps to assure candid or honest voting. Under such a rule of secrecy, people vote according to their best judgment, rather than to avoid political ostracism or penalty, or to seek approval or favors, or to pay off political or monetary bribes.[182]

---

178. *See* Address by Stephen A. Herman, 1976 Annual Federal Bar Convention, in 45 U.S.L.W. 2160-61 (1976).
179. 354 U.S. 234 (1957).
180. *Id.* at 266 (Frankfurter, J., concurring).
181. *Id.* at 266-67.
182. The distinguishing feature [of the secret ballot] is, that every voter is thus enabled to secure and preserve the most complete and inviolable secrecy in regard to the persons for whom he votes, and thus escape the influences which,

Citizens govern not only by voting, but by assisting in the law enforcement and judicial processes.[183] Individuals provide information for law enforcement directly to the police or prosecutor, or to grand juries. The practice of informing to the police is widespread and, however subject to abuse[184] and emotionally repugnant under many circumstances, it is necessary. Informing almost constitutes a profession —a profession, however, which requires as a condition of its practice that confidentiality be provided.[185] The legal assurance of that confidentiality consists of an informer's privilege, which permits the prosecutor to withhold the name of an informer at trial.[186] The privilege is qualified or limited, however, and gives way "[w]here the disclosure of an informer's identity, or of the contents of his communication, is relevant and helpful to the defense of an accused, or is essential to a fair determination of a cause . . . ."[187] The decision to grant the privilege in any particular case is made after "balancing the public interest in protecting the flow of information against the individual's right to prepare his defense."[188]

The third context in which the individual citizen requires the protection of confidentiality in order to assure the candid performance of a governmental function is in our jury system. A witness before a grand jury is given a temporary guarantee against the compulsory disclosure of his testimony, which continues until an indictment is handed down.[189] The grand juror[190] and the petit juror[191] are themselves per-

---

under the system of oral suffrages, may be brought to bear upon him with a view to overbear and intimidate, and thus prevent the real expression of public sentiment.

2 T.M. Cooley, Treatise on the Constitutional Limitations Which Rest Upon the Legislative Power of the States of the American Union 1373-74 (8th ed. 1927); see C. Beard, American Government and Politics 573 (1944). See also N.Y. Const. art. 2, § 7; Pa. Const. art. 7, § 4; N.J.S.A. 19:15-26 (1964).

183. See Worthington v. Scribner, 109 Mass. 487, 488 (1872).

184. See United States ex rel. Knauff v. Shaughnessy, 338 U.S. 537, 551 (1950) (Jackson, J., dissenting). It is interesting to note that this opinion, which scathingly characterizes informer's testimony as "abhorrent to free men," was written by Justice Jackson, who also wrote the opinion cited infra note 185 when he served as Attorney General, implying that such testimony was necessary for law enforcement purposes. See R. Berger, Executive Privilege 224 (1974).

185. See 40 Op. Att'y Gen. 45 (1941); 8 J. Wigmore, supra note 50, at § 2374.

186. Roviaro v. United States, 353 U.S. 53, 60-61 (1947).

187. Id.

188. Id. at 62. Compare this with the balancing process in Wigmore's analysis of other testimonial privileges. See text accompanying notes 61-63 supra.

189. See 8 J. Wigmore, supra note 50, § 2362, at 736-37.

190. Id., § 2361, at 735-36; see text accompanying notes 229 & 237 infra.

191. 8 J. Wigmore, supra note 50, § 2346, at 678; see text accompanying notes 229 & 237 infra.

manently protected against compulsory disclosure of what went on in the jury room.[192]   Justice Cardozo, speaking for a unanimous Supreme Court, justified these privileges in *Clark v. United States*:[193] "Freedom of debate might be stifled and independence of thought checked if jurors were made to feel that their arguments and ballots were to be freely published to the world."[194]

We see in the protection the law affords to a citizen's participation in acts of governing the same public interest in the protection afforded confidentiality in nongovernment associations: confidentiality of communication between the members of the group is frequently necessary to accomplish the group's purposes.

(2)   The Legislature

The legislature operates within very well-defined and well-recognized bounds of privacy.   In discussing confidentiality in congressional proceedings, we are fortunate to have the scholarly opinions of Justices White, Stewart, Douglas, and Brennan in the recent case of *Gravel v. United States*.[195]   In *Gravel*, a grand jury was studying the possibility of criminal conduct in the release and publication of the "top-secret" Pentagon Papers.   It subpoenaed one of Senator Gravel's aides, who had been hired the very day the Senator had read extensively from the Pentagon Papers before a hearing of a Senate subcommittee he chaired. The subpoenaed aide was known to have assisted the Senator in preparing for and conducting the hearing.

Senator Gravel moved as an intervenor to quash the subpoena and to require the prosecutor to specify the particular questions to be addressed to his aide.   In sustaining the Senator's motion to quash, the Court unanimously agreed[196] that the speech or debate clause of the Constitution[197] incontrovertibly "protects [a congressman or his aide] from criminal or civil liability and from questioning elsewhere than in

---

192. Voluntary disclosure presents a different and very significant set of problems with which the law has not yet begun to cope.

193. 289 U.S. 1 (1933).

194. *Id.* at 13; *see* Branzburg v. Hayes, 408 U.S. 665, 684 (1972); *cf.* text accompanying notes 248-66 *infra*.

195. 408 U.S. 606 (1972).

196. Four Justices dissented, but because they would have gone further in establishing congressional immunity.   *See id.* at 629 (Stewart, J., dissenting in part); *id.* at 633 (Douglas, J., dissenting); *id.* at 648 (Brennan, J., joined by Douglas & Marshall, JJ., dissenting).

197. U.S. Const. art. 1, § 6, cl. 1.

the [Congress]," with respect to any speech or debate in either House.[198] All the Justices further agreed that the speech or debate clause "[forbids] questioning any witness, including [a congressman's aide], . . . concerning communications between the [congressman] and his aides during the term of their employment and relat[ing] to . . . [a] legislative act of the [congressman]."[199]

Thus, immunity for the confidential communications of legislators is even stronger than that of the husband-wife privilege. The latter privilege only prevents a spouse from testifying regarding a confidential communication with another spouse.[200] The legislative privilege defined in *Gravel* bars *any* witness from testifying to the communications between legislators and their aides relating to their legislative acts. Moreover, the Court's language in *Gravel* broadly grants immunity from questioning as to "communications," without restricting it to *confidential* communications, as in the case of spousal immunity. Finally, it should be noted that the immunity provided is against *any* prosecution, civil or criminal, for "all things generally done in a session of [Congress],"[201] and not merely a testimonial privilege.

What public policy underlies such a broad grant of immunity from questioning in *any* forum for *any* purpose as to "all things generally done" by legislators in the course of legislative business, including communications with fellow legislators or aides? The policy is designed to foster the Congress' purposes; it is intended "to prevent intimidation of legislators by the Executive and accountability before a possibly hostile judiciary."[202] The rule of legislative privilege is designed to ensure "the independence of the legislature;"[203] it protects legislators "from deterrents to the uninhibited discharge of their legislative duty."[204]

The four dissenters in *Gravel* read the speech or debate clause —rightly so, I believe—more broadly than the majority. They interpreted it as protecting the "informing function" of Congress by extending to all communications with third parties,[205] not solely those between legislators and their aides.[206] Justice Brennan, in dissent, quoted

---

198. 408 U.S. at 615.

199. *Id.* at 628-29.

200. *See* note 51 *supra* and accompanying text.

201. 408 U.S. at 617, *quoting* Kilbourne v. Thompson, 103 U.S. 168, 204 (1881).

202. 408 U.S. at 617, *citing* United States v. Johnson, 383 U.S. 169, 181 (1966).

203. United States v. Johnson, 383 U.S. 169, 179 (1966).

204. Tenney v. Brandhove, 341 U.S. 367, 377 (1951).

205. The dissenters did not expressly refer to confidential as well as nonconfidential communications, but that was obviously the intent.

206. *See* 408 U.S. at 629-31 (Stewart, J., dissenting in part); *id.* at 636-37 (Douglas.

Thomas Jefferson's statement that in order for legislators to effectively discharge their duties they "should be free from the cognizance or coercion of the co-ordinate branches, Judiciary and Executive; and . . . their communications with their constituents should of right, as of duty also, be free, full and unawed by any."[207]

It should be noted that legislative privilege goes so far in federal law that citizens do not have access to congressional documents deemed confidential.   Indeed, Congress has thus far effectively resisted proposals, prompted by recent disclosures of payroll padding, double billing of expenses and the like,[208] requiring its members to report regularly on certain aspects of their conduct in office. Neither the FOIA[209] nor the newly enacted Government in the Sunshine Act[210] applies to Congress. And a court subpoena will not be "complied with by the Congress or its committees without a vote of the house concerned to turn over the documents willingly . . . ."[211] As a House Committee has said: "[N]o evidence of a documentary character under the control and in the possession of the House of Representatives can, by the mandate of process of the ordinary courts of justice, be taken from such control or possession but by its permission."[212]

Thus, it is plain that confidential communications, at least between legislators or between legislators and their aides, in the course of and in pursuit of their legislative business, are immune from disclosure under any circumstances and for any purpose. As with other such forms of protection of group confidentiality thus far discussed, protection of legislators' confidential communications assures the success of the group's purpose.

The necessity for candor in the conduct of legislative business and the role that confidentiality plays in assuring it is apparent in the protection afforded to executive sessions of congressional committees. The precedent for such legislative secrecy is in the early practice of the English Parliament, our own colonial legislatures and the meetings of the Constitutional Convention in 1787, all of which were conducted

---

J., dissenting); *id.* at 648-64 (Brennan, J., joined by Douglas & Marshall, JJ., dissenting).

207. 408 U.S. at 653.

208. *See* Malbin, *Many Races for Congress are Contests in Morality*, N.Y. Times, Oct. 31, 1976, § 4, at 3, col. 1.

209. *See* 5 U.S.C. § 552(e) (Supp. V, 1975).

210. 5 U.S.C.A. § 552b (Supp. 1976).

211. Soucie v. David, 448 F.2d 1067, 1081-82 (D.C. Cir. 1971) (Wilkey, J., concurring).

212. H.R. Res. 427, 81st Cong., 2d Sess., 96 CONG. REC. 565-66 (1950).

in complete privacy.[213] Indeed, participants at the Constitutional Convention were enjoined from taking certain documents outside the hall where deliberations took place. Moreover, the records of the Convention were sealed for more than 30 years,[214] and most of the framers acknowledged that the secrecy was necessary to the success of the enterprise.[215] James Madison reportedly believed that secret discussion permitted men the luxury of yielding to the force of a superior argument and that no Constitution would ever have been adopted by the Convention if the debate had been public.[216]

The right of Congress, at its discretion, to deliberate and debate in secrecy is constitutionally protected in Article I, section 5, clause (3), which provides that Congress shall keep and publish "a Journal of its Proceedings . . . , excepting such Parts as may in their Judgment require Secrecy . . . ." Madison observed, in fact, that "[t]here never was any legislative assembly without a discretionary power of concealing important transactions the publication of which might be detrimental to the community."[217]

It may well be that this constitutional provision for secrecy is intended mostly for the protection of military secrets. Provision for dealing with them has been recognized by Congress in its rules of procedure;[218] moreover, there has been a longstanding practice by the executive of consulting with Congress on such matters through the chairpersons or members of appropriate congressional committees.[219] Even as vigorous an opponent of secrecy in government as Raoul Berger recognizes the necessity of secrecy in such cases.[220]

213. For the English and American common-law experience see H. CROSS, THE PEOPLE'S RIGHT TO KNOW: LEGAL ACCESS TO PUBLIC RECORDS AND PROCEEDINGS 25-29, 180-89 (1953). See also 1 M. FARRAND, THE RECORDS OF THE FEDERAL CONVENTION OF 1787 xi-xxv (rev. ed. 1937).
214. 3 Stat. 475, 15th Cong., 1st Sess., Res. 8 (1818), cited in the Nixon case, 418 U.S. at 705.
215. C. WARREN, THE MAKING OF THE CONSTITUTION 134-39 (1937). Thomas Jefferson and Patrick Henry both regretted the secrecy, though.
216. Jared Sparks, Journal, April 19, 1830, in 3 M. FARRAND, supra note 213, at 479. See Bi-Metallic Inv. Co. v. State Bd. of Equalization, 239 U.S. 441, 445 (1915), in which Justice Holmes observed that the "Constitution does not require all public acts to be done in town meeting or an assembly of the whole." See also City of Madison, Joint School Dist. No. 8 v. Wisconsin Employment Relations Comm., 97 S. Ct. 421 (1976).
217. 3 J. ELLIOT, DEBATES IN THE SEVERAL STATE CONVENTIONS ON THE ADOPTION OF THE FEDERAL CONSTITUTION 409 (2d ed. 1836), quoted in R. BERGER, supra note 184, at 206.
218. H.R. REP. No. 271, 27th Cong., 3d Sess. 7 (1843).
219. See R. BERGER, supra note 184, at 291.
220. Id. at 291-92.

Secrecy in Congress, however, is not limited to cases of military matters.[221] Under well-established rules of Congress, some committee meetings are held in executive session, with the press and the public excluded,[222] in order to interview individuals outside the glare of publicity and the attendant danger of unfairly besmirching their reputations. This danger was imprinted in the public mind by Joseph McCarthy's outrageous manner of conducting congressional hearings and Attorney General Herbert Brownell, Jr.'s, televised testimony before the Jenner subcommittee in the 1950's.[223]

A third and significant justification for such executive sessions is that they promote clear thinking and open minds. Oliver Wendell Holmes, Sr., observed that "the very minute a thought is threatened with publicity it seems to shrink towards mediocrity."[224] Scientists, artists and scholars, for example, require the temporary seclusion of the laboratory, studio and study in which to explore their ideas without having to communicate them publicly and, perhaps, being embarrassed by them.[225] The free play of the mind, its openness to new or even wild and unconventional ideas, requires "the individual to find himself in an atmosphere where he is not being evaluated, not being measured by some external standard."[226] Ultimately, artists, scientists and scholars must make their work public, and expose their ideas to the test of truth in the market place. But the temporary seclusion serves a valuable purpose as a way station to truth.

221. See G. GALLOWAY, THE LEGISLATIVE PROCESS IN CONGRESS 570-71 (1953); R. LUCE, CONGRESS, AN EXPLANATION 12-13 (1926); R. YOUNG, THE AMERICAN CONGRESS 189-92 (1958).
222. See Branzburg v. Hayes, 408 U.S. 665, 684 (1972); G. GALLOWAY, supra note 221, at 298.
223. See A. BARTH, GOVERNMENT BY INVESTIGATION 58-61, 91-92 (1955); T. TAYLOR, GRAND INQUEST 85-87 (1955).
224. O.W. HOLMES, THE POET AT THE BREAKFAST-TABLE 344 (1872).
225. See CREATIVITY (P. Vernon ed. 1970); G. WALLAS, THE ART OF THOUGHT ch. 4 (1926).
226. Rogers, Towards a Theory of Creativity, in CREATIVITY 147 (P. Vernon ed. 1970). A quotation from Mozart, found in the Vernon book, makes the same point: "When I am, as it were, completely myself, entirely alone, and of good cheer . . . my ideas flow best and most abundantly." Id. at 55. A similar observation has been made regarding scientific creativity:
  [T]he typical research scientist of genius appears introverted . . . . On the whole, therefore, one could expect that the ability, characteristic of introverts, to withdraw, to exclude the outside world in long periods of concentrated thought and speculation, would outweigh in creative scientists (and even more in creative artists) the superior ability of the extr[o]vert to communicate socially. This is indeed what is generally found.
Cattel & Butcher, Creativity and Personality, in CREATIVITY, supra at 313.

This distinction between a private way station and a public stopping place applies, it seems to me, to legislators as well.[227] Constituents will ultimately hold their legislators accountable for their votes. But a temporary way station for private deliberation and frank exchange of opinion with staff and legislative colleagues is essential to informed legislative decisionmaking. "Men are averse to changing their positions or yielding anything when many eyes are watching."[228] Risktaking, probing, bargaining, negotiation and accommodation are all necessary to the resolution of conflict and disagreement. To require that all legislative meetings be open to public view would thwart these essential elements of the democratic process.

Justice Cardozo thought that "freedom of debate" and "independence of thought" were served by keeping the jury room a private place;[229] seclusion also serves a valuable purpose in artistic, scientific and scholarly work. Individual jurors, scientists, artists and scholars are under no compulsion to make known what they believe; congressmen, however, are under a political obligation to justify their legislative position. Theirs is a public and representative calling which, as a "rule of the game," requires them to stand accountable before those they represent and the public at large.

The public need to hold legislators to account, and the legislative need to maintain limited spheres of confidentiality, have recently sought accommodation in the national legislature and in almost all the states which have by now adopted, or are considering, so-called "Sunshine Laws."[230] The accommodation between privacy and publicity in this legislation is instructive of the purposes served by group privacy. For example, the New Jersey statute declares as the public policy of the state that "secrecy in public affairs undermines the faith of the public in government and the public's effectiveness in fulfilling its role in a democratic society."[231] Significantly, however, the statute also pro-

---

227. Lord Devlin has recently provided a very reasonable interpretation of what President Wilson meant by "open Covenants of Peace openly arrived at." According to Devlin, he "meant to say . . . that international agreements should be published; he did not mean that they should be negotiated in public." P. DEVLIN, TOO PROUD TO FIGHT: WOODROW WILSON'S NEUTRALITY 33 (1975).

228. R. LUCE, *supra* note 221, at 12-13.

229. Clark v. United States, 289 U.S. 1, 13 (1933).

230. *See* The Committee on Federal Legislation, *Government in the Sunshine Act*, 30 RECORD OF N.Y.C.B.A. 376 (1975); Wickham, *Let the Sun Shine!*, 68 NW. U.L. REV. 480 (1973). For examples of specific legislation see Mitchell, *Public Access to Governmental Records and Meetings in Arizona*, 16 ARIZ. L. REV. 891, 892 n.6 (1974).

231. N.J.S.A. 10:4-7 (1976).

vides exceptions to its open meeting provisions which preserve limited legislative privacy.[232] Thus, for instance, "any political party committee" falls outside the purview of the statute.[233] Moreover, the statute does not cover meetings of public bodies "attended by less than an effective majority of the members of a public body . . . ."[234]

A similar balance of the values of privacy and publicity appears in other state statutes and in recent federal legislation.[235] Without entering into a detailed analysis of these exceptions and exemptions, it is clear that they represent, in general terms, a vindication of legislative confidentiality under a variety of circumstances.

(3) The Judicial Branch

The courts require confidentiality in some of their proceedings, and statutory law provides forms of protection similar to those extended to legislative proceedings. Thus, the New Jersey "Sunshine Law" exempts "the judicial branch of the government,"[236] including grand and petit juries,[237] from its open hearing provisions in order to protect the confidentiality of conferences among judges, communications between judges and law clerks, and jury deliberations.

In dictum in the *Branzburg* case, the Supreme Court said that "the press [and, obviously, the public generally] is regularly excluded from . . . our own conferences . . . ."[238] The same justification we have seen in other contexts is at work in the judicial setting as well: "[F]ree give and take of a secret conference may dry up if the justices feel that what may be highly biased accounts by some of their brothers are going to find their way into the history books."[239]

---

232. *Id.* 10:4-8, -9, -12.

233. *Id.* 10:4-8.

234. *Id.* There are nine other subjects of discussion which the Act specifies may be considered at meetings of a public body from which the public is excluded. Among them are "matter . . . rendered confidential" by law; "material the disclosure of which constitutes an unwarranted invasion of individual privacy . . . ;" "[a]ny collective bargaining agreement;" "[a]ny pending or anticipated litigation;" and "[a]ny matter involving the employment . . . of any . . . public officer or employee employed or appointed by the public body . . . ." *Id.* 10:4-12.

235. *See* note 230 *supra.* As I have already noted, neither the FOIA nor the Federal Sunshine in Government Act applies to the legislative branch.

236. *See* N.J.S.A. 10:4-8 (1976).

237. *Id.; cf.* notes 190-91 *supra* and accompanying text.

238. 408 U.S. at 684.

239. J. Frank, Marble Palace 110-11 (1958). *See also* A. Westin, *supra* note 2, at 46.

(4)   The Executive Branch

The need to maintain the confidentiality of some executive proceedings has been the subject of a vast amount of discussion.[240] Unfortunately, some of this discussion, such as that by Raoul Berger,[241] is in my judgment somewhat marred by the fact that it was written in the throes of the extraordinary political tensions surrounding the Watergate affair. Justice Holmes' wonderful apothegm, "Great cases, like hard cases, make bad law,"[242] suggests a corollary: Political crises make poor scholarship.

Rational discussion of the executive's need for confidentiality is made difficult because of President Nixon's gross abuse of his office while flying the political flag of "executive privilege." As former Attorney General Levi has recently said: "[The] emotive value [of the term] presently exceeds and consumes what cognitive value it might have possessed."[243]

Another difficulty with the discussion of confidentiality in the executive branch of government is that its full analytic context has sometimes been neglected. As has been demonstrated thus far in the discussion of other forms of group privacy, it is useless to ask simply whether an executive privilege of confidentiality exists. The appropriate issues are: what members of the executive branch may maintain confidentiality of their discussions with what people, for what purposes, before what tribunals and in what legal contexts, over what period of time. It is only in this framework that seemingly irreconcilable views of executive confidentiality can be made compatible. Fortunately, the work of reconciling such differences is made easier by the decisions of three recent Supreme Court cases[244] and by the 1974 amendments

---

240.   *See, e.g.,* R. BERGER, *supra* note 184; Bishop, *The Executive's Right of Privacy: An Unresolved Constitutional Question,* 66 YALE L.J. 477 (1957); Hardin, *Executive Privilege in the Federal Courts,* 71 YALE L.J. 879 (1962); Schwartz, *Executive Privilege and Congressional Investigatory Power,* 47 CALIF. L. REV. 3 (1959); Younger, *Congressional Investigations and Executive Secrecy: A Study in the Separation of Powers,* 20 U. PITT. L. REV. 755 (1959). *See also Hearings on the Availability of Information to Congress Before a Subcomm. on H.R. 4938, 5983, 6438 of the House Comm. on Government Operations,* 93d Cong., 1st Sess. 113-39 (1973) [hereinafter cited as *Information Hearings*]; House Foreign Operations and Government Information Subcommittee, *The Present Limits of "Executive Privilege," reprinted in* 119 CONG. REC. 10079-83 (1973) [hereinafter cited as *Present Limits*].

241.   R. BERGER, *supra* note 184.

242.   Northern Sec. Co. v. United States, 193 U.S. 197, 400 (1904) (dissenting opinion).

243.   Levi, *supra* note 4, at 323.

244.   United States v. Nixon, 418 U.S. 683 (1974); EPA v. Mink, 410 U.S. 73 (1973); New York Times v. United States, 403 U.S. 713 (1971).

to the Freedom of Information Act.[245]

(a) Executive Privilege Under the Constitution

Professor Berger begins his excellent study of confidentiality in the executive with the pronouncement that "Executive Privilege . . . is a myth."[246] Immediately after publication of his book, however, his thesis was undermined by the unanimous Supreme Court decision in *United States v. Nixon.*[247] The Court there reiterated that the President of the United States bears a privilege in respect to "the confidentiality of his conversations and correspondence, [which] like the . . . confidentiality of judicial deliberations . . . is fundamental to the operation of government and inextricably rooted in the separation of powers under the Constitution."[248] Thus, it is established that the Constitution provides for executive privilege; the issue is under what precise circumstances it may be exercised.

If in calling executive privilege a "myth," Professor Berger meant to deny that an unqualified or absolute claim of privilege exists, he is correct. It is undoubtedly true that executive privilege is not absolute in the sense that President Nixon and his attorneys claimed before the public and the courts.[249] The *Nixon* Court decided that the privilege was qualified in two senses. First, at least "absent a claim of need to protect military, diplomatic or sensitive national security secrets,"[250] the President is subject to a "judicial subpoena in an ongoing criminal prosecution;"[251] the President's "generalized interest in confidentiality . . . cannot prevail over the fundamental demands of due process of law in the fair administration of criminal justice."[252] Secondly, the privilege is also qualified to the extent that, even when it is asserted, the trial judge has the right and the duty to inspect, *in camera*, all material claimed to be privileged, except that of a sensitive military

---

245. 5 U.S.C. § 552 (Supp. V, 1975), *amending* 5 U.S.C. § 552 (1970).
246. R. BERGER, *supra* note 184, at 1.
247. 418 U.S. 683 (1974).
248. *Id.* at 708.
249. *Id.* at 706; *see* Respondent's Brief, United States v. Nixon, 418 U.S. 683 [41 L. Ed. 2d 1039, 1320-21] (1974); R. BERGER, *supra* note 184, at 254-64; Westin, *The Case for America,* in UNITED STATES V. NIXON, THE PRESIDENT BEFORE THE SUPREME COURT xvii (L. Friedman ed. 1974).
250. 418 U.S. at 706.
251. *Id.*
252. *Id.* at 713.

nature. It is the trial judge,[253] then—not, as had been claimed,[254] the President himself—who must determine which material meets the tests of relevance and admissibility in the criminal proceeding at hand, excising all other material and restoring it to "its privileged status."[255]

In carving out these limitations on executive privilege, the Court indirectly also raised questions about some of the positive dimensions of the privilege. For instance, the Court was careful to limit its decision to "subpoenaed materials sought for use in a criminal trial,"[256] leaving open, among other things, the questions of a citizen's request under the FOIA,[257] a subpoena by Congress[258] or a subpoena in a civil suit.[259] The Court also expressly excluded from availability in a criminal prosecution the subpoena of, and even *in camera* inspection of, "military, diplomatic or sensitive national security secrets."[260] Finally, quoting Chief Justice Marshall in the *Burr* case, the Court was careful to note the importance of a " 'guard, furnished to [the President] to protect him from being harassed by vexatious and unnecessary subpoenas.' "[261] It also remarked that the President cannot be treated as just another "ordinary individual."[262]

Thus, although the unanimous Court placed limits on its scope, the extent of the executive privilege under the Constitution that emerges from the *Nixon* case, by overtone and express language, is considerable. Putting aside for the moment questions about the exact dimension of the privilege, let us consider its rationale. The Court found the privilege embedded in an interest "common to all governments," the need for candor in deliberation.[263] It also found it to be an incident of the American constitutional doctrine of separation of powers:

> A President and those who assist him must be free to explore alternatives in the process of shaping policies and making decisions and to do so in a way many would be unwilling to express except privately. These are the considerations justifying a presumptive privilege for Presidential communications. The privilege is funda-

---

253. *Id.* at 713-16.
254. *See* Respondent's Brief at 1320.
255. 418 U.S. at 716.
256. *Id.* at 713.
257. 5 U.S.C. § 552 (1970), *as amended*, 5 U.S.C. § 552 (Supp. V, 1975).
258. *See* text accompanying notes 368-77 *infra*.
259. *See* 418 U.S. at 712 & n.19.
260. 418 U.S. at 706; *see* text accompanying notes 358-67 *infra*.
261. 418 U.S. at 714, *quoting* United States v. Burr, 25 F. Cas. 187, 190, 191-92 (No. 14,694) (C.C.D. Va. 1807).
262. 418 U.S. at 715.
263. *Id.* at 705-06.

mental to the operation of Government and inextricably rooted in the separation of powers under the Constitution.[264]

In sum, the protection afforded Presidential communications, like that afforded communications between spouses, and communications in corporate life, or in legislative, judicial and jury deliberations, is rooted in the necessity of candor of communication for the success of the association. The question arises as to how far in the executive hierarchy the privilege extends. The answer is far from clear.

The language of the *Nixon* opinion is extremely guarded; it refers to a *"President's* privilege." Yet, the separation of powers doctrine, on which the *Nixon* doctrine of executive privilege rests, is certainly applicable beyond the President.[265] Equally applicable is the need for candor in deliberation; in fact, to support this proposition the *Nixon* Court cited *Carl Zeiss Stiftung v. V. E. B. Carl Zeiss, Jena,*[266] a case that concerned levels of executive communication lower than that of the President.

Extension of the privilege to those lower in the executive hierarchy than the President is also supported by the Court's reasoning in the *Gravel* case.[267] In deciding that a Senator's aide was entitled to the same privilege under the speech or debate clause as is a Senator, the Court drew on the rationale extending the privilege to lower executive levels: " '[The] privilege is not a badge or emolument of exalted office, but an expression of a policy designed to aid in the effective functioning of government. . . . [W]e cannot say these functions become less important simply because they are exercised by officers of lower rank in the executive hierarchy.' "[268] In other words, "for the purpose of construing the privilege a Member and his aide are to be 'treated as one.' "[269] The same rationale would be available to extend the privilege of the *Nixon* case to other members of the executive hierarchy. This is especially persuasive since much of the language and rationale of *Gravel*—involving congressional privilege—parallels that of *Barr v. Matteo,*[270] which involved, admittedly in another context, the executive branch.

---

264. *Id.* at 708 (footnote omitted). *See also* cases cited by the Court, *id.* at 708 n.17; Carl Zeiss Stiftung v. V.E.B. Carl Zeiss, Jena, 40 F.R.D. 318, 325 (D.D.C. 1966).
265. *See* Carl Zeiss Stiftung v. V.E.B. Carl Zeiss, Jena, 40 F.R.D. 318, 325 (D.D.C. 1966).
266. 40 F.R.D. 318 (D.D.C. 1966).
267. Gravel v. United States, 408 U.S. 606 (1972).
268. *Id.* at 617, *quoting* Barr v. Matteo, 360 U.S. 564, 572-73 (1959).
269. *Id.* at 616, *quoting* United States v. Doe, 455 F.2d 753, 761 (1st Cir. 1972).
270. 360 U.S. 564 (1959).

(b)   Common-Law and Statutory Protection of Executive Privilege

In the common-law cases, as in the cases involving constitutional interpretation, two issues must be distinguished: (1) is there a privilege; and (2) what agency, using what criteria, determines whether the privilege applies in a given case? As to the first of these questions, it is clear that the executive, at all levels of the hierarchy, is afforded a testimonial privilege at common law. The leading English case is *Duncan v. Cammell Laird & Co.*,[271] which held that documents retained by an executive authority which are "otherwise relevant and liable to production must not be produced if the public interest requires that they should be withheld."[272]   The court reasoned that "the public interest requires a particular class of communications . . . to be protected from production on the ground that the candour and completeness of such communications might be prejudiced if they were ever liable to be disclosed in subsequent litigation . . . ."[273]   A similar rule of executive privilege to protect candor in deliberation exists widely at common law in the American state courts.[274]

The question whether the courts or the executive agency should determine if the privilege applies in a given case is another matter, however. The English view in *Duncan* was that "[a ministerial] objection to production [of evidence] on the ground that this would be injurious to the public interest is conclusive."[275]   But this rule, broadly applied at all levels of executive bureaucracy, was subject to grave abuse.[276] As a result, it was sharply limited by the 1968 English case of *Conway v. Rimmer.*[277] There the court said that, when necessary, the application of executive privilege should be reviewed *in camera* by the court.[278]   Although there is some authority to the contrary, the same rule prevails at the state court level in the United States.[279]

The earliest statutory protection of confidential communications at all levels of the federal bureaucracy is found in the Housekeeping Stat-

---

271. [1942] A.C. 624.

272. *Id.* at 636.

273. *Id.* at 635.

274. *See, e.g.,* Mitchell, *supra* note 230, at 894; Comment, *Executive Privilege at the State Level,* 1974 Law Forum 631, 642-46.

275. [1942] A.C. 624, 641.

276. H. Wade, Administrative Law 308-09 (3d ed. 1971).

277. [1968] A.C. 910.

278. *Id.* at 996.

279. Comment, *supra* note 274, at 642.

ute of 1789.[280]   This statute empowered agencies of the federal government to regulate the custody and use of their records.   Since it afforded no judicial review of the agency decision, it "proved an ideal vehicle for refusing to disclose government documents to private citizens."[281]   A 1958 amendment limited to some extent the role that the statute may have had in legalizing government secrecy,[282] but the problem remained.

A new statutory approach to public access was undertaken by the Administrative Procedure Act (APA) of 1946,[283] which provided for disclosure of agency procedures, opinions and records.   An exception to disclosure was made, however, "to the extent that there is involved . . . any function of the United States requiring secrecy in the public interest."[284]   The determination of what records were to be kept confidential was left to the discretion of the agency and, although the Act provided for judicial review of agency decisions,[285] there was no provision for specific relief.[286]

The next and most comprehensive congressional attempt to promote public access to government records was undertaken in 1966 in the Freedom of Information Act (FOIA).[287]   As the Supreme Court has noted, this Act "seeks 'to establish a general philosophy of full agency disclosure unless information is exempted under clearly delineated statutory language.' "[288]   Thus, under the Act each federal agency must make all nonexempt records available to "any person" who requests them.[289]   Moreover, for the first time, the FOIA provides a

---

280.   Ch. 14, § 7, 1 Stat. 68 (1789), *as amended*, Rev. Stat. § 161 (1875), *as amended*, 5 U.S.C. § 301 (1970).

281.   Note, *National Security and the Public's Right to Know: A New Role for the Courts Under the Freedom of Information Act*, 123 U. Pa. L. Rev. 1438, 1441 (1975).

282.   Act of Aug. 12, 1958, Pub. L. No. 85-619, 72 Stat. 547, *amending* Rev. Stat. § 161 (1875) (codified at 5 U.S.C. § 301 (1970)); *see* NLRB v. Capital Fish Co., 294 F.2d 868, 875 (5th Cir. 1961).

283.   Administrative Procedure Act of 1946, ch. 324, 60 Stat. 237.

284.   *Id.* § 3.

285.   *Id.* § 10.

286.   *Id.*

287.   5 U.S.C. § 552 (1970), *as amended*, 5 U.S.C. § 552 (Supp. V, 1975).   For the different but related problem of what data executive agencies may collect, and how they may share it, see 44 U.S.C. §§ 3503-07 (1970), which grant broad authority to the Director of the Office of Management and Budget in this regard.

288.   NLRB v. Sears, Roebuck & Co., 421 U.S. 132, 136 (1975), *quoting* S. Rep. No. 813, 89th Cong., 1st Sess. 3 (1965).

289.   5 U.S.C. § 552(a)(3) (Supp. V, 1975), *amending* 5 U.S.C. § 552(a)(3) (1970).

judicial remedy empowering the federal district courts to order the production of any identifiable record which is improperly withheld.[290]

The philosophy of disclosure embodied in the FOIA is central to its purpose; however, recognition that the confidentiality of specified government records and communications is necessary to the effective operation of government is clearly reflected in the exemptions to its provisions.[291]   Indeed, most of these exemptions are comparable in spirit and purpose to some of the other forms of protection of group confidences already examined.   Thus, there are exemptions for: (1) "national defense or foreign policy" secrets; (2) "internal personnel rules and practices of an agency;" (3) information "exempted from disclosure by statute;" (4) "trade secrets and commercial and financial information obtained from a person and privileged or confidential;" (5) "inter-agency or intra-agency memorandums or letters;" (6) "personnel . . . and similar files the disclosure of which would constitute a clearly unwarranted invasion of personal privacy;" (7) "investigatory records compiled for law enforcement purposes;" (8) records "contained in or related to examination, operations, or condition reports prepared by, on behalf of, or for the use of an agency responsible for the regulation or supervision of financial institutions;" and (9) "geological and geophysical information and data, including maps, concerning wells."[292]

Because detailed studies of the FOIA have been published,[293] I will not attempt an extensive treatment of the Act.   Nor will I attempt to judge whether each of the exemptions of the Act properly balances the public interest in knowing how its government operates against the public interest in protecting the confidences necessary to the effective functioning of government.   I merely express my agreement with the suggestion by Congress and others that, on the whole, the FOIA exemptions are probably too broadly written.   They still leave too much room for "the games bureaucrats play" to protect themselves from embarrassment.[294]

---

290. *Id.* § 552(a)(4)(B).

291. *Id.* § 552(b).

292. *Id.*

293. *See, e.g.,* Davis, *The Information Act: A Preliminary Analysis,* 34 U. CHI. L. REV. 761 (1967); Katz, *The Games Bureaucrats Play: Hide and Seek Under the Freedom of Information Act,* 48 TEXAS L. REV. 1261 (1970); Note, *The Freedom of Information Act and the Exemption for Intra-Agency Memoranda,* 86 HARV. L. REV. 1047 (1973).

294. *See* Katz, *supra* note 293; Lardner, *Series on the FOIA,* The Washington Post, July 25-29, 1976.   One "abuse" of the Act, it should be noted, takes place at the hands

Some observations concerning the character of the exemptions, and the peculiarities of three of them in particular, are necessary to my thesis, however. First, exemption (3) merely incorporates by reference exemptions from disclosure of confidential communications found, for example, in the Census Act and the income tax laws.[295] In these instances, protection of the privacy of citizens or of businesses is a legitimate basis for maintaining confidentiality. Without passing judgment on every such form of statutory protection,[296] it is fair to conclude that an omnibus provision such as that found in exemption (3) is required in the FOIA.[297]

Other exemptions in the FOIA plainly protect specific privacy interests of individuals and groups outside government who provide information to the government on a confidential basis. Thus, exemption (4) protects "trade secrets;" exemption (6) protects personal privacy interests embodied in "personnel and medical files;" exemption (8) protects the records of financial institutions; and exemption (9) protects geological information.[298]

Exemptions (1), (5) and (7) are of a different character. As originally enacted, exemption (7) maintained in very general terms the confidentiality of investigatory files "compiled for law enforcement purposes."[299] The Act was amended in 1974, however, to require specific grounds for invoking the exemption.[300] The obvious intent of these provisions was to broaden protection of the public's right to know, while continuing to guard the effectiveness of the government's prosecutorial function by maintaining the confidentiality of specific governmental communications.

In originally enacting the FOIA, Congress recognized that at "the same time that a broad philosophy of 'freedom of information' is enacted into law, it is necessary to protect *certain equally important*

---

of businessmen, who use it for what the Food and Drug Commissioner terms "industrial espionage." See note 138 *supra.*

295. *See* notes 171 & 175 *supra.*

296. It has been estimated that there are some 100 statutes or parts of statutes affected by exemption (3). *See* FAA Administrator v. Robertson, 422 U.S. 255, 265 (1975).

297. *Id.* at 266-67; *see Hearings on S. 1666 Before the Subcomm. on Administrative Practice and Procedure of the Senate Comm. on the Judiciary,* 88th Cong., 1st Sess. 6 (1963).

298. 5 U.S.C. § 552(b) (1970).

299. 5 U.S.C. § 552(b)(7) (1970), *as amended,* 5 U.S.C. § 552(b)(7) (Supp. V, 1975).

300. 5 U.S.C. § 552(b)(7) (Supp. V, 1975), *amending* 5 U.S.C. § 552(b)(7) (1970).

rights of privacy with respect to certain information in government files."[301]   As we have seen, some of that confidential information consists of investigatory files used in government prosecutorial work; some of it consists of "inter-agency or intra-agency memorandums or letters which would not be available by law to a party other than an agency in litigation with the agency."[302]   This is so-called exemption (5) material.   By the terms of this exemption, the FOIA invokes the common law of executive testimonial privilege.   This would seemingly import a degree of precision to the exemption, except for the fact that as Moore,[303] Wigmore[304] and Davis[305] have observed, the common law is not terribly precise in respect of the matter.

However great the difficulty of defining the precise scope of exemption (5), the supporting public policy is plainly expressed in its legislative history and in recent Supreme Court cases.   Congress recognized that

> it would be impossible to have any frank [inter- and intra-agency] discussion of legal or policy matters in writing if all such matters were to be subjected to public scrutiny. . . . [E]fficiency of Government would be greatly hampered if . . . agencies were . . . forced to "operate in a fish bowl."[306]

In two recent cases, the United States Supreme Court has reiterated this rationale.   In *EPA v. Mink*,[307] the Court identified the exemption (5) policy as that of " 'open, frank discussion between subordinate and chief concerning administrative action.' "[308]   In *NLRB v. Sears, Roebuck & Co.*,[309] the Court indicated that "Congress had the Government's executive privilege specifically in mind" in enacting the exemption.[310]   Quoting legislative history and lower court cases, the Court went on to say that the privilege rests "on the policy of protecting the 'decision making processes of government agencies.' "[311]   " '[T]here

---

301. S. Rep. No. 813, 89th Cong., 1st Sess. 3 (1965) (emphasis supplied); *see* H.R. Rep. No. 1497, 89th Cong., 2d Sess. 6 (1966).

302. *See* 5 U.S.C. § 552(b)(5) (1970).

303. 4 J. Moore, Federal Practice § 26.60 (rev. 2d ed. 1976).

304. 8 J. Wigmore, *supra* note 50, at §§ 2378-79.

305. Davis, *supra* note 293, at 764.

306. S. Rep. No. 813, *supra* note 301, at 9; H.R. Rep. No. 1497, *supra* note 301, at 10.

307. 410 U.S. 73 (1973).

308. *Id.* at 87, *quoting* Kaiser Aluminum & Chem. Corp. v. United States, 157 F. Supp. 939, 946 (Ct. Cl. 1958).

309. 421 U.S. 132 (1975).

310. *Id.* at 150.

311. *Id.; see* United States v. Morgan, 313 U.S. 409, 422 (1941).

are enough incentives as it is,' " added the Court, " 'for playing it safe and listing with the wind.' "[312] Without " 'frank discussion' . . . , the 'decisions' and 'policies formulated' would be the poorer as a result."[313] Finally, the Court referred to the *Nixon* case as involving an analogous context in which " '[h]uman experience teaches that those who expect public dissemination of their remarks may well temper candor with a concern for appearances . . . to the *detriment of the decision making process.*' "[314]

Thus, executive privilege for confidential intra- and inter-agency communications is established by exemption (5) in order to protect the efficacy of administrative decisionmaking. The FOIA thereby incorporates by statute a theory of privilege at all levels of the federal administrative hierarchy similar to that afforded to the President under the Constitution in the *Nixon* case.

There are, however, limitations on the exercise of the privilege. If, under the rule of *Nixon*, a criminal defendant can require the production of confidential communications that do not involve foreign policy and military security matters, against the President's claim of executive privilege, the same weighing of public values should mandate that any officer of the government produce such communications in a criminal proceeding. The statute does not expressly require this result; its language refers, however, to material "which would not be available by law . . . in litigation with the agency."[315] This statutory language invokes the common law of executive privilege in which "different rules have been held to apply"[316] depending upon whether the Government was prosecuting in a criminal case or appearing as a plaintiff or a defendant in a civil case. The common-law test in criminal prosecutions has been one of "the public interest."[317] This brings us back to the observation made above that it would be difficult to believe that

---

312. 421 U.S. at 150, *quoting* Ackerly v. Ley, 420 F.2d 1336, 1341 (D.C. Cir. 1969).
313. 421 U.S. at 150, *quoting* S. REP. No. 813, *supra* note 301, at 9.
314. 421 U.S. at 150-51, *quoting* United States v. Nixon, 418 U.S. at 705.
315. 5 U.S.C. § 552(b)(5) (1970).
316. EPA v. Mink, 410 U.S. 73, 86 n.13 (1973).
317. While we must accept it as lawful for a department of the government to suppress documents, even when they will help determine controversies between third persons, we cannot agree that this should include their suppression in a criminal prosecution, founded upon the very dealings to which the documents relate, and whose criminality they will, or may, tend to exculpate. So far as they directly touch the criminal dealings, the prosecution necessarily ends any confidential character the documents may possess; [the prosecution] must be conducted in the open, and will lay bare their subject matter.
United States v. Andolschek, 142 F.2d 503, 506 (2d Cir. 1944) (L. Hand, J.).

the weighing of the "public interest" involved in *Nixon* would be any different at a level of government below that of the President.

Although the executive privilege rule of exemption (5) is apparently unavailable in a criminal proceeding, it appears not only to be available, but to be unqualified or indefeasible in response to a citizen's request for information under the FOIA. In this respect, the rule of executive privilege applicable to nonlitigant applicants for information under the FOIA is stronger than the British common-law rule or the APA provisions that controlled the release of privileged executive communications to litigants prior to the enactment of the FOIA. It will be recalled that, under the current British rule of the *Conway* case, the "final responsibility" in a civil action lies with the court to determine whether the public interest dictates maintaining the confidentiality of a government document.[318] A similar rule was applied in civil litigation under the APA; the claim of executive privilege could be defeated when, in the judgment of the court, the litigant proved "extraordinary need."[319] The FOIA provision seems to create an absolute privilege for all information requested by a nonlitigant applicant which is not "routinely available" in civil litigation;[320] no showing of "extraordinary need" will defeat it. Although one writer suggests otherwise,[321] there is good reason to believe that a litigant—rather than a mere applicant—*will* have the same opportunity to show "extraordinary need" under the FOIA as was previously available under the APA.

Another similarity of approach under the APA and the FOIA is that they both require "different treatment for materials reflecting deliberative or policy-making processes on the one hand, and purely

---

318. *See* text accompanying note 277-78 *supra.*
319. Note, *supra* note 293, at 1051 n.22.
320. For example, in EPA v. Mink, 410 U.S. 73, 86 (1973), the Court stated that the Act does not "permit inquiry into the particularized needs of the individual seeking information, although such an inquiry would be made of a private litigant." *See also* Sterling Drug, Inc. v. FTC, 450 F.2d 698, 704-05 (D.C. Cir. 1971); Note, *supra* note 293, at 1051 n.22.
321. See Note, *supra* note 293, at 1051 n.22, in which the rule of absolute privilege is justified on the grounds that the "sheer size of the job" of assessing "extraordinary need" for every applicant under the FOIA precludes application of the APA rule. There is no reason why the old APA rule should not apply to litigants, as opposed to mere applicants for information, since the number of litigants will not necessarily grow under the FOIA. Moreover, the contrary result would suppose Congress intended to restrict availability of information rather than loosen it under the FOIA. It is plain, however, that Congress "expressly intended 'to delimit the exception [5] as narrowly as consistent with efficient Government operation.'" EPA v. Mink, 410 U.S. 73, 89 (1973), *quoting* S. Rep. No. 813, *supra* note 301, at 9.

factual, investigative matters on the other."[322]   The latter are subject to disclosure, while the former are not. An analogous distinction will probably also be made under both Acts between "predecisional communications, which are privileged . . . and communications made after the decision and designed to explain it, which are not."[323]   Underlying both distinctions is the theory that little or no inhibition to the candor of the decisional process will result from the potential disclosure of purely factual material or post-decisional communications. Moreover, the release of such post-decisional communications serves the public interest in discovering "the basis for an agency policy actually adopted" and in avoiding the growth of "secret [agency] law."[324]

(c)   National Defense and Foreign Relations: A Common-Law, Statutory and Constitutional Issue

National defense and foreign relations materials are covered by the last of the exemptions to the free availability of information under the FOIA, which I shall discuss.[325]   Exemption (1), as originally enacted, provided that material not be disclosed to the public if it was "specifically required by Executive order to be kept secret in the interest of the national defense or foreign policy."[326]   The "executive order" referred to is a system of classifying documents, for the purpose of maintaining military security, which originated under President Roosevelt during World War II and culminated in President Nixon's Executive Order Number 11,652, as amended by Executive Order Number 11,714, the order currently operative.[327]   Prior to the enactment of the FOIA, there was no statutory authority for review of classification decisions, but the FOIA seemed to promise such review by expressly providing for de novo judicial review.[328]

---

322. EPA v. Mink, 410 U.S. 73, 89 (1973). Although the *Mink* Court did not say so, the basis of the fact-opinion difference is that only a disclosure of the latter induces a lack of candor.

323. NLRB v. Sears, Roebuck & Co., 421 U.S. 132, 151-52 (1975) (footnotes omitted).

324. *Id.* at 152-53; *see* Davis, *supra* note 293, at 797; Note, *supra* note 293, at 1057-63.

325. The confidentiality of these materials is protected by common-law and constitutional doctrine as well.

326. 5 U.S.C. § 552(b)(1) (1970), *as amended,* 5 U.S.C. § 552(b)(1)(B) (Supp. V, 1975).

327. *See* Note, *supra* note 281, at 1442-43.

328. 5 U.S.C. § 552(a)(3) (1970), *as amended,* 5 U.S.C. § 552(a)(4)(B) (Supp. V, 1975).

This promise was thwarted in *Epstein v. Resor*,[329] in which a district court refused to review, even *in camera,* a Defense Department "Top Secret" classification of a file on the forced repatriation of anti-communist Russians; the court extended review only to determine whether the classification was "clearly arbitrary and unsupportable."[330] Confirming the restrictive interpretation of the *Epstein* court, the Supreme Court in *Mink* avoided de novo review under section 552(a)(3) by concluding, as a matter of statutory construction, that the applicability of exemption (1) turned solely on whether the documents were classified according to the procedure specified in the President's executive order.[331] *Mink* specifically held, as well, that exemption (1) does not "permit *in camera* inspection of such documents to sift out so-called 'nonsecret components.' "[332]

The reaction to the *Mink* case in Congress was sharp, however, and in 1974 the FOIA was amended. As amended, it provides a change in exemption (1) requiring a showing that documents sought to be kept confidential are "specifically authorized *under criteria established by an Executive order* to be kept secret in the interest of national defense or foreign policy."[333] It also now provides that a showing must be made that such documents *"are in fact* properly classified pursuant to such Executive order."[334] Finally, the 1974 amendments changed the judicial review provisions of the Act to provide that the court not only review de novo, but that it have the authority to review *in camera* all of the documents in question.[335]

There is considerable doubt whether the 1974 amendments, any more than the original enactment, will yield aggressive and comprehensive judicial review of claims to privilege on the ground of national defense or foreign policy.[336] The explanations for such judicial passivity, in the face of congressional prodding, are that the public interest in the maintenance of confidentiality in this area is extremely

---

329. 296 F. Supp. 214 (N.D. Cal. 1969), *aff'd,* 421 F.2d 930 (9th Cir.), *cert. denied,* 398 U.S. 965 (1970).

330. 296 F. Supp. at 217.

331. *See* 410 U.S. at 81.

332. *Id.*

333. 5 U.S.C. § 552(b)(1) (Supp. V, 1975), *amending* 5 U.S.C. § 552(1) (1970) (emphasis supplied).

334. 5 U.S.C. § 552(a)(4)(B) (Supp. V, 1975) (emphasis supplied). For a good discussion of the legislative history of the 1974 amendments see Note, *supra* note 281, at 1446-50.

335. 5 U.S.C. § 552(a)(4)(B) (Supp. V, 1975), *amending* 5 U.S.C. § 552(a) (1970).

336. *See* Note, *supra* note 281, at 1463-72.

high, that the executive is given special authority under the Constitution in this area, and that the judiciary feels ill-equipped to resolve the complex questions at issue in what would necessarily be *in camera* proceedings.[337]

In 1798 George Washington stated that "[t]he nature of foreign negotiations requires caution, and their success must often depend on secrecy."[338] This principle applies to the conduct of national defense as well. The extraordinary value placed by Congress upon confidentiality in the conduct of national defense and foreign affairs is apparent in the enactment of espionage statutes,[339] the implicit authorization for a national security classification system[340] and, of course, the enactment of exemption (1) of the FOIA. The Supreme Court in *Totten v. United States*,[341] *United States v. Reynolds*[342] and in the recent *Pentagon Papers*[343] and *Nixon*[344] cases, clearly recognized the same fundamental value.

The problem posed by this well-recognized and highly valued interest is that it is difficult or impossible to define with precision and that, as Justice Jackson once said, "Security is like liberty in that many are the crimes committed in its name."[345] This possibility of abuse, fully documented in recent times,[346] would seem to cry out for judicial review. Why have the courts hesitated?

In the first place, judicial review itself, even *in camera*, may be seen as a form of breach of the need for secrecy. Thus, in the *Reynolds* case the Supreme Court cautioned against courts jeopardizing "the security which the privilege [against disclosure of military secrets] is meant to protect by insisting upon an examination of the evidence,

---

337. *See id.*
338. 1 J. RICHARDSON, MESSAGES AND PAPERS OF THE PRESIDENTS 194 (1896). *See generally* SECRECY AND FOREIGN POLICY (T. Franck & E. Weisband eds. 1974); Republic of China v. National Union Fire Ins. Co., 142 F. Supp. 551 (D. Md. 1956).
339. *See, e.g.,* 18 U.S.C. § 792 *et seq.* (1970). *See also* Atomic Energy Act of 1954, 42 U.S.C. § 2011 *et seq.* (1970); Subversive Activities Control Act of 1950, 50 U.S.C. § 781 *et seq.* (1970).
340. *See, e.g.,* 5 U.S.C. § 552(b)(1) (1970), *as amended,* 5 U.S.C. § 552(b)(1) (Supp. V, 1975); 18 U.S.C. § 798 (1970); 22 U.S.C. §§ 1934, 2585 (1970); 50 U.S.C. §§ 781-83 (1970).
341. 92 U.S. 105 (1875).
342. 345 U.S. 1 (1953).
343. New York Times Co. v. United States, 403 U.S. 713 (1971).
344. 418 U.S. at 710-11.
345. United States *ex rel.* Knauff v. Shaughnessy, 338 U.S. 537, 551 (1950) (dissenting opinion).
346. *See* R. BERGER, *supra* note 184, at 288, 366-72.

even by the judge alone, in chambers."[347]   Beyond this concern, the courts have also realized that the executive has "confidential sources of information" and "agents in the form of diplomatic, consular, and other officials,"[348] necessary to the appraisal of military security and foreign relations questions.   This leads the courts to conclude that "[i]t would be intolerable that [they], without the relevant information, should review and perhaps nullify actions of the Executive" in this area.[349]   In the Supreme Court's judgment, military security and foreign relations involve "decisions of a kind for which the Judiciary has neither [the] aptitude [nor the] facilities . . . ."[350]

The final reason why the courts hesitate to intrude into foreign relations and military security questions is that they call for determinations which not only "lie outside sound judicial domain in terms of aptitude [and] facilities," but also lie outside "sound judicial domain" in terms of "responsibility."[351]   The foundation of this constitutional doctrine was laid in *Marbury v. Madison*,[352] which distinguished certain "political powers" in the exercise of which the President could use "his own discretion."[353]   Applying this doctrine in *United States v. Curtiss-Wright Export Corp.*,[354] the Supreme Court noted that the President is "the constitutional representative of the United States with regard to foreign nations . . . . For his conduct he is responsible to the Constitution."[355]   And in *Nixon*, the Court characterized "military, diplomatic or sensitive national security secrets" as article II responsibilities of the President[356] in relation to which "the courts have traditionally shown the utmost deference."[357]

As will be recalled, the unanimous Court in the *Gravel* case granted to a senatorial aide immunity from testimony before a grand jury investigating espionage, in respect of a communication which was

347. United States v. Reynolds, 345 U.S. 1, 10 (1953).
348. United States v. Curtiss-Wright Export Corp., 299 U.S. 304, 320 (1936).
349. Chicago & S. Air Lines, Inc. v. Waterman S.S. Corp., 333 U.S. 103, 111 (1948).
350. *Id.*
351. Curran v. Laird, 420 F.2d 122, 129 (D.C. Cir. 1969). *See also* Chicago & S. Air Lines, Inc. v. Waterman S.S. Corp., 333 U.S. 103, 111 (1948). For the historical origins of the "presidential power" mystique, see C. ROSSITER, THE AMERICAN PRESIDENCY 53-67 (1956).
352. 5 U.S. (1 Cranch) 137 (1803).
353. *Id.* at 166.
354. 299 U.S. 304 (1936).
355. *Id.* at 319, *quoting* 8 U.S. Sen. Reports, Committee on Foreign Relations 24 (1816); *see* Spacil v. Crowe, 489 F.2d 614, 617-18 (5th Cir. 1974).
356. 418 U.S. at 706.
357. *Id.* at 710.

not affected with the high value of military security or foreign relations.[358] The decision rested on the separation of powers doctrine. Given the unique Article II responsibilities of the executive in respect of foreign relations and military security, and given the extraordinary public interest in secrecy in such matters, one must conclude that the Court would read into the separation of powers doctrine at least as strong a privilege of confidentiality for the executive as it did for the legislative branch in *Gravel*.

Indeed, in the *Nixon* case, although *in camera* inspection was ordered as to documents outside the military security and foreign relations area, the Court clearly intimated a different view of communications of the latter type when it said: *"Absent a claim of need to protect military, diplomatic, or sensitive security secrets, we find it difficult to accept the argument that even the very important interest in confidentiality of Presidential communications is significantly diminished by production of such material for in camera inspection."*[359] And, as previously indicated, the legal basis on which the *Nixon* decision rests is the doctrine of separation of powers.[360]

Wigmore asks about judicial *in camera* disclosure: "Is it to be said that even this much of disclosure cannot be trusted? Shall every subordinate in the department have access to the secret, and not the presiding officer of justice?"[361] The question takes on greater force, of course, in light of the recent grave abuses by the executive of the doctrine of privilege.[362] But what basis for review do judges have? Are they really in a position to challenge military and foreign relations decisions made by the executive "taken on information properly held secret"?[363] Was the Supreme Court in *Chicago & Southern Air Lines, Inc. v. Waterman Steamship Co.*[364] right or wrong in concluding that courts have "neither [the] aptitude, [nor the] facilities" for such review?[365] The Senate Judiciary Committee that recommended the 1974

---

358. 408 U.S. at 616-17.
359. 418 U.S. at 706 (emphasis supplied).
360. *Id.* at 704-06.
361. 8 J. Wigmore, *supra* note 50, § 2379, at 812 n.6, *quoting* J. Wigmore, Evidence § 2379 (3d ed. 1940).
362. *See, e.g.,* R. Berger, *supra* note 184, at ch. 9; Note, *supra* note 281, at 1438-39.
363. Chicago & S. Air Lines, Inc. v. Waterman S.S. Corp., 333 U.S. 103, 111 (1948).
364. 333 U.S. 103 (1948).
365. *Id.* at 111. But compare Youngstown Sheet & Tube Co. v. Sawyer, 343 U.S. 579 (1952), in which the Supreme Court did exercise powers of review in respect to executive judgments in the fields of military and foreign affairs.

FOIA amendments, designed to overcome the *Mink* prohibition of *in camera* inspection, thought that "someone other than interested parties —officials with power to classify and conceal information—must be empowered to [review foreign relations and military security judgments]."[366] It believed that "the courts [were] qualified to make such judgments."[367]

This difference of opinion between Congress and the Court on the issue of judicial competence to review foreign affairs and military security judgments identifies a much more basic conflict. Is executive privilege a constitutional facet of the separation of powers doctrine, or a creature of the FOIA and other statutes preserving forms of confidentiality in executive business? The *Nixon, Gravel* and *Reynolds* cases strongly suggest a constitutional basis for the doctrine; the 1974 FOIA amendments, especially those to exemption (1), suggest that the issue is within the legislative sphere.

My own view, briefly stated, is that the issue cannot be answered without reference to the specific nature of the communication and its purpose, the parties to it, the identity and purpose of the person who seeks to share it, the time period during which secrecy is sought to be maintained and the context in which it is sought. Factual information not part of an investigative file, which is in the hands of a low-level bureaucrat, does not reflect on the nature of the decisional process of the bureau and is required by a defendant in a criminal proceeding in the interest of justice, is clearly beyond separation of powers protection. A request by Congress in an ordinary legislative inquiry for military secrets held by the President, or even a request by the courts for *in camera* inspection in a criminal prosecution, might well face constitutional barriers to disclosure. The answer would undoubtedly differ if the request from the court involved a criminal prosecution of the President.

The principle that the legal protection afforded the confidences among associates will vary with *who requests* the information and *for what purposes* is highlighted by a recently proposed amendment to the FOIA intended "to require that all information be made available to Congress except where Executive Privilege is involved."[368] The executive has exercised its privilege against requests for information

---

366. S. REP. No. 854, 93d Cong., 2d Sess. 31 (1974).
367. *Id.*
368. *Information Hearings, supra* note 240, at 5 (Preamble to H.R. 4938).

from Congress numerous times in recent years.[369]   The FOIA as originally enacted left open the question of the rights of Congress under its provisions.[370]   Congressman Erlenborn, one of the sponsors of H.R. 4938, said that the purpose of the bill is to "declare the policy that Congress shall have access to all information in the possession of the executive branch."[371]   Instead of being limited by all the exemptions under subdivision (b) of the FOIA, there would be only one exemption:

> [T]he President may prevent the disclosure [only] by invoking executive privilege . . . within the restrictions of the bill, namely: [w]hen a policy recommendation had been made to the President or the head of one of the executive agencies; and [w]hen the President certifies that disclosure of such advice would seriously jeopardize the national interest and the ability of the President or the agency head to get forthright advice in the future.[372]

The bill, in Congressman Erlenborn's words, thus "recognizes the general right and need of Congress to receive information" as being no less than "the President's right and need to receive in confidence advice from trusted advisers who will not be inhibited by the possibility that such advice will become a matter of public debate at some future date."[373]

The bill would substitute one exemption for the nine which currently are found in the FOIA, but only for the purpose of congressional inquiry; it would, in other words, considerably broaden the availability of information to Congress, as opposed to that available to the general public. The recognition that Congress may have a need for information from the executive, which is greater than that of the general public, and which outweighs the need for confidentiality in executive affairs, is already recognized in at least seven statutes.[374] I believe that the principle is sound. It recognizes the constitutional obligation of congressional oversight, gives meaning to the notion of separate but co-equal powers of the executive and legislative branches and provides a practical tool for congressional inquiry into executive operations.

Putting aside the question whether the executive has a constitutional right to refuse confidential information beyond that found codi-

---

369. *See Present Limits, supra* note 240.
370. *See* 5 U.S.C. § 552(c) (1970), *as amended,* 5 U.S.C. § 552(c) (Supp. V, 1975).
371. *Information Hearings, supra* note 240, at 14.
372. *Id.*
373. *Id.*
374. *Id.* at 101.

fied in the exemptions of the FOIA, and putting aside whether that constitutional right could extend to all levels of the executive,[375] it seems wise and appropriate to have the executive share as much information as possible with the Congress.   Indeed, overcoming the reluctance of the judiciary to intervene in clashes between the executive and the legislature may well have been one of the strong motivating forces behind the enactment of the FOIA.   Two questions must be answered, however.   First, may the President be judicially compelled to give Congress the information if there is a difference of opinion as to whether executive privilege may be invoked?   Congressman Erlenborn's bill offers no remedy beyond those methods of enforcement that now exist.[376]   Secondly, can Congress assure that what it receives in confidence will not be shared with the public generally, defeating the purposes, for instance, of the individual privacy protection provided in the current FOIA exemption (6)?   The evidence on this score is mixed.[377]

In summary, the FOIA is in some measure a codification of constitutional principles and of common law, as much as it is a purely legislative initiative.   It offers an avenue of access to knowledge of government affairs in the form of a judicial remedy to all citizens, which could previously be obtained only by persons properly and directly concerned.[378]   Moreover, it is intended "to strengthen the disclosure requirements of the Administrative Procedure Act"[379] by substituting in subdivision (b) a set of standards more precise than the vague standards of exemption under the APA.[380]

But the very existence and form of those exemptions to disclosure tell us that the Congress recognizes the public interest in limited confidentiality in government.   In addition, it recognizes the delicate balance between such a limited public interest in governmental confidentiality and the public right to know how its government operates.   Finally, the exemptions underscore the fact that the protection to be afforded government confidences depends, among other things, on the subject matter of the confidences.   A similar recognition of the delicate balance between the necessity for confidentiality in the affairs of the executive branch of government and the necessity for public disclosure

375. *Id.* at 15.
376. *Id.*
377. *See* R. BERGER, *supra* note 184, at 286-303.
378. Administrative Procedure Act of 1946, ch. 324, § 10, 60 Stat. 237.
379. Soucie v. David, 448 F.2d 1067, 1072-73 (D.C. Cir. 1971).
380. EPA v. Mink, 410 U.S. 73, 82 (1972).

is reflected in the federally enacted Privacy Act,[381] the recently enacted Government in the Sunshine Act[382] and in most state sunshine laws and public records acts.[383]

III.   REPRISE AND CONCLUSION

1.   The law of group privacy determines under what circumstances a confidence shared by two or more people will be protected against the desires of a party to the confidence or of some third person. The contexts in which rules of group privacy are applied range from the casual sharing of a bit of neighborhood gossip over a fence, which a columnist or a litigant might inquire about, to a congressional inquiry directed to the President of the United States concerning negotiations with a foreign power.

2.   By contrast, the law of individual privacy concerns the circumstances under which individuals may refuse to share aspects of their lives with others.   The law of individual privacy determines whether the sharing is to take place at all; it describes the conditions under which a "right to be let alone" is recognized.   The law of group privacy determines the character of the sharing which takes place, if any is to take place at all; it determines the conditions under which a "right to huddle" is recognized.

As the conditions of life grow increasingly complex, and as the state and other social and economic organizations begin to serve more and more complex needs, individuals are called upon to sacrifice more

---

381. 5 U.S.C. § 552(a) (Supp. V, 1975). *See generally* Note, *An Introduction to the Federal Privacy Act of 1974 and Its Effect on the Freedom of Information Act*, 11 N. ENG. L. REV. 463 (1976); Getman v. NLRB, 450 F.2d 670 (D.C. Cir. 1971) (privacy-disclosure balancing).   It is reported that there are 3 billion, 9 hundred million federal agency records on individuals which are to be protected under the Privacy Act and the FOIA.   Address by Stephen A. Herman, *supra* note 178, at 2161.

382. 5 U.S.C.A. § 552b (Supp. 1976). See also The Federal Advisory Committee Act of 1972, 5 U.S.C. App. I (Supp. V, 1975), which requires that meetings of all advisory committees be open to the public.

383. It is interesting to note that the Federal Government in the Sunshine Act has an exemption for meetings which relate "solely to the internal personnel rules and practices of an agency." 5 U.S.C.A. § 552b(c)(2) (Supp. 1976).   Most state sunshine laws neglect such an exemption. *See, e.g.,* N.J.S.A. 10:4-6 *et seq.* (1975).   The federal sunshine law takes account of the fact that many public agencies serve executive rather than legislative functions.   The same justification that applies to the exemption for inter- or intra-agency memoranda under the FOIA applies to meetings of executive agencies. *See* The Committee on Federal Legislation, *supra* note 230, at 381.   State sunshine laws like that of New Jersey seem in this respect to do a disservice to bodies such as Boards of Freeholders, which perform both legislative and executive functions.

and more of their privacy. If you want insurance, or a job, or a car loan, or social security payments or free health care, if you are to pay your income tax or participate in a farm price support program, you must be willing to share information about yourself and your family with others.   The law of group privacy concerns itself with the terms under which such sharing is to take place.

3.   Confidentiality of communication in one's associations serves different purposes depending upon the nature of the association. Secret societies achieve cohesiveness and identity by sharing a mystique of signs, rituals and passwords that is zealously hidden from the general community.   The Agriculture Department induces farmers to share information about their crop yields by promising that the information will not in turn be shared with the Internal Revenue Service.   The football huddle and the political caucus use their seclusion to plan their attacks against opponents and to generate battle esprit.   Lovers fashion intimacy by telling each other things about themselves that they would not share with anyone else.   Business associates seek a competitive advantage by keeping secret from competitors their industrial technology, the names of suppliers of goods or profit margins on sales.

Each of these associations illustrates confidentiality serving a different group purpose.   But what they have in common is that, in each, confidentiality serves to assure the success and preserve the integrity of the association. In sociologist Robert Merton's terms, each of these illustrates the principle that privacy is essential to a properly functioning social structure.[384]

4.   Here, then, is the link between individual and group privacy: The right to be let alone protects the integrity and the dignity of the individual.   The right to associate with others in confidence—the right of privacy in one's associations—assures the success and integrity of the group purpose.

5.   Permeating much of the law of group privacy is an awareness that confidentiality assures associational success or efficacy by enabling individuals to be candid with each other.   Most people are reticent; they avoid positions which place them in the public eye.   They express their feelings and opinions more fully and forthrightly if they can be assured of confidentiality, particularly when emotional and controversial issues are involved.   The views expressed by grand and petit jurors to

---

384. R. MERTON, SOCIAL THEORY AND SOCIAL STRUCTURE 397-400 (enlarged ed. 1968).

one another and the advice given to a responsible business or governmental official by a staff advisor are fuller and more frank when confidentiality is assured. Of course, this full and frank communication assures greater success of the enterprise. Indeed, the law and our common sense recognize that many of our most socially valued associations would not exist without strong assurances of confidentiality. Competitive sports and businesses, love and marriage, advisors and assistants to people holding positions of power and responsibility all depend to an extraordinary degree on confidentiality.

6. Group privacy is also important in a democracy for the preservation of centers of initiative and power outside the ambit of government. Totalitarian governments control the total social and political environment by intruding in unlimited fashion into family life, the church, charitable, economic and social organizations and political parties. This wholesale governmental intrusion into individual spheres generates an aura of invincibility and domination, which induces compliance and submissiveness. The individual finds that there is no place to turn for practical help or emotional and moral support in any disagreement with the totalitarian state.

By contrast, the democratic state is characterized not only by the electoral accountability of its political leadership and the constitutional guarantees of individual liberty, but by a deep-rooted respect for group privacy, for independent centers of group power and authority. The first and fourth amendments and numerous provisions of statutory and common law protect the autonomous relationships of the family, the church and the school, and business, social, political and charitable organizations by assuring, among other things, group privacy.

7. A primary means of creating autonomous institutions is to grant them a degree of immunity from inquiry concerning their affairs. Dissenters from established political and social ways, business enterprises seeking competitive advantages and wanting to take entrepreneurial risks, the church and the family all find that their capacity to act independently of the state and society depends upon a degree of remove from public scrutiny. But institutions in the democratic state vary in the degree to which they can and should be free of public scrutiny. Government officials should be as fully accountable to the public as is consistent with effective fulfillment of their roles. Some social groups—the family, the church and some schools, for example— which are not directly funded by tax dollars, should be allowed to maintain a very high degree of privacy in their affairs because they affect

primarily their own members. Other social groups, with varying degrees of impact on the life and well-being of the nation, fall somewhere in between the two extremes.

8. There is a strong public interest in scrutinizing the affairs of some organizations and in maintaining the confidences of others. The degree to which confidences among associates should be maintained and public scrutiny avoided varies with the degree to which organizations affect the public interest. This is a way of defining the state, and it explains, in part, why the distinction between governmental and nongovernmental organizations is one of degree rather than kind.

9. Thus, there are good reasons of public policy for the law to favor confidences among associates. But there are also social values which sometimes outweigh these reasons. Among the most important are: (1) the liberty of individuals to abandon a pledge of confidentiality, unless its abandonment constitutes a breach of contract, a breach of a legally constituted relationship of trust or a violation of the espionage laws; (2) the search for truth and justice in legal proceedings; (3) the right and necessity of a democratic people to understand how organs of government operate and to hold political officers and civil servants accountable; and (4) the right and necessity of a democratic government to regulate and hold accountable in the people's name businesses and other organizations whose operation strongly affects the public welfare.

10. In addition to countervailing public interests, there are factual circumstances which should give us pause about condoning unqualified confidentiality in government or business. Secrecy is the occupational disease of bureaucrats; they tend to keep more secrets than the public interest requires; they tend to keep them not only to serve the public interest, but to shield their own incompetence and dereliction of duty. We have the right to expect public servants and officers of businesses vested with the public interest to be more candid than they have heretofore been about what they do, and why. People cannot work well in a fish bowl, but democracy cannot work well if important decisions are made and forever kept behind closed doors.

11. In reaching an appropriate balance of the interests involved, we must distinguish between the way station and the stopping place on the path to public accountability. Woodrow Wilson's principle of "open covenants, openly arrived at," once applied only to diplomacy, but now a slogan common to all of politics, is misused if it is taken to leave no room for confidential deliberation and negotiation in public life.

Labor, corporate and political leaders must account for their views before a public trade union, stockholder or constituency at some appropriate time. But they should be free to engage in preliminary negotiations and to develop their ideas in privacy. People who are responsible to the public for their conclusions should have the benefit, as artists, scientists and scholars do, of secluded periods of time to arrive at those conclusions. Such a way station on the road to accountability stimulates creativity and thoughtfulness and also promotes rational accommodation of conflict.

12. A decision by the legal system to maintain confidentiality between associates may take many forms under the authority of a variety of legal sources. Thus, in *Griswold* and *NAACP v. Alabama*, the first amendment was invoked by the defense in a criminal proceeding to declare criminal statutes void. In *Gravel* and *Nixon*, articles I and II of the Constitution were invoked in the attempt to quash a subpoena in a criminal proceeding. The common law provides testimonial privileges against breaches of confidence in legal proceedings. Tort and contract law provide causes of action for breaches of confidence, and numerous statutes, like the Freedom of Information Act and the Sunshine Law, afford causes of action for certain disclosures, as well as defenses against disclosure of certain kinds of confidences.

13. Whether a cause of action or a defense lies to protect group privacy in any particular case depends upon 1) the subject covered by the confidence, 2) how long the confidence is intended to be maintained, 3) the nature of the legal proceeding, 4) who seeks to breach the confidence and for what reason, and 5) whose confidence it is and what purpose it serves.

A spouse is required to provide certain information about her husband to the Welfare Department which could not be required in a courtroom or by a newspaper reporter. Under the FOIA, a government agency can defend against a request for defense information which might serve a potential enemy's purposes, a defense not available for other types of information—but only so long as the information would truly embarrass the national defense at the time it is sought. Certain information is available in criminal prosecutions but not in civil proceedings. Business information available to agencies of government, or to a shareholder upon request, or in civil or criminal litigation, is not available to a business competitor. The President of the United States may have certain defenses to disclosure not available to subordinates. A legal remedy may protect a confidence entered into by contract, although no remedy would exist in the absence of the contract. *In camera* disclosure may be available in court or before Congress where full public disclosure might not be. Congress may have certain rights to executive information to which neither the courts nor the public at large has rights.

14.   Although it is not possible to provide a single formula which comprehends the variety of circumstances and social values involved in group privacy, Wigmore's criteria for testimonial privilege seem to be applicable beyond the testimonial area. It seems obvious that only communications that are normally undertaken on the express or implied assumption of confidentiality should find protection, and that protection should be afforded only if the relationship could not flourish without confidentiality. For instance, factual data that does not reflect a difference of opinion and is not the subject of current contention is shared among government agencies and officers without any thought of a confidence being involved. There is no reason, then, why it should not be available publicly. Moreover, such data would and could be shared publicly without impairing the nature of the government decisionmaking process, because no public officer's personal reputation is at stake in sharing it. In other cases, however, these two criteria would favor confidentiality. Thus, for instance, people normally vote in government elections supposing their vote is secret, and the secret ballot is an essential element of our democracy.

Wigmore's other two criteria can also be applied beyond the testimonial process. Maintaining the relationship of confidence between congressmen and their aides is an important public value. The slight improvement to public knowledge of the legislative process is not worth the damage that would be done to that process if congressmen could be compelled, under a provision like that found in the FOIA, to disclose the confidences they share with their aides. A different result is to be reached in deciding whether memoranda about an agency policy, written after the agency has adopted it, and as part of the process of applying it, should be shared with the public. Here the need of those subject to regulation to know the policy's meaning outweighs the harm to the operations of the agency arising from the personal sensitivity to criticism of agency officers who have written the memoranda.

15.   Finally, a word more about privacy in government. Consideration of the issue is obviously bedeviled in the aftermath of the worst abuse of secrecy our nation has known. But it would be folly to go from one extreme to the other. One person's legitimate newsbriefing

is another's outrageous newsleak; one person's essential confidence is another's obnoxious secret.   The people who regard marital and confessional secrets as sacrosanct, the public opinion journals which maintain business secrets as sound business practice and urge the adoption of a journalist's privilege, the businessmen and political theorists who urge protection of the confidences of private corporate bodies as a necessity of their strength and autonomy, the labor leaders who know the value of confidentiality in negotiations and the congressmen and judges who could not operate effectively without maintaining a confidential relationship with their colleagues and their staffs—none of these should be heard to condemn a qualified executive privilege as an unmitigated evil.

Executive privilege may be a destructive myth if it claims unqualified privilege before all tribunals for all communications with all government employees for all time.   But executive privilege is a necessity of sound government—it protects limited kinds of executive communications for limited purposes and limited periods of time against limited forms of disclosure.   We could not survive as a nation without it.